VINE'S

EXPOSITORY COMMENTARY ON

1 & 2 THESSALONIANS

W.E. VINE

WITH C. F. HOGG

VINE'S

EXPOSITORY COMMENTARY ON
1 & 2
THESSALONIANS

W.E. VINE
with C. F. HOGG

THOMAS NELSON PUBLISHERS
Nashville ▪ Atlanta ▪ London ▪ Vancouver

Published in Nashville, Tennessee, by Thomas Nelson, Inc. and distributed in Canada by Nelson/Word, Inc.

Library of Congress Cataloging-in-Publication Data

Vine, W. E. (William Edwy), 1873–1949.
    [Expository commentary on 1 & 2 Thessalonians]
    Vine's expository commentary on 1 & 2 Thessalonians / W. E. Vine
with C. F. Hogg.
        p.   cm.
    ISBN 0-7852-1171-3
    1. Bible. N.T. Thessalonians—Commentaries.   I. Hogg, C. F.
II. Title.
BS2725.3.V56   1997
227'.8107—dc20   96–36200
                                                                     CIP

Printed in the United States of America.
1 2 3 4 5 — 00 99 98 97 96

Thessalonians

with

C. F. Hogg

· CONTENTS ·

1 and 2 Thessalonians

Abbreviations viii
Publisher's Preface ix
Preface 1

1 Thessalonians

Chapter 1 19
Chapter 2 41
Chapter 3 69
Chapter 4 83
Chapter 5 109

2 Thessalonians

Chapter 1 161
Chapter 2 178
Chapter 3 204

· LIST OF ABBREVIATIONS ·

The undernoted abbreviations are used in the Notes.

A.V.	Authorized Version
chh.	chapters
ca., circa	about the year
cp.	compare
ct.	contrast
e.g.	for example
Eng.	English
et al.	and other passages
Gk.	Greek
Heb.	Hebrew
i.e.	that is
in orig.	in the original
lit.	literally
LXX.	the Septuagint, a translation of the Old Testament from Hebrew into Greek, made between 250 and 150 B.C.
marg.	margin
MS., MSS.	manuscript(s)
N.T.	New Testament
O.T.	Old Testament
R.V.	Revised Version
vv.	Verses
viz.	namely

|| at the end of a paragraph or note indicates that all the New Testament occurrences of the Greek word under consideration are mentioned in it.

"Qualified in Many Fields, Narrow in None"

Undoubtedly William Edwy Vine was qualified in many fields. As well as being a theologian and a man of outstanding academic intellect, he had a heart for all humanity that made him a master of communication.

Born in 1873, at the time when C. H. Spurgeon, D. L. Moody and F. B. Meyer were enjoying popularity on both sides of the Atlantic, Vine was brought up in a boarding school owned by and governed by his father as its headmaster. This factor was a major contribution to his interest in teaching. At the age of 17 he was a teacher at his father's school while attending the University College of Wales in preparation for his eventual London University degree, an M.A. in classics.

At the age of twenty-six he spent an Easter vacation at the home of a godly couple, Mr. and Mrs. Baxendale, where he met their daughter Phoebe; a few years later, they married. It was a marriage made in Heaven. They had five children: Helen, Christine, Edward (O.B.E.), Winifred, and Jeanette. During the time of their engagement, Vine's reputation as a clear Bible expositor was growing. It was not long before he accepted the joint headmastership of the school with his father. In 1904, after his father died, his brother Theodore then became joint headmaster with him.

It was during this time, in conjunction with Mr. C. F. Hogg, that he produced three classic works which are contained in this collection: Commentaries on 1 and 2 Thessalonians, followed by Galatians. These master works display the full scope of Vine's scholarship.

While Vine was teaching in the school, preparing for his M.A. and writing in-depth commentaries, he also developed a lifetime habit of teaching classes in New Testament Greek grammar. This laid the foundation for his all-time classic work, *An Expository Dictionary of New Testament Words,* and later, *An Expository Dictionary of Old Testament Words.* His Dictionaries are classics—copies are in excess of three million worldwide. They are available today in the best-selling *Vine's Complete Expository Dictionary of Old and New Testament Words* (published in a separate volume by Thomas Nelson Publishers)—proof that his scholarship and clarity of expression is as relevant as when first published.

"One who, in his less humble moments fancies himself to be something of a specialist in this field, must bear witness that the reading of the greater part of the *Expository Dictionary* in typescript and in proof before publication was for him a real education in New Testament usage." Professor F. F. Bruce

A Bridge Builder between this Century and the Next Millennium

To own this extensive library is to have tools that can only bring practical and spiritual insight both for new and mature Christians.

Expository Commentaries

Vine applies a "microscopic" approach to expository teaching—a word approach that takes into consideration every reference to that word in the Bible as well as its use in contemporary and classic Greek.

The value of these books alone make this collection a must. They stand up with other great commentaries, such as J. Armitage Robinson on Ephesians, Lightfoot on Colossians, and Westcott on John's Gospel and Hebrews, to name but a few.

"For the student of the English New Testament these commentaries will long remain standard works." Professor F. F. Bruce

Vine's verse-by-verse exposition reveals a depth of understanding that commentaries many times their size fail to give. He explains the meaning of the key words in each verse and links them with the complete passage.

"Here we have some of the most distinctive features of Mr. Vine's exegesis, which stamp him as a truly biblical theologian." Professor F. F. Bruce

A Bridge Builder between Mind and Heart

Concerning the man himself, I have come to know more of him through two of his daughters as well as from the local Christian church that he and his wife attended for so many years. Many of the members still remember the Vines, known for their hospitality, humor, hard work, and commitment to the Word of God and missionary enterprise. The writings of W. E. Vine come from the finest intellect in combination with a devoted missionary heart, truly a rare combination.

"The Scriptures' chief function is to bear witness of Christ, and the chief end of their study and exegesis is to increase our inward knowledge of Him, under the illumination of the Spirit of God. Nor would Mr. Vine, in all his study and writing, be content with any lower aim than this, for himself and his readers alike." Professor F. F. Bruce

Robert Hicks Bath, England
1996

• PREFACE •

This volume is an outcome of the preparation of some Notes on these Epistles for the use of a circle of Bible students during 1908–11.* The reception accorded to the Notes on their original publication has encouraged the writers to reissue them, revised and expanded, in a more permanent form, and with a wider circle of readers in view. They are not intended for the scholar, but for the Christian man or woman who, aware that only through the letter can the spirit of the word find access to the mind and heart, desires some assistance in obtaining a more accurate knowledge of the Scriptures.

The epistles to the Thessalonians present few critical problems, historical or textual; in these pages the few that do emerge are neither emphasized nor ignored. But the aim of the writers is primarily, if not exclusively, edification. In this indeed they do but attempt to conform to the pattern of Scripture, for doctrine in the Bible is always set out in relation to life. God reveals Himself to men in order that they may become like Him.

Originality will be sought for here in vain. We have had no ambition to put into circulation anything that is not current coin in the Kingdom of God. But it would be impossible to acknowledge specifically all our obligations to those Bible students, past and present, who, in speech and in writing, have helped us to a better understanding of the Scriptures.

Broadly speaking there are two methods of studying the Scriptures, one, the telescopic, following the wide sweep of the development of the purpose of God in history and prophecy. The other, the microscopic, occupied rather with the detail of that development, and particularly with the words in which it is expressed. Nature certainly shows the same perfection in the leaf of the tree as in the forest, in the grain of sand as in the stars, and each is an equally worthy subject of investigation; who would think of pitting one against the other? So must it be with the Scriptures, if so be that in them also is the handiwork of God. In a letter to his publisher the late Dr. Westcott, then a young man, declared that since it had pleased God to reveal His mind to men through the medium of words he intended to devote his life to their study. In humbler fashion, but in the same spirit, we have used the microscope on this portion of Holy

---

*The Exeter Correspondence School of Bible Study.

Writ; but not to the exclusion of the telescope, for indeed the two are not rivals, each is good and one the complement of the other.

The epistles to the Thessalonians are not isolated documents, they are specimens of a literature unique in its origin, character, purpose and authority, and must therefore be interpreted by constant reference to the whole of which they form a part. Hence the continual appeal to, and comparison with, the other Scriptures which is a prominent feature of the Notes.

This method assumes the integrity of the Bible, the diverse parts of which are unified by a purpose to the development of which each separate writing makes its own distinctive contribution. The presence of such a purpose—and it is readily discerned—is, moreover, evidence of a superintending and controlling Mind. In the pages that follow, therefore, these Epistles have been treated as genuine writings of the apostle Paul, the product of his own mind in its normal working, but also and no less, as inspired of God, and, in all matters of which they treat, as of final authority, with the other Scriptures, to all who name the name of the Lord Jesus Christ.

With us it has been axiomatic, then, that the words upon which we have ventured to comment (always, we hope, with reverence for the Divine Author and with respect for the human agent) are "words that the Spirit teacheth." And if so, it follows that since they are sanctified by the touch and use of God, they may not be lightly esteemed. Moreover, has it not pleased God to call His own Son "the Word"?

The Bible is essentially Missionary Literature, laying the foundation of, and providing authority and direction for, the Missionary enterprise which is to be the agelong occupation of the people of God. And these letters are the oldest Missionary correspondence of the Christian Era. They were written by one of the earliest missionaries while our own continent was still an unexplored field of operations. As such they afford a due to the nature and direction of a force which has since worked an unparalleled upheaval in the world. It was, moreover, in the propagation of Christianity that its doctrines were formulated. The Faith was beaten out on the anvil of Paganism by the Missionaries of the Cross.

For the exposition herein presented the writers alone are responsible. They represent no school, they speak with no authority save that authority which is inherent in truth. They not merely recognize a "right of private judgment," they insist upon the responsibility of every man to whom, in the Providence of God, the Scriptures come, and in whatever tongue, to read them for himself as he shall one day answer to God therefor. The direct responsibility of man to God is the foundation of human freedom.

It may not be out of place here to say a few words about the method of the dual authorship of this book. Draft notes were prepared by one of the collaborators; over these the other worked, adding the results of his own study. This combination thereupon formed the subject of correspondence—the writers living far apart and meeting but seldom. From the outset there was an explicit understanding that nothing should appear in print under their joint names that did not carry the cordial approval of both. The Notes are now published, without reserve or exception, as conveying the united judgment of the writers.

Since the book is intended for readers of the Bible in English, where reference is made to the original tongues the words are presented in Roman letters *(italicized)* instead of the Hebrew and Greek script. This plan will, it is hoped, facilitate the use of such concordances as the "Englishman's," Strong's "Exhaustive," or Young's "Comprehensive."

Our thanks are due to several friends who, during the publication of the earlier drafts of the Notes, kindly favored us with criticisms and suggestions, all of which received careful consideration. Had they been more numerous the book would doubtless have been even more advantaged.

To Mr. W. S. Payne, of Cordoba, Argentina, we offer our hearty thanks for much labor given to the preparation of the MS. for the press, and especially for the verification of the large number of references. And to Mr. T. Alan Hogg for help rendered in the preparation of the Indexes. The text of the epistles is printed from the Revised Version of 1881, with the kind permission of the Syndics of the University Presses.

Above all we acknowledge with reverent gratitude the good hand of God upon us in permitting the task to be brought to a conclusion. Full well are we persuaded that our labor is acceptable to Him, and likely to be useful to His people, only as it is sanctified by the Holy Spirit (Rom. 15:12).

The motto chosen at the inception of the work was the charge of Moses to Israel concerning the Law: "It is no vain thing for you; because it is your life" (Deut. 32:47). These words are equally applicable to the whole Bible, the completed Revelation of God, and to the Christian of the day now present. We shall be thankful indeed if our readers, with ourselves, are by anything written herein helped the more deeply to reverence, and the more closely to follow, Holy Scripture, and the more steadfastly "to serve a living and true God, and to wait for His Son from Heaven."

C.F.H. W.E.V.   November, 1914.

The Restrainer

Additional note to second epistle, chapter 2, verse 7.

Some esteemed correspondents (among them the late Dr. Griffith Thomas) wrote inquiring why we had not, in our note on this verse, mentioned the suggestion that the restrainer might be Satan. This suggestion was before us, indeed, but we did not perceive any reason why, if Satan were intended, the apostle should not have said so, categorically. However, aiming to put all available material before the reader, to enable him to form his own judgment, we feel that this view also should be briefly described.

The suggestion is that "one that restraineth" *(ho katechōn)* is Satan, and "that which restraineth" *(to katechon)* his power. We are indebted to another for a reasoned presentation of this interpretation, of which we give a resume, as follows.

(1) Verse 6. "to the end that" describes the purpose of the restrainer in imposing the restraint, not the consequence of relief from that restraint. That purpose is that the Man of Sin may be revealed "in his own season," that is, at the moment the restrainer judges to be opportune, not before.

(2) Such purpose could be attributed with propriety only to God or to Satan.

(3) *Katechō* can hardly mean restraint in the sense of repelling some hostile or repugnant person or thing or to restrain them from approaching. The use of the word in Luke 4:42 perfectly illustrates its only legitimate meaning: "the multitude . . . would have stayed (i.e., restrained) Him, that He should not go from them." Romans 1:18 affords another illustration.

In the first epistle, moreover, the apostle had already used another word *(enkoptō)* in the sense of repelling, or keeping a person out of a place, "Satan hindered us" (2:18). If that were his meaning why not use the same word here? See *Galatians 5:7.*

Then again *katechō* is used in 1 Thessalonians 5:21 in the sense of holding fast by what one has, not in the sense of repelling anything. It is, at least, unlikely that the apostle would use the same word here in an opposite, and unusual, sense.

(4) That the Lawless One (= the Man of Sin, the Son of Perdition, v. 3) is controlled by Satan is specifically stated in v. 9.

(5) If *ho katechōn* is properly translated by such a term as the controller, it is a descriptive title of Satan, to be compared with *ho peirazon,* the Tempter, in 1 Thessalonians 3:5. Incidentally, this would dispose of the difficulty to which reference is made above, that the apostle must have had some reason for not expressing his meaning in plain terms. On the other hand Satan is never elsewhere so described in the New Testament.

(6) There seems to be an antithesis intended between the revelation of the Lord Jesus Christ in God's time, to suit His purpose (cp. Ps. 2:6; 110:1; Mark 1:15; Gal. 1:4; 1 Tim. 2:6), and the revelation of the Lawless One by Satan in a time to suit his purpose.

(7) "Until he be taken;" as shown in the *Notes,* there is nothing in the text to justify "taken." *Ginomai* means to become, to come to be (2 Thess. 2:8).

Naturally then, the meaning of the phrase is to come into being, or to appear, rather than to be removed, or to disappear.

This interpretation may be expressed in the following paraphrase, which should be compared with those given on 2 Thessalonians 2:8.

"And (in consequence of what I told you, though, of course, you cannot identify the Man of Sin, yet even) now you know what it is that controls him (holding him in leash, as it were) with the intention that he may be revealed at the time of Satan's own choosing (and not before). For the secret (spirit) of lawlessness is already working; only (there is) the Controller at present (who will hold it in check) until he (the Man of Sin) may become (successfully manifested) out of the (very) midst (of the situation that will develop, so not risking defeat by a premature attempt to capture the key position). And then (but not till then) the Lawless One shall be revealed whom the Lord Jesus shall slay, etc."

Introductory Notes

The Writer

Paul, a Roman name, "Little," always used by the apostle himself, cp. 2 Peter 3:15. His Hebrew name was Saul, "asked for," Acts 13:9, cp. Simon Peter, Matthew 10:2, Jesus Justus, Colossians 4:11, cases in which a Greek or Latin name is attached to a Hebrew name; Saul and Paul, however, are never found together. In Paul's case, the double name may be explained in one of four ways: *(a)* he had both from childhood; *(b)* being short of stature, 2 Corinthians 10:10, the contrast with his Old Testament namesake, 1 Samuel 9:2, suggested the second name; *(c)* he took it from Sergius Paulus, the Roman proconsul whom he met at Paphos, Acts 13:4-12; it is in this context that the name Paul first occurs; *(d)* in self-depreciation, cp. 1 Corinthians 15:9, and Ephesians 3:8, *et al.* Of these *(a)* is, perhaps, to be preferred. While he is presented as laboring among the Jews, Luke refers to him by his Jewish name, but as soon as the apostle has fairly begun his work among the Gentiles, the historian drops the Jewish name and speaks of him henceforth exclusively as Paul, Acts 13:9.

It is not possible, of course, to fix with certainty the dates of Paul's birth, conversion, and death, but 1 B.C., A.D. 32 and 67 respectively may be taken as approximating closely to them. He would thus be slightly younger than the Lord Jesus, Who was born from four to eight years before the account called A.D.* Paul may have seen the Lord in the days of His flesh, though there is no record that he ever did; 1 Corinthians 9:1 refers to the incident of Acts 9:1-18, cp.

_____
*The beginning of the present era, which errs by some years was fixed in A.D. 525 by Dionysius Exiguus, an abbot of Rome.

1 Corinthians 15:8. He was probably put to death at Rome. If the above dates are approximately correct, Paul must have been about fifty years old, and must have had about eighteen years' experience in missionary work when he wrote the Thessalonian epistles. With the possible exception of his own epistle to the Galatians and the more general epistle written by James, "the Lord's brother," Galatians 1:19, these are the oldest Christian documents extant.

In all his writings, save those to the Thessalonians, the apostle adds some descriptive words to his name. But this church was young and unsophisticated; error had not yet crept in, nor was Paul's apostleship questioned; hence the simplicity of the salutation.

His Companions

SILVANUS. = Silas, was a Jew, Acts 16:20, "a chief man among the brethren" at Jerusalem, 15:22, a prophet, 32, and a companion of Paul on his first missionary journey into Europe, 40; later, a companion of Peter also, 1 Peter 5:12.

TIMOTHY, a younger man, the son of a Jewish Christian mother and a Gentile father, Acts 16:1. These three had preached the gospel together at Thessalonica under the leadership of the first, a godly association of maturity and youth. The elder did not fear to acknowledge the younger men and to associate them with himself, they, in their turn, did not assert independence of him, cp. Philippians 2:5, 6.

The City

Thessalonica was a very ancient maritime city, situated, approximately, lat. 41 N., long. 23 E., built in 315 B.C. by Cassander, brother-in-law of Alexander the Great. The Romans conquered Macedonia in 168 B.C. and made the city a naval station, furnishing it with docks. In the apostles' day it was a "free," or self-governing, city, administratively, strategically, and commercially important. Under the name Saloniki, it was, until recently, reckoned the second city in the Turkish Empire; now it belongs to Greece.

The People

The natives of Thessalonica, like those of Philippi, were of Thracian race, and Paul speaks of the churches in these cities as "of Macedonia," 2 Corinthians 8:1, since both cities lay within the Roman province of that name. Historians have rated the race characteristics of the Thracians more highly than those of the Greeks, to whom the Corinthian Epistles were written, or of the Asiatics, to whom the Ephesian and Colossian Epistles were written. Paul seems to have found the Thracian converts reliable and devoted. That they had deeply engaged his affections his writings testify.

FIRST EPISTLE

The Occasion

At a port of such importance as Thessalonica, foreigners were certain to be found in large numbers. Among these was a colony of Jews, large and wealthy enough to possess a synagogue. To this Paul had resorted on three successive Sabbaths, opening and alleging from the Scriptures: *(a)* that the Messiah must suffer and rise again from the dead; *(b)* that Jesus of Nazareth is the Messiah. Some believed and cast in their lot with the preachers. But the work grew beyond the bounds of the synagogue, and apparently the missionaries remained in the city much longer than the fortnight or so mentioned in Acts 17:2, for a great number of "devout Greeks" of both sexes, among them some described as being "of the chief women," v. 4, also believed. These were, of course, native Thracians. The word here translated "devout" is used both of the worship of God, Acts 18:13, and of an idol, 19:27. "Greek" (a different word is found in 6:1; 9:29) was used by the Jews to describe all who were not of their own race, Romans 1:16, 1 Corinthians 1:22, 23, just as the Greeks used it to distinguish themselves from the "barbarians," or, as we say, "foreigners," Romans 1:14, 1 Corinthians 10:32. Of these some were probably proselytes, or at least were interested in the Jews' religion; hence, as the epistle itself shows, 1:9; 2:14, et al., the Thessalonian church was mainly composed of Gentiles.

The jealousy of the Jews was aroused; they attacked the house of Jason, apparently the apostle's host, and made such a turmoil, that, alike out of consideration for the municipal authorities, and for their own safety and that of the converts, Paul and Silas left the city the same night. Finding further opportunity for gospel testimony at Berea, a town a little distance to the southwest, the missionaries remained there, but were speedily disturbed by the Thessalonian Jews. This time Paul alone left the city, Silas and Timothy remaining at Berea, while he went to Athens, where, though he reasoned with the Jews in the synagogues, their enmity does not seem to have been aroused. Here, probably, Timothy joined him, and was sent back to Thessalonica, 1 Thessalonians 3:1, while Paul went on to Corinth, whence he wrote this letter to express his anxiety for the converts whom he had so lately left, to explain his absence from them in their troubles, and to instruct them further in the faith. It is possible, moreover, that in this brief interval he had heard tidings from Thessalonica of the falling asleep of some of those who had so recently received Christ Jesus the Lord, see 4:13.

The Epistle

"Epistle" is a less common word for a letter. A letter affords a writer more freedom, both in subject and in expression, than does a formal treatise. A letter is usually occasional, that is, it is written in consequence of some circumstance which requires to be dealt with promptly. The style of a letter depends largely on the occasion that calls it forth. That to the Galatians, for example, is full of force, alike of argument and feeling. In parts of the Corinthian epistles Paul waxes warm, becomes almost passionate, denouncing his enemies and yearning over his children. In Romans he is all logic, though he soars at times, as in ch. 8. In Ephesians and Colossians he is carried along by the very majesty and glory of his exalted theme, though he is nowhere more simply practical in any of his writings. But in this epistle he is fervent, simple, natural, just talking to his beloved children in the Lord, much as, ten years later, he spoke to those at Philippi.

Paul frequently used the letter form for the purpose of conveying instruction and counsel, but he was not the earliest writer to do so, cp. Jeremiah 29, and Acts 15:23-29. Both prophet and apostle used the services of an amanuensis, or secretary, to commit their thoughts to paper, see Jeremiah 36:4, 18, 32; 45:1; Romans 16:22; 1 Corinthians 16:21; Colossians 4:18; 2 Thessalonians 3:17. The epistles to the Galatians, 6:11, and to Philemon, v. 19, seem to have been written by the apostle's own hand.

Analysis

I. *Introduction* (1:1-10)

    (a) The Reception of the Gospel—faith. The past (2:1-12).
    (b) The Fruit of the Gospel—love. The present (2:13—4:12).
    (c) The Anticipations of the Gospel—hope. The future (4:13—5:11).
    (d) Conclusion (5:12-28).

II. *Introduction* (1:1)

A. *Historical and Personal*

    (a) Effect of the Gospel at Thessalonica (1:2-10).
    (b) The missionary's retrospect of his labors there (2:1-16).
    (c) His care for, and desire to be with, the converts (2:17—3:10).
    (d) His prayer for them (3:11-13).

B. *Doctrinal and Hortatory*

    (a) Exhortations to the converts to "maintain good works" (4:1-12).
    (b) Teaching concerning the coming of the Lord (4:13—5:11).
    (c) Further exhortations to the converts (5:12-22).
    (d) And prayer for them (5:23, 24).
    (e) Conclusion (5:25-28).

III. Chapters 1 and 2

Evidences of the Election
of the Thessalonian Converts

(a) The experience of the missionaries as reported by the missionaries (1:4, 5).

(b) The experience of the converts as reported by the missionaries (6–8).

(a) The experience of the missionaries as reported by the people generally (9a).

(b) The experience of the converts as reported by the people generally (9b, 10).

(a) The experience of the missionaries as reported by the converts themselves (2:1–13).

(b) The experience of the converts as reported by the converts themselves (14–16).

IV. Chapter 1:2–5

An Illustration of the Figure
Chiasmos, *or* X-form

See note at 5:5. The sections prefaced by the same letter are to be read together.

(a) We give thanks to God always for you all,

(b) making mention of you in our prayers without ceasing;

(c) remembering your work of faith and labor of love and patience of hope in our Lord Jesus Christ,

(c) before our God and Father,

(b) knowing, brethren beloved of God, your election,

(a) how that [because] our gospel came not unto you in word only, but also in power, and [even] in the Holy Spirit ['s power], and [even] in much fullness [of the Holy Spirit's power].

SECOND EPISTLE

On the occasion of his first visit the apostle spent eighteen months at Corinth, Acts 18:11, and apparently the second letter to the Thessalonian church, as well as the first, was written during this period, for Silas (Silvanus) who does not appear as an associate of Paul at any later stage, is again included in the salutation. Moreover the conditions at Thessalonica reflected in the first letter are the conditions reflected in the second, cp. 1 Thessalonians 3:3, 4 with 2 Thessalonians 1:3–7, and this is true also of the circumstances of the writer, cp. 1 Thessalonians 2:15, 16; with 2 Thessalonians 3:2, and with Acts 18:6.

How the first letter reached its destination is not related, neither is any hint given of the length of time that elapsed before the reply reached the apostle, nor can we learn whether that reply was oral or written. Meantime evangelistic work in Corinth and the neighborhood had been vigorously prosecuted, and churches had been formed as a result, cp. 1:4 with Romans 16:1 and 2 Corinthians 1:1. When the reply arrived, Paul learned that the faith of the converts had increased, and their brotherly love also. They were still distressed by persecutions, which, indeed, had grown rather than diminished in severity, but their endurance had not failed. By these tokens of spiritual progress the missionaries were cheered and encouraged. But the apostle learned at the same time that certain expressions in his letter had either been misunderstood or willfully wrested by his readers, as indeed was the case elsewhere and in later days with others of this writings, 2 Peter 3:16. Moreover, a letter, or letters, not written by him, had been circulated in his name, 2:2. It became necessary, therefore, to write again without delay, and, by supplementing what he had already written, to correct the erroneous notions about the coming of the Lord which some had adopted with consequences certain to be disastrous to the church and derogatory to the Name of the Lord. On the one hand the excitement of a false hope had to be allayed, on the other the true hope must be encouraged for its sanctifying power.

Thus the main purpose of this second letter was to say that the day of the Lord was not then present, as their persistent afflictions and the misunderstanding of the words of the first letter had led the less stable, and the ill-regulated in mind, to conclude. Before that day comes certain things must take place, and certain effects be produced, 2:3; the germ of these indeed, was already present, and silently working in the world, v. 7.

There was another feature at Thessalonica concerning which further instruction was necessary. The "disorderly," who were to be "admonished" at an earlier stage, 1 Thessalonians 5:14, must now be dealt with in a more drastic way, 3:6–12. And, generally, all of the longer letter that is repeated in the shorter, is amplified and expressed in more emphatic language: cp., 1 Thessalonians 1:2, 3 with 2 Thessalonians 1:3; 1 Thessalonians 1:4 with 2 Thessalonians 2:13; 1 Thessalonians 2:6 with 2 Thessalonians 3:8; 1 Thessalonians 2:12 with 2 Thessalonians 1:5; 1 Thessalonians 5:25 with 2 Thessalonians 3:1; 1 Thessalonians 5:27 with 2 Thessalonians 3:17.

In the second epistle reminiscences of labor in the gospel at Thessalonica are few, 1:10; 2:5, 14, 15; 3:7, 10. That there is no mention of the desire, so fervently expressed in the first Epistle, 2:17–20; 3:11, to revisit the scene of his labors, is probably a result of the vision the Lord had vouchsafed to him in the interval, Acts 18:9, 10.

Analysis

Introduction (1:1, 2)

A. *Personal*

    (a) Thanksgiving for their faith, love, and patience (1:3, 4).
    (b) The end of persecution for the saints (1:5–7).
    (c) The end of persecution for the world (1:8–10).
    (d) Prayer for their individual well-being (1:11, 12).

B. *Doctrinal*

    (a) Concerning the Parousia; the Apostasy; the Lawless One; the Day of the
    Lord; the Judgment (2:1–12).

C. *Personal*

    (a) Confirmatory of their election and calling (2:13–15).
    (b) Prayer for their testimony—service (2:16, 17).
    (c) The writer—his desire (3:1, 2).
    (d) The readers—his confidence (3:3, 4).
    (e) Prayer for their spiritual progress—experience (3:5).

D. *Hortatory*

    (a) Concerning discipline (3:6–15).
    (b) Prayer for their collective well-being (3:16).
    (c) Conclusion (3:17).

Authenticity of the Epistles

a. *Internal Evidence*

The authenticity of these letters is very well attested. The intensely personal elements which characterize the first letter and which would be quite impossible to imitate, are prominent in the second. The apostle's circumstances, as they are to be learned from Acts 18:1–11, are again reflected, as are those of the converts at Thessalonica. A forger writing at a later date could not have succeeded in excluding from his letter some slight but discernible reference to the altered circumstances of his own time. Moreover, had a forger been at work he would certainly have avoided the language of the first letter which leaves it an open question whether Paul would or would not be alive and on the earth at the coming of the Lord, for no forgery could have been attempted until after Paul had fallen asleep.

As the years passed men began to ask "where is the promise of His Parousia?" so that it became necessary for the surviving apostles, John, in his Gospel, and Peter, in his second epistle, to stimulate the hope that threatened to become dormant among the saints, whereas these epistles were written at a much earlier period, when it was still necessary to curb a too eager anticipation of the fulfillment of the promise "I come again."

b. *External Evidence*

Approaching the subject from a different standpoint, it does not appear that the authenticity of the Thessalonian Epistles was questioned in ancient times. Eusebius, *circa* A.D. 350, classifying the books of the New Testament, includes them both among those universally received, though he has another list for those of which the authenticity had been questioned by some.

The earliest list of books of the New Testament that has been preserved is that of Marcion, *circa* A.D. 140, and though it is incomplete these Epistles find a place in it, as they do also in what is known as the "Muratorian Fragment," which dates, probably, from the end of the second century.

Polycarp, who was burnt *circa* A.D. 180, says "He (Antichrist) shall come . . . not as a righteous king, neither in lawful submission to God, but in impiety, unrighteousness, and lawlessness. . . . He shall put down idols so as to persuade men that he is God. He shall exalt himself as the only object of worship. . . . Concerning him the apostle in his second epistle to the Thessalonians thus speaks. . . ." (*Against Heresies*, v. 25:1).

Origen, *circa* A.D. 185–264, speaks of Paul's instruction concerning "this being who is called Antichrist," and proceeds to quote 2 Thessalonians 2:1–12.

Clement of Alexandria, and Tertullian, writing about the same time as Origen, accept both epistles as authentic writings of Paul. The earliest translations of the New Testament into Syriac and Latin also contain them. Thus the Pauline authorship of both is fully established.

The Gospel Preached at Thessalonica

A letter, if of any length, usually contains a number of allusions to matters known equally to the writer and to those whom he addresses. The epistles to the Thessalonians present this characteristic; Paul had preached the gospel to them, and they had responded heartily to his message; thereupon he had done among them the work of pastor and teacher. Circumstances shortly separated them, but the attachment that had sprung up between them was strong, and as he wrote he was filled with recollections of the gracious work of God in which they had shared. These overflowed through his pen, so that it is possible not only to gather from his letters much of the circumstances of sorrow and of joy attendant on his labors in their city, but also to learn from them something of what he had taught there. And as these epistles are among the very earliest Christian documents, and certainly older than any of the four Gospels, their testimony to primitive Christianity is of great interest and importance.

We turn to them, then, to learn what Paul and his friends preached at Thessalonica eighteen hundred and sixty years ago. But these letters are brief, and contain no hint that Paul intended to restate everything believed and practiced in the church to which they were written. We must not be surprised, therefore, that many important matters are not referred to at all. It would be unreasonable to conclude, for example, that the Christians at Thessalonica had not been taught the necessity for a new birth, or the doctrine of justification by faith, or of the priesthood of all believers, and the privilege of access and worship, or that they had not been baptized, or that they did not observe the Lord's Supper, because none of these things are referred to in these letters.

We inquire, then, what we may learn from the epistles, concerning (1) God; (2) the Lord Jesus; (3) the Holy Spirit; (4) the Gospel; (5) the Way of Salvation; (6) Believers; (7) the World; (8) Satan.

1. Concerning God

a. His unity, 1:9; *b.* His Fatherhood, 1:1; 3:13; 2 Thessalonians 2:16; *c.* He is God of peace, 5:23; *d.* He reigns over a glorious kingdom, 2:12; 2 Thessalonians 1:5; *e.* He makes choice among men, 1:4; 2 Thessalonians 2:13; *f.* He loves those who receive His gospel, 1:4; *g.* He knows the hearts of men, 2:4, 5; *h.* He communicates His mind through men to men, 5:20; *i.* He is righteous, 2 Thessalonians 1:5, 6; *j.* He will visit the world in judgment, 1:10; 5:9; 2 Thessalonians 2:12.

2. Concerning the Lord Jesus

a. He is the Son of God, 1:10; *b.* and equal with God, 1:1; 3:11; 2 Thessalonians 1:12; *c.* He is Lord, 1:1; 4:1, 2 Thessalonians 3:6; *d.* and Savior, 1:10; 5:9, 10; *e.* He is the Christ, the Messiah of the Jews, 2:14, 15; *f.* He died (and His death testified to the reality of His manhood), 1..); 4:14; *g.* a violent death, 2:15; *h.* in the interests of those who believe on Him, 5:10; *i.* He was raised from among the dead and is now in Heaven, 1:10; 4:14; *j.* He is coming again, 2:19; 5:23; *k.* to deliver believers from impending calamity, 1:10, by taking them to be with Himself 4:17; 2 Thessalonians 2:1; *l.* and thereafter, in circumstances of great majesty, to execute the judgments of God, 2 Thessalonians 1:7, 8; 2:8.

3. Concerning the Holy Spirit

a. He is the agent in carrying out the elective purposes of God, 2 Thessalonians 2:13; *b.* He gives power to the preacher of the gospel, 1:5; *c.* He is given by God to all believers, 4:8; *d*. He produces joy in the hearts of afflicted believers, 1:6.

4. *Concerning the Gospel*

a. It has its origin in God, 2:2, 8, 9; *b*. it is preached with His authority, 2:4; *c*. it has an energy peculiar to itself which differentiates it from every human religion, 2:13; *d*. its subject is Christ, 3:2.

5. *Concerning the Way of Salvation*

a. It is made known through the preaching of the gospel, 2:16; *b*. it is found by those who love the truth, 2 Thessalonians 2:10; *c*. it is available only to those who believe, 2:13; *d*. its essential is that Jesus died and rose again, 4:14.

6. *Concerning Believers*

a. They are chosen of God, 1:4; 2 Thessalonians 2:13; *b*. to walk worthily of Him, 2:12; *c*. they shall not all die, 4:15; *d*. and those who die shall be raised from among the dead, 4:16; *e*. the rest who are alive when the Lord Jesus comes, shall together with the raised dead be caught up to meet the Lord in the air, 4:17; 2 Thessalonians 2:1; *f*. thus all believers shall be delivered from the wrath of God that is to come upon the earth, 1:10; 5:9; *g*. but shall themselves undergo a judgment in what is called the Parousia of the Lord Jesus, 2:19, 20; 3:13; 5:23; *h*. when He comes to execute judgment, believers, since their salvation is due entirely to Him, will add in great and peculiar measure to His praise, 2 Thessalonians 1:10.

7. *Concerning the World*

a. In spite of a false sense of security, 5:3; *b*. the world is to suffer, suddenly and inevitably, the judgments of God, 1:10; 5:3; 2 Thessalonians 1:9; *c*. Jew and Gentile alike, 2:16; *d*. the Jews because of the characteristic sins of the mind, 2:14, 15; *e*. for, notwithstanding their knowledge of God, they believe not the truth, 2 Thessalonians 2:12; *f*. and obey not the gospel, 1:8; *g*. the Gentiles who know not God, 2 Thessalonians 1:8, because of the characteristic sins of the flesh 4:5; *h*. and because they had pleasure in unrighteousness, 2 Thessalonians 2:12; *i*. hence this judgment is an act of justice (vengeance), 2 Thessalonians 1:8; *j*. and the consequent suffering just (punishment, lit., justice), 2 Thessalonians 1:9; *k*. its character ruin, conscious loss of blessedness, banishment from the presence of the Lord, His glory and His power, 2 Thessalonians 1:9; *l*. and its duration endless, 2 Thessalonians 1:9.

8. *Concerning Satan*

A person with great and mysterious powers, always used with malignant purpose; *a*. he hinders the missionaries, 2:18; *b*. and tempts the converts to evil ways, 3:5; *c.* in the future his power will be freed from some present restraint, the character of which is not explicitly stated, 2 Thessalonians 2:6, 7; *d.* consequently a mysterious figure is foretold, called "the Man of Sin," "the Son of Perdition," "the Lawless One," 2 Thessalonians 2:3, 8; *e.* who will be the ultimate and concrete representative of a lawless spirit even then at work, 2 Thessalonians 2:8; *f.* and who will appear in the energy of Satan himself, 2 Thessalonians 2:9; *g.* this Lawless One shall be slain and his power brought to nought when the Lord Jesus assumes His own place of supremacy, 2 Thessalonians 2:8.

1 Thessalonians

1 THESSALONIANS

▪ CHAPTER ONE ▪

Verses 1–10

1:1 Paul and Silvanus, and Timothy—see Introduction. Paul mentions Timothy in all his epistles, save Galatians, Ephesians, Titus, Silvanus in 1 and 2 Thessalonians only.

unto the church—Gk *ekklesia,* cp. Eng. "ecclesiastical," from *ek,* out of, *kaleō,* I call; lit., "a company called out." In his five earlier epistles, viz.— Thessalonians, Galatians, Corinthians, Paul addresses the assembly, in the four later, viz.—Romans, Philippians, Ephesians, Colossians, the saints. *Ekklesia is* used:

a, of Israel, Deuteronomy 18:16, Nehemiah 13:1, LXX, Acts 7:38:

b, of a lawfully convened assembly of citizens in a Greek city, Acts 19:39:

c, of a riotous mob, Acts 19:32, 41:

d, of an assembly consisting exclusively of professed believers, 1 Corinthians 1:2, cp. Acts 5:11, 14:

e, of the whole company of the redeemed of this age, described as "the church which is His [Christ's] body," Matthew 16:18; Ephesians 1:32, 33.

Acts 9:31 is an isolated instance of its use in the singular to include all believers in a country—Palestine.

In most, if not all, of the cities in which Paul and his companions had preached, men had turned to God. In his brief resumé of these missionary labors Luke sometimes mentions the results in general terms, Acts 14:21, sometimes he describes particular cases, 16:1, 14, 15, 27–34, but in no case does he describe in detail the character of these labors or their results. Where they are mentioned at all the converts are sometimes viewed in their relation to the Lord and called "disciples," Acts 14:20, 21; sometimes in relation to one another and called "brethren," 15:36; sometimes in their corporate capacity and called "the church," 20:17. The organization of the converts to which the last words point, seems to have received attention, however brief the stay of the missionaries, as at Philippi, where the time spent is described as "certain days," 16:12, yet shortly after they had left that city the converts, as a church, expressed their fellowship with Paul in his labors in the gospel by sending him a gift, see Philippians 4:15. At Thessalonica also their stay was limited to a brief period and was unexpectedly cut short, but immediately after leaving them Paul addressed a letter "to the church of the Thessalonians."

It is not stated that Peter formed a church in the house of Cornelius, Acts 10:44–48, but Paul "when he landed at Caesarea" a few years later "went up and saluted the church," 18:22.* The Apostolic Council addressed its decrees to "the brethren," 15:23, and to the "brethren" Paul delivered them, with the result that the "churches" were strengthened and increased, 16:4, 5. In the opening of his epistle to the Philippians Paul addressed "all the saints which are at Philippi, with the bishops and deacons," 1:1, but toward the close wrote "no church—but ye only," 4:15. The epistle to the Colossians is addressed to "the saints and faithful brethren," 1:1, but in the brief letter that accompanied it "the church" is saluted, Philemon 2, cp. Colossians 4:15, 16. The epistle to the Ephesians opens in the same manner, yet in Colossians 4:16 we read of "the church of the Laodiceans." It is highly probable that the letter sent to the Laodiceans is that preserved as "Ephesians." On these grounds it may be safely assumed that wherever there were believers there was a church.

Below is appended a list of the places mentioned in the New Testament in which churches existed in apostolic days. Not all of these were established when the epistles to the Thessalonians were written, but no attempt is here made to determine the order of their foundation. The church at Rome, e.g., may or may not have been in existence at that time, A.D. 51, but it was certainly flourishing five years afterwards, A.D. 56, when Paul addressed an epistle to the saints there.

The list is not exhaustive. Paul had spent some years in Syria and Cilicia, in which province Tarsus is situated, see Acts 9:30; 11:25; Galatians 1:21. Of his labors during this period Luke says nothing, but later it is recorded that "he went through Syria and Cilicia confirming the churches," Acts 15:41, churches that were apparently the fruit of labors in which in earlier years he had at least borne a part. In Acts 9:31, R.V. has "church," referring to the church which had been scattered from Jerusalem, see Acts 8:1. The churches "throughout all Judaea, Galilee and Samaria," Acts 9:31, are not particularized, nor are those of Phoenicia, Acts 15:3; nor those in Phrygia, 16:6; 18:23; nor those in Galatia, Galatians 1:2; nor those "in the whole of Achaia," i.e., Greece, 2 Corinthians 1:1, language which seems to contemplate more than the three places specified, viz., Corinth, Cenchrea and Athens. Cp. also Acts 13:49; 16:4–5, Romans 16:4; 1 Corinthians 4:17; 14:33.

Jerusalem, Acts 5:11; Damascus, Acts 9:19; Lydda and Sharon, Acts 9:32–35; Joppa, Acts 9:43; Cyrene (Africa), (?) Acts 11:20; Antioch (Syria), Acts 11:26; Cyprus (Paphos and Salamis), Acts 13:4–12; Lystra, Derbe, Iconium, "the cities of Lycaonia," Antioch (Pisidia), Acts 14:6, 20–23 (these four, with

---

*This may refer to Jerusalem, but not necessarily so.

others, were probably "the churches of Galatia" to which Paul addressed an epistle).

"The churches of Macedonia," 2 Corinthians 8:1, of which there is reference, direct or indirect, to those at Philippi, Thessalonica, Berea, Acts 16:12—17:15, and Nicopolis, Titus 3:12; Athens, Acts 17:3; Corinth, Acts 18:8, and Cenchrea, Romans 16:1; Troas, Acts 20:6-11; Tyre, Acts 21:4; Ptolemais, Acts 21:7; Caesarea, Acts 21:8, 16; Rome, Acts 28:15; Puteoli, Acts 28:13, 14; Colossae, Philemon 2; Hierapolis, Colossians 4:13; Crete, Titus 1:5. "The churches of Asia," 1 Corinthians 16:19, cp. Revelation 1:4, of which Ephesus, Smyrna, Pergamum, Thyatira, Sardis, Philadelphia, and Laodicea, are particularized in Revelation 1:11;* Pontus, Cappadocia, Bithynia, 1 Peter 1:1; Babylon, 1 Peter 5:13. See further at 2:14.

of the Thessalonians—the local description, cp. Colossians 4:16, the only New Testament parallel.

in—this preposition is frequently used by Paul to express intimacy of union, and is not readily explained by any simpler term. Here it introduces the spiritual description and may be paraphrased thus: "in relationship with God, as Father, and with Jesus Christ as Lord"; cp. Colossians 3:3. The first part marks the assembly at Thessalonica as non-heathen, the second as non-Jewish. The single preposition "in," governing both phrases, suggests the unity of the Son with the Father, cp. Galatians 1:1, 1 Timothy 6:13.

God the Father—the everlasting power and divinity of God are manifest in creation, Romans 1:20; His Fatherhood is the subject of revelation, Matthew 11:27, John 17:25; 20:17; it is not universal, Matthew 13:38, John 8:23, 41-44; but is asserted only in relation to those who have been born anew, 1:12, 13, Galatians 3:26, 1 John 3:1; 5:1. Being "our Father" God looks to His children for honor, Malachi 1:6, and confidence, Matthew 6:25, 34, while He deals with them in pity, Psalm 103:13, 14, and in love, John 16:27.

and the Lord—*kurios,* variously translated in the New Testament "lord," "Lord," "master," "Master," "owner," "Sir," a title of wide significance, occurring in each book of the New Testament save Titus and the epistles of John. It is used:

a, of an owner, as in Luke 19:33, cp. Matthew 20:8, Acts 16:16, Galatians 4:1; or of one who has the disposal of anything, as the Sabbath, Matthew 12:8:

b, of a master, i.e., one to whom service is due on any ground, Matthew 6:24; 24:50, Ephesians 6:5:

---

*"Asia," is not the continent, but the Roman Province of that name situated in the West of what is now Asia Minor. The name was subsequently extended to denote the continent.

c, of an emperor or king, Acts 25:26, Revelation 17:14:

d, of idols, ironically, 1 Corinthians 8:5, cp. Isaiah 26:13:

e, as a title of respect addressed to a father, Matthew 21:30, a husband, 1 Peter 3:6, a master, Matthew 13:27, Luke 13:8, a ruler, Matthew 27:63, an angel, Acts 10:4, Revelation 7:14:

f, as a title of courtesy addressed to a stranger, John 12:21; 20:15, Acts 16:30; from the outset of His ministry this was a common form of address to the Lord Jesus, alike by the people, Matthew 8:2, John 4:11, and by His disciples, Matthew 8:25, Luke 5:8, John 6:68:

g, kurios is LXX and New Testament representative of Hebrew Jehovah ("LORD" in Eng. versions), see Matthew 4:7, James 5:11, e.g.; of *adon,* Lord, Matthew 22:44, and of *Adonay,* Lord, 1:22; it also occurs for *Elohim,* God, 1 Peter 1:25.

Thus the usage of the word in the New Testament follows two main lines: one, *a—f,* customary and general, the other, *g,* peculiar to the Jews, and drawn from the Greek translation of the Old Testament.

Christ Himself assumed the title, Matthew 7:21, 22; 9:38; 22:41–45; Mark 5:19 (cp. Ps. 66:16, the parallel passage, Luke 8:39, has "God"), Luke 19:31; John 13:13, apparently intending it in the higher senses of its current use, and at the same time suggesting its Old Testament associations.

His purpose did not become clear to the disciples until after His resurrection, and the revelation of His deity consequent thereon. Thomas, when he realized the significance of the presence of a mortal wound in the body of a living man, immediately joined with it the absolute title of deity, saying, "My Lord and my God," John 20:28. Thereafter, except in Acts 10:4 and Revelation 7:14, there is no record that *kurios* was ever again used by believers in addressing any save God and the Lord Jesus, cp. Acts 2:47 with 4:29, 30.

How soon and how completely the lower meaning had been superseded is seen in Peter's declaration in his first sermon after the resurrection, "God hath made Him—Lord," Acts 2:36, and that in the house of Cornelius, "He is Lord of all," 10:36; cp. Deuteronomy 10:14; Matthew 11:25; Acts 17:24.

In his writings the implications of his early teaching are confirmed and developed. Thus Psalm 34:8, "O taste and see that Jehovah is good," is applied to the Lord Jesus, 1 Peter 2:3, and "Jehovah of Hosts, Him shall ye sanctify," Isaiah 8:13, becomes "sanctify in your hearts Christ as Lord," 3:15.

So also James, who uses *kurios* alike of God, 1:7, cp. v. 5; 3:9; 4:15; 5:4; 10:11, and of the Lord Jesus, 1:1 (where the possibility that *kai* is intended epexegetically, i.e. = even, cp. 1 Thessalonians 3:11, should not be overlooked), 2:1 (lit., "our Lord Jesus Christ of glory," cp. Pss. 24:7; 29:3; Acts 7:2; 1 Cor. 2:8), 5:7, 8, while the language of 4:10; 5:15, is equally applicable to either.

Jude, v. 4, speaks of "our only—Lord, Jesus Christ," and immediately, v. 5, uses "Lord" of God (see the remarkable marg. here), as he does later, vv. 9, 14.

Paul ordinarily uses *kurios* of the Lord Jesus, 1 Corinthians 1:3, e.g., but also on occasion, of God, in quotations from the Old Testament, 1 Corinthians 3:20, e.g., and in his own words, 1 Corinthians 3:5, cp. v. 10. It is equally appropriate to either in 4:6, 1 Corinthians 7:25, 2 Corinthians 8:21, 2 Thessalonians 3:16, and if 1 Corinthians 11:32 is to be interpreted by 10:21, 22, the Lord Jesus is intended, but if by Hebrews 12:5-9, then *kurios* here also = God. 1 Timothy 6:15-16, is probably to be understood of the Lord Jesus, cp. Revelation 17:14.

Though John does not use "Lord" in his epistles, and though, like the other evangelists, he ordinarily uses the personal name in his narrative, yet he occasionally speaks of Him as "the Lord," John 4:1; 6:23; 11:2; 20:20; 21:12.

The full significance of this association of Jesus with God under the one appellation, "Lord," is seen when it is remembered that these men belonged to the only monotheistic race in the world. To associate with the Creator one known to be a creature, however exalted, though possible to pagan philosophers, was quite impossible to a Jew.

It is not recorded that in the days of His flesh any of His disciples either addressed the Lord, or spoke of Him, by His personal name. Where Paul has occasion to refer to the facts of the gospel history he speaks of what the Lord Jesus said, Acts 20:35, and did, 1 Corinthians 11:23, and suffered, chh. 2:15; 5:9, 10. It is our Lord Jesus Who is coming, 2:19, etc. In prayer also the title is given, 3:11, Ephesians 1:3; the sinner is invited to believe on the Lord Jesus, Acts 16:31; 20:21, and the saint to look to the Lord Jesus for deliverance, Romans 7:24, 25, and in the few exceptional cases in which the personal name stands alone a reason is always discernible in the immediate context.

The title "lord" as given to the Savior, in its full significance rests upon the resurrection, Acts 2:36; Romans 10:9; 14:9, and is realized only in the Holy Spirit, 1 Corinthians 12:3.

While He is still rejected alike by Jew and Gentile, angels, Matthew 28:6, and saints, Romans 10:9, acknowledge Him in it, but in the day of His manifested glory every tongue in the universe shall confess "that Jesus Christ is Lord, to the glory of God the Father," Philippians 2:11.

Those who own Him as Lord now are His servants, 1 Corinthians 7:22; Ephesians 6:6, and to them He looks for obedience, Luke 6:46, cp. Romans 6:16, and on that condition graciously admits them to His friendship, John 15:14, 15.

Other titles by which the Lord Jesus was known, or by which He was addressed, in the days of His flesh and which are recorded in the gospels are:

- *rabbi*, Aramaic, = teacher, Matthew 26:25; Mark 9:5; John 4:31, et al.;
- *rabboni*, a modification of *rabbi*, Mark 10:51; John 20:16;||
- *didaskalos*, the Gk. equivalent of *rabbi*, Luke 9:38; John 1:38, et al.;
- *epistates*, lit, "one who stands over," i.e., a superior, Luke 5:5; 8:24, 45; 9:33, 49; 17:13;||
- *kathegetes*, a guide, occurs Matthew 23:10.||

In 2 Peter 2:1; Jude 4, cp. 2 Timothy 2:21, *despotes* = one who has absolute dominion, is used of the Lord Jesus; elsewhere it is a title of God, Luke 2:29; Acts 4:24, cp. Revelation 6:10.

Jesus—the English form of the Greek *Iēsous*, which is, in turn, a transliteration of the Hebrew *Joshua* = "Jehovah is salvation," i.e., "the Savior," a common name among the Jews, see Exodus 17:9; Luke 3:29; Colossians 4:11, et al. It was given to the Son of God in Incarnation as His personal name in obedience to the command of an angel to Joseph, the husband of His mother, Mary, shortly before He was born, Matthew 1:21. By it He is spoken of throughout the Gospel narratives generally, but not without exception, as in Mark 16:19, 20; Luke 7:13, and a dozen other places in that Gospel, and a few in John; see note on "Lord," above. "Jesus Christ" occurs only in Matthew 1:1, 18; 16:21, marg.; Mark 1:1; John 1:17.

In Acts the name "Jesus" is found alone in Luke's narrative only in ch. 1 and in 7:55: later it occurs in the utterances of His adversaries, human or demoniacal; 19:13, 15 and 25:19, are typical cases. It is also found where His claim to be Messiah is asserted, as in 8:35, and once in the words of an angel, 1:11, cp. Revelation 14:12; 19:10. "Lord Jesus" is the normal usage, as in Acts 8:16; 19:5, 17; see also the reports of the words of Stephen, 7:59, of Ananias, 9:17, and of Paul, 16:31; though both Peter, 10:36, and Paul, 16:18, also used "Jesus Christ."

In the epistles of James, Peter, John and Jude, the personal name is not once found alone, and in Revelation only in 14:12; 17:6; 19:10; 20:4.

In the epistles of Paul "Jesus" appears alone just thirteen times, and in the Hebrews eight times; in the latter the title "Lord," is added once only, at 13:20.

Only twice is it on record that the Lord spoke of Himself by this Name, on both occasions from heaven, Acts 22:8, Revelation 22:16; in each case the response of the person addressed is "Lord."

While He was on earth not one of His disciples is recorded as having addressed Him, or spoken of Him, by His personal name. However the usage in the Gospel narratives is to be accounted for, it is plain that the custom of confessing with the mouth Jesus as "Lord," Romans 10:9, was universal among believers in apostolic days; it is, therefore, the pattern for Christians unto the end of the age.

Christ:—*Christos* = Heb. Messiah, John 1:41. "Messiah" = one who has been ceremonially anointed, occurs in the Old Testament over thirty times, and is used sometimes in a literal, sometimes in a figurative sense, of:

a. the priests, Leviticus 4:3:

b. Abraham, Isaac, Jacob, and the patriarchs, 1 Chronicles 16:22:

c. the same, but enlarged to include the Nation in the wilderness, Habakkuk 3:13:

d. the kings of Israel, 1 Samuel 2:10; 16:6; Psalm 89:38, i.e., Saul, 1 Samuel 12:3; David, 2 Samuel 19:21, cp. Psalm 89:20; Solomon, 2 Chronicles 6:42, cp. 1 Kings 1:39; Zedekiah, Lamentations 4:20, cp. 2 Kings 25:5, 6:

e. Cyrus, King of Persia, Isaiah 45:1, cp. Ezra 1:1:

f. the ideal Priest-King, in Whom the hope of Israel was bound up and Who is to reign over the Nation and over the earth, Psalm 2:2, cp. 45:7; Daniel 9:25, 26, cp. Zechariah 6:12, 13.

Christos is derived from *chriō* = to smear with oil, which occurs five times in the New Testament, always figuratively:

a. of the Lord Jesus, Luke 4:18; Acts 4:27; 10:38; Hebrews 1:9:

b. of the saints, 2 Corinthians 1:21, cp. 1 John 2:20, 27, where the Anointing (Gk. *chrisma*) is the Holy Spirit.

Since He Who anoints is God, Isaiah 45:1; 61:1; Acts 10:38; Hebrews 1:9, the Messiah is called:

a. the Lord's Christ, Luke 2:26:

b. the Christ of God, Luke 9:20:

c. His, i.e., God's, Christ, Acts 3:18; 4:26, Revelation 11:15; 12:10.

In the gospels "Christ" is used:

a. of the expected Messiah: by Herod, Matthew 2:4, John the Baptist, John 3:28, the High Priest, Mark 14:61, the Lord Jesus, Matthew 22:42; 24:5; Mark 13:21; Luke 24:26, the people generally, Luke 3:15; John 7:31:

b. of the newly-born Child, by the angel announcing Him to be the promised Messiah, Luke 2:11:

c. of the Lord Jesus:

by Himself claiming to be the promised Messiah, Matthew 16:20; 23:10; Mark 9:41; John 17:3; by His disciples, in acknowledgment of His claim, Matthew 16:1, 6; John 7:41; 11:27; by those in perplexity about His claim, John 4:29; 7:26, 27; 10:24; by others in direct and indirect denial of His claim, Matthew 26:63, 68; 27:17; Mark 15:32; Luke 23:35; John 9:22.

In Acts it is recorded that Peter, 2:31; 3:18, Philip, 8:5, and Paul, 17:3; 26:23, expounded the Old Testament teaching about the Messiah, as a preliminary to asserting that Jesus is the Person intended, cp. 2:36; 3:20; 8:12; 17:3; for that Jesus is the Messiah promised by God and expected by His people, was the gospel to the Jew, see further 5:42; 9:20–22; 18:5, 28, and John 20:31, whereas in evangelizing the Gentiles this testimony had no place, cp. Acts 14:8–18; 17:22–31.

Paul uses the phrases "in Christ Jesus," 2:14, and, but not so frequently, "in Christ," 4:16, never "in Jesus," see note at 4:14, nor "in Jesus Christ," to express the intimacy of the mystical union between the believer and the Lord in His death and resurrection. There are no simpler words available to explain the term, which is pregnant with meaning for those who have the mind of Christ. "In Christ" occurs also in 1 Peter 3:16; 5:14, in the same sense, and not elsewhere in the New Testament, but cp. 1 John 5:20.

In the epistles of James, Peter, John, and Jude, men who had companied with the Lord in the days of His flesh, "Jesus Christ" is the invariable order of the name and title, for this was the order of their experience; as "Jesus" they knew Him first, that He was Messiah they learnt finally in His resurrection. But Paul came to know Him first in the glory of heaven, Acts 9:1–6, and his experience being thus the reverse of theirs, the reverse order, "Christ Jesus," is of frequent occurrence in his letters, but, with the exception of Acts 24:24, does not occur elsewhere in the New Testament.

In Paul's letters the order is always in harmony with the context. Thus "Christ Jesus" describes the Exalted One who emptied Himself, Philippians 2:5, and testifies to His preexistence; "Jesus Christ" describes the despised and rejected One Who was afterwards glorified, Philippians 2:11, and testifies to His resurrection. "Christ Jesus" suggests His grace, "Jesus Christ" suggests His glory.

Grace to you and peace.—the latter was the usual greeting among the Jews, cp. Matthew 10:12, 13 with Luke 10:5, as *chairete* = "rejoice!" was among Greeks, cp. Acts 15:23, James 1:1, see marg. and 2 John 10:11. This latter, however, the apostle Paul does not use, but for it substitutes *charis* = grace.

Taken by the Holy Spirit into the service of God the words were greatly enlarged and deepened in meaning. Grace is God's favor toward man, free and unmerited; peace is the result to all who receive that favor in Christ. Thus these two words sum up the gospel, its cause and its effect, cp. Romans 3:24 with 5:1. They are used by Paul in each of his epistles; writing to Timothy he adds "mercy," but not to Titus or Philemon, nor to any assembly: but cp. Galatians 6:16. See further at 5:28, 2 Thessalonians 3:18.

Grace is associated with God, 2 Corinthians 1:12, and with Christ, Galatians 1:6, and with both, Romans 5:15; see further at 2 Thessalonians 1:12. For "peace" see notes at 5:3, 23, and 2 Thessalonians 3:16.

1:2 We give thanks to God—making mention *of you* **in** (*epi* = on) **our prayers;**—the missionaries would feel their need of united prayer in their work at Corinth, whence the apostle wrote; on every such occasion they thanked God for the fruit of the gospel at Thessalonica. Thanksgiving, Romans 1:8;

1 Corinthians 1:4; Philippians 1:3; Colossians 1:3; 2 Thessalonians 1:3; 2 Timothy 1:3; Philemon 4, or blessing, 2 Corinthians 1:3; or both, Ephesians 1:3, 16, or some ascription, Galatians 1:5, stands at the beginning of each of the epistles, save 1 Timothy and Titus. The ground of praise varies. Here, and in 2 Thessalonians, Romans, Ephesians, Colossians, it is personal, "for you," and so, practically, Philemon; in Philippians, for their fellowship, clearly an advance; in 1 Corinthians, for God's gifts to them; in 2 Corinthians, for His mercy to himself, in 2 Timothy, that He is able to remember his younger colleague. But in Galatians the ground of praise is the death of Christ.

always,—*pantote* = on all occasions, see at 2:16, and cp. Luke 18:1.

for you all,—Christians differ in attainment, but there is always something of Christ in each, and hence always something for which to thank God, since Christ is the oil that feeds the lamp of praise.

1:3 remembering—before our God and Father,—the new revelation of God (already revealed as Creator, Eccl. 12:1; Preserver, Ps. 104:27; Savior, Is. 45:15; Judge, Eccl. 12:14) as Father is always present in Paul's mind when he prays, ch. 3:11; 2 Thessalonians 2:16, Ephesians 1:17; 3:14; Colossians 1:3; cp. 1 Peter 1:17, the Lord's direction to His disciples, Matthew 6:9, and His own example, John 17:1.

without ceasing—*adialeiptōs,* see also chh. 2:13; 5:17, and Romans 1:9. The corresponding adjective occurs in Romans 9:2, and 2 Timothy 1:3.|| An old papyrus letter, lately discovered in Egypt but written as far back as the apostles' days, speaks of an "incessant cough." Thus not uninterrupted prayer, but constantly recurring prayer is the thought here.

your work of faith—described, v. 9, as a turning to God, Who is unseen, from idols, which are palpable. This association of work and faith, cp. John 6:29, is significant in view of Paul's rejection of the former, which was characteristic of the dispensation of law, and his proclamation of the latter, which, as the condition of salvation, is characteristic of the dispensation of grace. Faith is the response of the soul to the life-giving word of God, Romans 10:8–17; the work of faith is the initial act of belief on the part of one who hears the voice of the Son of God, John 5:24. Faith is contrasted with sight, 2 Corinthians 5:7, cp. 4:18. See also at 2 Thessalonians 1:11.

and labor of love—described, v. 9, as the service of God. Labor, *kopos* = toil resulting in weariness, cp. John 4:6, 38; and see note at 5:12. Work refers to what is done, and may be easy and pleasant; labor refers to the doing of it, the pains taken, the strength spent. Where love is the motive, labor is light.

The supreme expression of love is the Cross, Romans 5:8, where "commendeth" = proves, cp. Galatians 2:18. This is the type to which our love is to be conformed, 1 John 3:16. Love to God is expressed in obedience, John 14:15, 21, 23; 1 John 5:2, 3; 2 John 6; to man in considering the interests of others rather than our own, Philippians 2:4, cp. Romans 15:2. The latter is exhaustively described in 1 Corinthians 13. Love is contrasted with selfishness. See also at 3:12.

and patience of hope in [lit., "of," cp. 2 Thess. 3:5] **our Lord Jesus Christ,**—described, v. 10, as "waiting for His Son from heaven." Patience is more than waiting, cp. Romans 2:7, and Hebrews 12:3, where the corresponding verb is translated "endured." Thus "patience of hope" is that endurance under trial which is the effect of waiting for the coming of the Lord Jesus Christ. That the Thessalonian saints had shown this endurance is seen in v. 6; 2:14; 2 Thessalonians 1:4, where see note; see also at 5:14.

Hope has to do with the unseen, Romans 8:24, and the future, 25. It may be objective, as 1 Timothy 1:1, or subjective, as Romans 15:4. These uses must be distinguished, the latter preponderates in the New Testament. In Romans 5:4 the order is reversed; "patience, through probation, i.e., trial or proving (cp. 2 Cor. 8:2; 9:13) works, i.e., accomplishes, results in, hope." Both are true; hope encourages patience: patience strengthens hope.

Faith, love, hope recur at 5:8, 1 Corinthians 13:13; Colossians 1:4, 5, and, with "patience" instead of "hope," 2 Thessalonians 1:3, 4; 1 Timothy 6:11; Titus 2:2. Hope is contrasted with worldliness.

1:4 knowing,—the reason for the thanksgiving. The word used, _oida,_ intimates that this knowledge came not by revelation, nor by intuition, but from observation; hence the rest of the chapter recounts what led Paul to conclude that these Thessalonians were among the elect of God.

brethren—in the New Testament _adelphos_ is used of:
    a. male children of the same parents, Matthew 1:2; 14:3:
    b. male descendants of the same parents, Acts 7:23, 26; Hebrews 7:5:
    c. male children of the same mother, Matthew 13:55; 1 Corinthians 9:5; Galatians 1:19, where see note:
    d. people of the same nationality, Acts 3:17, 22; Romans 9:3; with "men" (_anēr_ = "male"), prefixed, it is found, in addresses only, Acts 2:29, 37; 7:2, etc.:
    e. any man (= neighbor, Luke 10:29), Matthew 5:22; 7:3:
    f. persons united by common interests, Matthew 5:47:
    g. persons united in a common calling, Revelation 22:9:
    h. mankind, Matthew 25:40; Hebrews 2:17. (Primarily one nation is contemplated, the Jews, but it is true of the rest of the race as of them, that they are

partakers of flesh and blood, whereof the Lord Jesus also partook; cp. Galatians 4:4, "born of a woman," i.e., He was man, and, "born under [the] law," i.e., He was a Jew; 1 Timothy 2:5, "(Himself) man, Christ Jesus"; 2 Timothy 2:8, "of the seed of David"; and see further that part of the genealogy, Luke 3:34–38, which asserts His relation to the human race; cp. John 8:40, and note the recognition of the Gentile element in Matthew 1:5:

i. the disciples, and hence, by implication, of all believers, by the Lord Jesus after His Resurrection, Matthew 28:10; John 20:17, cp. Romans 8:29; Hebrews 2:11:

j. believers, without distinction of sex, Matthew 23:8; Acts 1:15; Romans 1:13; Revelation 19:10, and here; this is the usual description and mode of address in the New Testament, where the word "sisters" is never used of believers save at 1 Timothy 5:2:

k. believers, with *aner* = male, prefixed, and with "or sister" added, 1 Corinthians 7:15; James 2:15, male as distinguished from female, Acts 1:16; 15:7, 13 (but not 6:3).

Philippians 1:14 should probably be read "most of the brethren, being confident in the Lord."

Other New Testament titles of those who obey the gospel are:

- holy brethren, Hebrews 3:1:
- faithful brethren, Colossians 1:2:
- the brotherhood, 1 Peter 2:17; 5:9, marg.:
- the household of the faith, Galatians 6:10:
- friends, 3 John 14, cp. John 15:13–15:
- God's elect, Titus 1:1: the elect, 1 Peter 1:1:
- the called, Romans 8:28:
- the people of God, 1 Peter 2:10:
- the Israel of God, Galatians 6:16:
- saints, Acts 9:32:
- those that call on (the Name of) the Lord, 1 Corinthians 1:2; 2 Timothy 2:22, cp. Romans 10:13:
- disciples, Acts 9:1:
- Christians, Acts 11:26:
- the believers, 1 Timothy 4:12 (see also at 1:7, below) (*hoi pistoi* each case)
- the faithful, Ephesians 1:1
- the sect of the Nazarenes, Acts 24:5, cp. 28:22:
- those of "the Way," "this Way," Acts 9:2; 22:4:
- sojourners, 1 Peter 2:11:
- pilgrims, 1 Peter 2:11.

beloved of God,—that God loves all men unconditionally, see John 3:16; that He loves in a special sense those who fulfill certain conditions, see 14:21, 23; 16:27. The measure of the latter is the Father's love to the Son, 17:23, cp. v. 26. Here the special sense is intended.

your election,—more fully in Ephesians 1:4, "He chose [i.e., elected] us in Him before the foundation of the world." For the meaning of the Gk. word see Luke 10:42; 14:7; Acts 6:5; 15:22, 25. This election must be understood not of the church collectively, but of the brethren individually, cp. Romans 16:13.

1:5 how that—*hoti* = because, as marg., which is to be preferred; connecting what follows with the beginning of v. 2, "we give thanks—because." The apostle uses the same form of words to describe the ground of his thanksgiving for the Thessalonian believers in three other places in these epistles, i.e., 2:13, "because . . . ye accepted . . . the word of God"; 2 Thessalonians 1:3, "because your faith groweth exceedingly"; 2:13, "because God chose you."

our gospel—the gospel they preached, as in 2 Thessalonians 2:14; in 2:2, 8, 9, "the gospel of God," i.e., the gospel which has its origin in and its authority from God; in 3:2 "the gospel of Christ," i.e., the gospel about Christ; cp. 2 Thessalonians 1:8. In each case the same gospel, the outlines of which may be gathered from these epistles, is intended.

came not unto you—*ginomai,* lit., "became," John 1:14; the same word is translated "shewed ourselves" below. See Acts 17:1-9.

in word only,—not merely as a statement of fact, though the gospel is always and essentially that, not merely in language of force and beauty, though the gospel moves the heart and tongue to eloquence, as Paul's own reported discourses and many parts of his extant letters testify.

but also in power,—no miracles are recorded in connection with the preaching of the gospel at Thessalonica; the preachers had freedom of utterance, and were conscious of divine help.

and—i.e., "even," but with an advance in the thought; "power, indeed, but the power of the Holy Spirit." These are frequently associated, Luke 4:14; Acts 1:8; Ephesians 3:16.

in the Holy Ghost,—the article is absent in orig.; yet this is sometimes the case where the reference is certainly to the Holy Spirit, Matthew 22:43, cp. Acts 4:25; 19:2, 6; Romans 14:17, and, conversely, the article may be present where the reference is not to the Holy Spirit, John 6:63. Arguments based on the presence or absence of the Gk. article are always precarious; doctrinal, literary or grammatical considerations frequently determine the form of a sentence. In these epistles, "Spirit" occurs twice with reference to the Holy Spirit, once with the article, 5:19, once without, 2 Thessalonians 2:13; "Holy Spirit" occurs three times, twice without the article, here and v. 6, once with it, 4:8. In v. 6 the Person is referred to, and this must rule the interpretation of v. 5; see 1 Corinthians 2:4, where the order is reversed, the article is absent, yet the reference is to the Person. The distinction between the Giver and His gifts is not always readily discerned, for the gift testifies to the presence of the giver.

Here the article is absent, because the apostle is writing of the character of the power that had been manifested, but not directly of the Spirit Himself.

and *in* **much assurance;**—*plērophoria,* lit., "complete carrying"; describing the spontaneity and liberty of spirit experienced by the missionaries at Thessalonica, an assuring evidence that the Holy Spirit was working through them. The inclusion of this with the preceding word under one preposition shows how intimately associated they are. There seems to be a kind of climax here, thus: "in power, even in Holy Spirit power, even in fullness of Holy Spirit power."

Plērophoria is used of the liberty of mind consequent upon an understanding in Christ, Colossians 2:2; of the absorbing power of the hope of the fulfillment of the promises of God, Hebrews 6:11; of the faith that excludes apprehension of the judgment of God, 10:22.||

The corresponding verb, *plērophoreō,* is used of the accomplished work of the Lord Jesus, Luke 1:1; of the preaching of the gospel, 2 Timothy 4:5, 17; this is the objective use of the word, in these places it is concerned with external things. In Romans 4:21 it describes the grasp by the mind of the promises of God and of His ability to make them good; in 14:5 it is used of the apprehension of the will of God for one's conduct, see also Colossians 4:12; this is the subjective use of the word, in these places it is concerned with an effect upon the mind.||

even as ye know—*oida,* as in v. 4; they themselves had observed the same facts.

what manner of men we showed ourselves—see on "came" above.

toward you—lit., among you.

for your sake.—the demonstration of the power of the Holy Spirit in the preaching was not given in the interests of the preachers but in the interests of the hearers, for they were the elect of God whose time to call them had now come; cp. Acts 18:10, God's encouragement to His servant, and 2 Timothy 2:10, the servant's purpose in consequence thereof.

The missionaries had acted on the same principle, they had not pleased themselves in their manner of life. They had not consulted their own convenience in the use of their liberty but had willingly surrendered it at the call of expediency. They had not only preached the gospel, they had given full proof that they were ready to "spend and be spent out" in the interests of the souls of those to whom they preached it, 2 Corinthians 12:15. The apostle speaks in some detail on this point in the section 2:1–12, below.

1:6 And ye became imitators of us,—*mimētēs ginomai,* an expression always used in a good sense in the New Testament. Here, and at 2:14, it is historic, i.e., it refers to the past, and the verb is in the aorist or "point" tense, indicating that conversion had taken place and that that conversion was not a gradual process but an act, cp. "ye turned," "point" tense, v. 9. In 1 Corinthians 4:16; 11:1; Ephesians 5:1; Hebrews 6:12, it is used in exhortation, and hence the verb is in the continuous tense, save in the last case. Thus, what we became at conversion we must give diligence to continue to be thereafter.||

The verb "to imitate" is found four times, 2 Thessalonians 3:7, 9; Hebrews 13:7; 3 John 11, always in exhortation and always in the continuous tense.

The point, or aorist, tense, "being a momentary tense," describes an event as a single whole, without regarding the time taken in its accomplishment. The present and imperfect are "continuous" tenses, i.e., they contemplate action as in progress, noting "the time taken in accomplishment" (J. H. Moulton, *Grammar of New Testament Greek, Proleg.* pp. 187, 190).

and of the Lord,—the order in orig. "and you imitators of us became and of the Lord," marks a climax and avoids the too close association of the apostles with the One who in the perfection of His example stands alone; cp. 1 Corinthians 11:1.

The statement is to be understood in a general sense. The Thessalonian believers had had other models, other masters before; from the time of their conversion to God they received the precepts and example of Christ, 1 Peter 2:21, and the example and precepts of those through whom they first heard of Him encouraged and guided them in so doing. Becoming followers of the missionaries, they found themselves following the Lord.

having received—point tense = "when you received the word, you became imitators": they had not merely heard the gospel, they had given heed to it as of vital concern to themselves; cp. note at 2:13, where *dechomai* is translated "accept." The word may be further studied in 2 Thessalonians 2:10; 1 Corinthians 2:14; Philippians 4:18; James 1:21, etc.; for the idea, cp. Deuteronomy 32:46; 2 Peter 1:19, "take heed . . . in your hearts."

the word—not the Living Word, only John uses *logos* in that sense; nor the Written Word, for the New Testament was not yet in existence, but the message, i.e., the gospel; cp. v. 8, Acts 4:29; 6:4; 8:4, *et al*. This is variously described as:

- the word of God, 2 Corinthians 2:17; 4:2:
- the word of the message of God, 2:13:
- the word of the Lord, Acts 15:36:
- the word of His grace, Acts 14:3:
- the word of the Cross, 1 Corinthians 1:18:
- the word of truth, 2 Corinthians 6:7:
- the word of the truth, Ephesians 1:13:
- the word of the gospel, Acts 15:7:
- the word of the truth of the gospel, Colossians 1:5:
- the word of this salvation, Acts 13:26:
- the word of reconciliation, 2 Corinthians 5:19:
- the word of life, Philippians 2:16:
- the word of righteousness, Hebrews 5:13.

A different word, *rhēma*, is used in the following passages:—

- the word of faith, Romans 10:8:
- the word of Christ, Romans 10:17:
- the word of God, Ephesians 6:17.

in much affliction,—the effect, external, see the history, Acts 17:6-9, and cp. 2:14; that the persecution did not soon cease, see 3:2, 3; 2 Thessalonians 1:4.

with joy of the Holy Ghost;—the effect, internal. The Holy Spirit works in a sphere the violence of man can never reach; cp. John 16:33; ct. Matthew 13:20, 21, where reception of the word, joy and affliction are again associated.

1:7 so that ye became—the latter part of v. 6 is a parenthesis, thus, "(having received . . . the Holy Ghost)," and the opening of v. 7 is to be read with the former part of v. 6. Following the example of the Lord Jesus and of the missionaries, they in turn became examples to others.

The point tense in v. 6 describes the initial act; the continuous tense here describes the subsequent course of the Christian life. See on "imitators" above.

an ensample—*tupos*, a mold, a pattern, a model; referring to their Christian conduct, v. 6, and to their Christian confession, v. 8. Cp. 2 Thessalonians 3:9; Philippians 3:17; 1 Timothy 4:12; Titus 2:7; 1 Peter 5:3, where the word appears again in the same connection.

to all that believe—present continuous tense and equivalent to a noun, lit., "all the believers," as in:

- John 3:36, the believer on [into] the Son hath eternal life.
- John 7:38, the believer on [into] the Son receives the Holy Spirit.
- John 11:25, the believer, though he die, shall live.
- John 11:26, the believer, living [at the return of the Lord?] shall never die.
- John 12:46, the believer does not abide in darkness.
- John 17:20, the believers were prayed for by the Lord Jesus.
- Acts 10:43, every believer on [into] Him receives remission of sins.
- Acts 13:39, every believer is justified.
- Romans 3:21, 22, a righteousness of God has been manifested—unto all the believers.
- Romans 9:33, the believer on Him shall not be put to shame.
- Romans 10:4, Christ is the end of the law for righteousness to the believers.
- Galatians 3:22, the promise—is given to the believers.
- 1 Thessalonians 2:13, the Word of God is active in the believers.
- 1 Peter 1:8, believers rejoice greatly with joy unspeakable.
- 1 John 5:10, the believer on [into] the Son hath the witness in him.
- 1 John 5:13, believers on [into] the Son know that they have eternal Life.

Thus the word is a common New Testament designation of the Christian, and expresses his present active relationship with God through the Lord Jesus Christ.

in Macedonia and in Achaia.—the former is now part of Turkey, the latter corresponds, nearly, to modern Greece. The epistle was sent from Corinth, the chief city of Achaia, to Thessalonica, the chief city of Macedonia.

1:8 For from you hath sounded forth—*exēcheomai* commonly refers to the sounding of a herald's trumpet. The Thessalonian converts had preached, their hearers had believed, and, in turn, had carried the gospel whither they went.||

The order is significant, example in v. 6, testimony in v. 8; cp. "work and word," 2 Thessalonians 2:17; "all that Jesus began both to do and to teach," Acts 1:1; cp. also Matthew 5:16.

the word of the Lord,—the phrase occurs over two hundred times in the Old Testament, and = the revealed will of God, cp. Isaiah 38:4. It occurs:

- in Acts 11:16, of words spoken by the Lord Jesus while on earth, cp. 20:35:
- in 1 Thessalonians 4:15, of a direct revelation, cp. 1 Kings 20:35:
- in 1 Peter 1:25, in a quotation from Isaiah 40:8, it is applied specifically to the gospel, to which it refers here and in 2 Thessalonians 3:1; Acts 8:25; 13:49; 15:35, 36; 16:32; 19:10.||

The word of the Lord is the message from the Lord which is delivered with His authority and made effective by His power, cp. 2:13, Acts 10:36 "the word which He sent . . . preaching good tidings of peace [lit., "gospeling peace"] by Jesus Christ," and Romans 1:1, 3, 16, "the gospel of God . . . concerning His Son . . . is the power of God unto salvation."

not only in Macedonia and Achaia—Thessalonica being a considerable seaport, made an excellent missionary center; the influence of the new converts traveled by sea as well as by land. Moreover, Corinth, from whence he wrote, was in constant communication with other ports; when Paul arrived there, he found Aquila and Priscilla "lately come from Italy," Acts 18:2; thus he would readily hear how the good work at Thessalonica had spread abroad.

but in every place—i.e., widely, generally, a figure of speech called hyperbole, in which the expression used should not be taken in its literal sense, cp. Acts 2:5; 19:10; Romans 1:8; 16:19; Colossians 1:6, 23.

your faith to God-ward—the preposition translated "to-ward," *pros,* is used with "faith" only here and Philemon 5. It occurs again in v. 9, "unto," and indicates the new direction given to minds which were formerly occupied with idols; cp. 2 Corinthians 3:4; 1 John 3:21.

is gone forth;—the apostle seems to have Psalm 19:4 in mind, as also in Philippians 2:15, 16, which see. The Thessalonian Christians afforded another example of the spirit of faith which animated the apostle, 2 Corinthians 4:13, and before him the Psalmist, 116:10; their preaching of the gospel testified to their confidence in it.

so that we need not to speak anything, 1:9 For they themselves report concerning us—i.e., "those to whom we might have told the news shewed that they were already acquainted with it." Not only had the remarkable religious movement at Thessalonica influenced believers elsewhere, v. 7, it had become a matter of general report, "a new thing." Acts 17:21, of sufficient interest to give a zest to conversation even among men for whom the story itself had little significance.

what manner—as described in v. 5; the first subject of the common report.

of entering in we had unto you;—i.e., of entrance upon gospel work, see 2:1; the word, *eisodos,* is used in a similar sense of the Lord Jesus, Acts 13:24, marg. Paul has a similar metaphor in 1 Corinthians 16:9, concerning a present opportunity at Ephesus, in 2 Corinthians 2:12, concerning a past experience at Troas, and in Colossians 4:3, desiring prayer for his ministry during his enforced stay at Rome; cp. also Acts 14:27; Revelation 3, 7, 8.

Eisodos is also used of the present access of the believer into the presence of God, Hebrews 10:19, and of his future "entrance into the eternal kingdom of our Lord and Savior Jesus Christ," 2 Peter 1:11.‖

and how—the second subject of the common report.

ye turned—*epistrephō*, momentary tense, indicating a change immediately consequent upon a deliberate choice; cp. 2 Corinthians 3:16. This word is often used literally of turning oneself round, Mark 5:30, and of returning to a place, Luke 2:20; and in the latter sense both of the human spirit, 8:55, and of a demon, Matthew 12:44. It is also used of man in his relationship with God, of Israelites who refused the gospel, Matthew 13:15, and of Gentiles who accepted it, Acts 15:19, as the Thessalonians did. The effect upon a man of this turning is to make him so completely different from what he was that he is said to become "as a little child," i.e., to begin life again, Matthew 18:3 (where *strephō*, a shorter form of the same verb indistinguishable from it in meaning, is used).

It is possible for a believer to turn back to the things from which he once turned away, Galatians 4:9, cp. 2 Peter 2:21, 22. The way remains open for such to return to the Lord and to His service, Luke 22:32.

It was part of the mission of the Baptist to turn "many of the children of Israel" to the Lord, Luke 1:16. One man may, by setting the truth before another, "convert" him, James 5:19, 20; men are also said to "turn again," i.e., to convert themselves, Luke 22:32; Acts 9:35. But in no case is God, or Christ, or the Holy Spirit, said to turn, or convert, anyone. Conversion is always the voluntary act of the individual in response to the presentation of truth.

"Turning" or "conversion," is sometimes associated with "repentance," as in Acts 3:19; 26:20; sometimes it is associated with "faith," as in Acts 11:21.

The noun "conversion" occurs in Acts 15:3.‖

unto God from idols,—the order is significant; the motive in this conversion was not that they were repelled by the grossness of their idols, but that they were attracted by the character of God; cp. 2 Peter 1:3.

"Idol," *eidōlon* = that which can be seen, and so, an image to represent an invisible deity. The corresponding Hebrew word = "vanity," Jeremiah 14:22; 18:15, "thing of nought"; Leviticus 19:4, marg., cp. Ephesians 4:17. Hence what represented a deity to the Gentiles, was to Paul a "vain thing," Acts 14:15, "nothing in the world"; 1 Corinthians 8:4; 10:19. Jeremiah calls the idol "scarecrow" ("pillar in a garden," 10:5, marg.) and Isaiah, 44:9–20, et al., and Habakkuk, 2:18, 19, and the Psalmist, 115:4–8, et al., are all equally scathing. It is important to notice, however, that in each case the people of God are addressed. When he speaks to idolaters, Paul, knowing that no man is won by ridicule, adopts a different line, Acts 14:15–18; 17:16, 21–31.

That there is a serious side to idolatry the apostle fully recognized. Over against "we know," 1 Corinthians 8:4, he sets "howbeit in all men there is not this knowledge," v. 7, and in 10:19 he declares that the sacrifices of the heathen were sacrifices to demons, that there was solemn reality in the cup and table of demons, and in the communion with demons held therein. See also Romans 1:22-25, where idolatry, the sin of the mind, Ephesians 2:3, directed against God, and immorality, sins of the flesh, working injury to the sinner and to his fellows, are linked together and directly traced to the failure to acknowledge God or to give Him thanks, Romans 1:21. The idolater is in bondage to the depraved ideas his idols represent, Galatians 4:8, 9, and, as a consequence, to divers lusts and pleasures, Titus 3:3.

This reference to idolatry shows that the bulk, at least, of the converts at Thessalonica were drawn from among the Gentiles.

to serve—*douleuo,* to discharge the duties of the purchased slave, to which there were no limitations either in the kind of service or in the time of its performance. The whole life of the Christian is to be lived in obedience to the will of God, an absolute law to which the gospel of the grace of God admits of no exception. For a full exposition of the nature of bond service see Romans 6:12-23; and cp. 2 Peter 2:19.

For an associated word, *douloō,* see at Galatians 4:3.

a living—for idols are lifeless, Psalm 135:17, *et al.;* frequently said of Jehovah by His servants when in contact with idolaters, as by Israel, just out of Egypt, Deuteronomy 5:26, by Joshua warring against the inhabitants of the Land, Joshua 3:10, by David when he saw Goliath and the Philistines, 1 Samuel 17:26, and by Hezekiah when the Assyrians threatened him, 2 Kings 19:4. See further at 5:10.

and true God,—i.e., real, "very God," cp. 2 Chronicles 15:3, LXX. "True" represents one of two similar Greek words so translated, this, *alēthinos* = real, signifying that God "fulfill the promise of His Name," He is true, not false; the other, *alēthēs* = veracious, that He "fulfills the promise of His lips," He is true, not a liar. The first, *alēthinos* = real, which occurs here only in Paul's writings, is used in Luke 16:11, and in John 1:9; 6:32; 15:1; Revelation 3:14, titles of Christ, and in Hebrews 8:2; 9:24; 10:22; the second *alēthēs* = veracious, in John 5:31, 32; 21:24; 2 Corinthians 6:8; Philippians 4:8. The difference can be studied in John 17:3, *alēthinos,* cp. with 3:33, *alēthēs;* so in 7:28 with 7:18, and in 8:16 with 8:14.

"Living" and "true" are found together in Jeremiah 10:10, and see 1 John 5:20.

1:10 and to wait—*anamenō,* only here in the New Testament; a closely related word *perimenō* appears in Acts 1:4 only, in both the thought of patience is predominant, as in expectancy in the more usual word, *apekdechomai,* Philippians 3:20, *et al.*||

for His Son—in Romans 8:32, "His own Son"; in John 3:16, "His only begotten Son"; in Matthew 3:17, "His beloved Son"; and in Colossians 1:13, "the Son of His love"; cp. Ephesians 1:6, "the Beloved." The Son is the eternal object of the Father's love, John 17:24, and the sole Revealer of the Father's character, John 1:14, Hebrews 1:3.

The words, "Father" and "Son," are never in the New Testament so used as to suggest that the Father existed before the Son; the prologue to the Gospel according to John distinctly asserts that the Word existed "in the beginning," and that this Word is the Son, Who "became flesh and dwelt among us."

From— = out of, see note at 4:16.

heaven,—lit., "the heavens." In His ascension Christ "passed through the heavens." Hebrews 4:14, "ascended far above all the heavens," Ephesians 4:10, cp. Psalm 8:1, marg., "into [the] heaven itself," Hebrews 9:24, and was "made higher than the heavens," 7:26, cp. 1:4, i.e., "far above all rule, and authority, and power, and dominion, and every name that is named," present or future, Ephesians 1:21, and, in fulfillment of the prophecy of Psalm 110:1, and of His own word, Luke 22:69, "sat down on the right hand of the Throne of the Majesty in the heavens," Hebrews 8:1, cp. 1 Peter 3:22.

The heavens are distinguished: the aerial, Matthew 6:26, the sidereal, 24:29, and the "third," 2 Corinthians 12:2.

whom He raised [*egeirō*] **from the dead,**—lit. "from among," This is the fact, which, when they knew it, brought Peter and the rest of the disciples into a new life of hope, 1 Peter 1:3; the fact, which, when he knew it, changed the persecutor of Christians into the bond servant of Christ, Acts 9:1–9; 1 Corinthians 9:1; Galatians 1:16. That the historic fact, "Jesus Christ risen from the dead," 2 Timothy 2:8, is the complete vindication of the truth of the gospel, is declared by the Lord Himself; Luke 24:46, and has been preached among Jews, Acts 17:3, and Gentiles, v. 31, from Pentecost till the present day, cp. 1 Corinthians 15:3. See further at 4:14.

even **Jesus,**—see at v. 1.

which delivereth us—lit., "the Deliverer," as in Romans 11:26.

from—*ek* = out of. In Romans 5:9, "saved from the wrath of God," where the subject is the same, "from" represents a different preposition, *apo.*

The words translated "deliver," *rhuomai,* and "save," *sōzō* (for which see note at 5:9) respectively, though they differ entirely in form, cover much the same ground in meaning. It may be said that while each means both "to rescue from" and "to preserve from," rescue is predominant in the former (see Matt. 27:43), preservation in the latter.

The word here translated "deliver" occurs with *apo* = "from," "away from," in Matthew 6:13; Romans 15:31; 2 Thessalonians 3:2; 2 Timothy 4:18, and with *ek* = "from," "out of," in Luke 1:74; Romans 7:24; Colossians 1:13, of bondage; in 2 Timothy 3:11, of persecutions, actually endured; and in 2 Corinthians 1:10; 2 Peter 2:(7), 9, of threatening danger. In 2 Timothy 4:17 *ek* is used, for the danger is more imminent than in v. 18, where *apo* appears. Thus, followed by *apo* this word means to preserve from evil persons, Satan or men, and their schemes, and followed by *ek,* as here, to rescue either out of actual distress or from imminent peril.||

the wrath to come.—lit., "the coming wrath"; the present tense is often used with a future meaning, cp. Matthew 26:2; John 14:3; 2 Corinthians 13:1.

Orgē, "wrath," is used in New Testament:

- of the wrath of man, Ephesians 4:31; Colossians 3:8; 1 Timothy 2:8; James 1:19, 20:
- of the displeasure of human governments, Romans 13:4, 5:
- of the sufferings of the Jews at the hands of the Gentiles, Luke 21:23:
- of the terrors of the Law, Romans 4:15:
- of the anger of the Lord Jesus, Mark 3:5:
- of God's anger with Israel in the wilderness, in quotation from the Old Testament, Hebrews 3:11; 4:3:
- of God's present anger with the Jews nationally, Romans 9:22; 1 Thessalonians 2:16:
- of His present anger with those who disobey the Lord Jesus in His gospel, John 3:36:
- of God's purposes in judgment, Matthew 3:7; Luke 3:7; Romans 1:18; 2:5, 8; 3:5; 5:9; 12:19; Ephesians 2:3; 5:6; Colossians 3:6, here and 5:9.

The earth is defined as the sphere of these judgments, Revelation 6:16, 17; 11:18; 14:10; 16:19; 19:15.||

This wrath is to be understood, then, of the calamities wherewith God will visit men upon the earth when the present period of grace is closed, and which will fall first upon the Jews, then upon the Gentiles, Romans 2:2, 9. The calamities of the Jews are referred to in Jeremiah 4:7; Zechariah 14:2; Matthew 24:15-21, and those of the Gentiles in Zechariah 14:3; Matthew 24:30; Luke 21:25-29, among many passages. The believer is assured of deliverance from both through the Lord Jesus Christ; cp. 5:9, and Romans 5:9. In these words the apostle reminds his readers of what he had taught them, while still with them, concerning the coming of the Lord. A further, and entirely new, revelation had been made to him in the meantime, and this he communicates to them in 4:13–18.

1 THESSALONIANS

· CHAPTER TWO ·

Verses 1–20

2:1 For yourselves, brethren, know—as 1:5.

our entering in unto you,—as 1:9.

that it hath not been found—lit., "hath not come to be," perfect tense denoting an abiding result; cp. John 15:16.

vain:—Paul had learned from Timothy that the assaults of Satan had not annulled their labors at Thessalonica.

Though the apostle well knew that no labor in the Lord is vain, 1 Corinthians 15:58, he also knew that only in the day of Christ, when all service is to be reviewed by the Lord, 1 Corinthians 3:12, 15, will it be finally manifest whether or no he had run and labored in vain, Philippians 2:16. He earnestly desired, therefore to assure himself of the stability of his work, and such tidings as Timothy had brought comforted and gladdened his heart, 3:6–8.

2:2 but having suffered before, and been shamefully entreated,—*hubrizō*, denotes either insult, Luke 11:45, or bodily ill treatment, Acts 14:5. These experiences of the missionaries had illustrated the parable of the despised feast, Matthew 22:6, and had brought them into closer fellowship with their Lord, Luke 18:32.||

as ye know, at Philippi,—a city one hundred miles, i.e., three or four days' journey, N.E. of Thessalonica. Men who could sing hymns unto God in jail after such treatment as they had received, Acts 16:25, were not likely to be deterred by physical suffering from further testimony in the district.

we waxed bold—*parrhēsiazomai,* in the New Testament always with reference to proclaiming the gospel, Acts 9:27, 29; 13:46; 14:3; 18:26; 19:8; 26:26; Ephesians 6:20. Notwithstanding the sufferings they had had to endure after preaching at Philippi, God had given them courage to resume His work at Thessalonica.||

in our God—shortly before writing these words, at Corinth, the apostle had been "in weakness, and in fear, and in much trembling," 1 Corinthians 2:3, a state of mind probably due in some measure, at least, to the absence of his fellow workers, for it seems to have passed with the arrival of Silas and Timothy from Macedonia, Acts 18:5. In the overruling providence of God, the wrath of the Jews, notwithstanding the conversion of the ruler of their synagogue, was at Corinth restrained, and the inevitable outbreak deferred for a year and a half whereas at Philippi, 16:19, and at Thessalonica, 17:5, and at Berea, 17:13, persecution began very shortly. It was about the time, too, of the writing of this epistle, that God encouraged His servant by a vision and reassuring words in the night, 18:9. Thus graciously did the Lord consider the frailty of the earthen vessel to which He had committed the treasure of His gospel, 2 Corinthians 4:7, and in the apostle's human weakness displayed His own divine power, 2 Corinthians 12:9, 10; see also at 3:7. Hence it is clear that the characteristic boldness of the apostle was not mere natural courage, though he was not devoid of that, but the calm fearlessness that comes of consciousness of the presence of God, cp. 1 Peter 2:19, marg.

to speak unto you the gospel of God—the gospel is variously described as of:

- God, concerning His Son, Romans 1:1–3:
- His Son, Romans 1:9:
- Jesus Christ, the Son of God, Mark 1:1:
- our Lord Jesus, 2 Thessalonians 1:8:
- Christ, Romans 15:19, etc.:
- the glory of Christ, 2 Corinthians 4:4:
- the grace of God, Acts 20:24:
- the glory of the blessed God, 1 Timothy 1:11:
- your salvation, Ephesians 1:13:
- peace, Ephesians 6:15.

Cp. also "the gospel of the Kingdom," Matthew 4:23; 9:35; 24:14; "an eternal gospel," Revelation 14:6, and see notes at 1:5, 6.

in much conflict.—*agōn* = a contest, as may be seen in 1 Timothy 6:12; 2 Timothy 4:7, where it is translated "fight," and in Hebrews 12:1, where it is translated "race." The corresponding verb = to contend in sports, 1 Corinthians 9:25, and to fight as soldiers do, John 18:36. Inward and outward conflict cannot be sharply divided one from the other. Here and in Philippians 1:30 the conflict is both inward and outward; in Colossians 2:1, the inward conflict of the soul in prayer is the thought. In each case the adversaries referred to in Ephesians 6:12 are implied.||

2:3 For—the apostle declares the integrity of the missionaries, and their innocence of the malicious charges made against them by the Jews in their jealous fury.

our exhortation—*paraklesis*, see at v. 11, and at 2 Thessalonians 2:16.

Having reasoned from the Scriptures, opening them, Psalm 119:130, and alleging, or setting forth, that the Messiah must suffer and that He must raise again from the dead, Paul had gone on to proclaim that in the Jesus of whom he had told them these things had been fulfilled, Acts 17:2, 3. On those who were persuaded of the truth of what they preached, the missionaries had urged certain practical considerations; this is here described as "our exhortation."

is **not of error,**—*planē* = a wandering, a forsaking of the right path, see James 5:20, whether in doctrine, 2 Peter 3:17; 1 John 4:6, or in morals, Romans 1:27; 2 Peter 2:18; Jude 11, though in Scripture doctrine and morals are never divided by any sharp line. See also Matthew 27:64, where it = "fraud."

The missionaries were confident theirs was a genuine gospel, standing out in contrast to the fatal delusion, for instance of which the apostle had already forewarned them, 2 Thessalonians 2:5. They had not themselves been carried away by any wiles of error, neither had they sought to mislead others by such wiles, Ephesians 4:14; they had not been deceived, neither were they deceivers, see 2 Timothy 3:13, where the corresponding verb, *planaō*, is used.||

nor of uncleanness,—cp. the description of the false teachers in 2 Peter 2:18, where sensuality and error are again associated. See also Jude 4, and Revelation 2:20. Both in Corinth and in Thessalonica gross vice was consecrated to the service of religion, cp. Romans 1:22–32, and see note on idolatry above.

nor in guile:—the preceding words deny a wrong source and a wrong motive; this denies a wrong method. The meaning of the word is best seen in its first New Testament occurrence, Matthew 26:4, or from the use of the corresponding verb in 2 Corinthians 4:2, "not handling the word of God deceitfully," or craftily, that is, with some personal end in view. Such a charge was afterwards made against Paul at Corinth, 2 Corinthians 12:16, "being crafty I caught you with guile" words quoted, apparently, from the language of his detractors.

2:4 but even as we have been approved of God—as at 3:5. No one of the three missionaries was a novice. Like Jeremiah, 1:5, and John the Baptist, Luke 1:15, Paul had been set apart for his life work, in the purpose of God, even before his birth, Galatians 1:15. Nevertheless he must be proved, i.e., tested; and he must be approved, i.e., found to have stood the test, before he can be permitted to engage in it. About ten years (32 or 33–42 or 43 A.D.) elapsed between Paul's conversion and the day that Barnabas came to Tarsus to find a colleague and to introduce him to a wider sphere of service, Acts 11:25, 26. During these years he had visited Arabia, had returned to Damascus again, and thence after three years, had gone to Jerusalem, where he first came under the notice of Barnabas. Of his residence in Tarsus, say, 35–43 A.D., nothing is recorded, but that he had commended himself, and had become widely known, is evident from the fact that Barnabas sought his help at a critical stage of the important work at Antioch. This was a period of testing, but his probation was not yet fulfilled. Three full years of new and varied experience had still to elapse before Paul was definitely called by the Holy Ghost and separated by his brethren, Acts 13:1–3, to that work among the Gentiles for which he had been set apart by God, and concerning which the Lord had spoken to him at the moment of his conversion, Acts 9:15, perhaps fourteen years before.

When Silas is first mentioned, Acts 15:22, he had already gained for himself a good standing, 1 Timothy 3:13, among his brethren at Jerusalem, who, recognizing in him one fitted of God to be "a chief man" or leader, made choice of him for an important mission. And now, as Barnabas had chosen Paul, so Paul chose Silas, as a fellow worker in the gospel, Acts 15:40.

Of Timothy we hear first in Acts 16:1, where albeit a young man, he is presented as one who had deserved the commendation of his brethren at places as far apart as Lystra and Iconium, eighteen miles, or, say, a six hours' journey. Learning something of him by personal contact, knowing of the esteem in which he was held by godly brethren, knowing, too, of his acquaintance with the facts of the gospel 2 Timothy 3:14, and his lifelong acquaintance with the Old Testament Scriptures, v. 15, Paul had chosen Timothy to be one of his band of fellow workers.

Thus, though they differed in age, training, and experience no one of these missionaries was a novice. Each was a believer of some years' standing, and each had been proved, and approved, in the actual work of the gospel locally before he undertook service in a wider sphere. And each had been chosen as a colleague by a worker of experience and standing superior to his own.

Now, after two years' joint labor, Paul could say confidently, "We have been approved of God to be intrusted with the gospel," and, ten years later, could write to the Philippians concerning Timothy, "Ye know the proof of him, that, as a child serveth a father, so he served with me in furtherance of the gospel," Philippians 2:19–22. Later still Peter puts on record that, in his judgment also, Silas is "our faithful brother," 1 Peter 5:12.

to be intrusted with the gospel,—this ministry had not been of his own choosing, he speaks of it elsewhere as a "stewardship intrusted" to him, 1 Corinthians 9:17; cp. Galatians 2:7; 1 Timothy 1:11; Titus 1:3.

The essential qualification for any service is trustworthiness, Matthew 25:21; 1 Corinthians 4:2. It is in the mercy of God His servants are enabled to be trustworthy, 1 Corinthians 7:25, and to continue so, Acts 26:22, unto the end, Acts 20:24; 2 Timothy 4:7.

so we speak;—cp. 2 Corinthians 2:17; 12:19.

not as pleasing men,—present continuous tense = "not seeking to please men," cp. Ephesians 6:6, etc.

This tense often expresses an aim, what one has in view in pursuing a certain course. For example Romans 2:4, "the goodness of God leadeth thee to repentance" (if you will follow it); 2 Corinthians 5:19, "reconciling the world" (if the world is willing to be reconciled); Galatians 5:4, "ye who would be," i.e., who seek to be, "justified by the law."

but God—i.e., but seeking to please God; otherwise they would not have been servants of Christ, Galatians 1:10, cp. 2 Corinthians 5:9. Here the choice is between pleasing God and pleasing men, and the Lord Jesus Himself is the pattern; He always did the things that were pleasing to His Father, John 8:29.

In Romans 15:1, 2; 1 Corinthians 10:33 (which is to be interpreted by v. 24) the choice is between pleasing ourselves and pleasing others. Here again Christ is the pattern, He pleased not Himself, Romans 15:3, cp. Philippians 2:4, 5.

which proveth—the same word as that translated "approve" above. Here it means "to examine" or "test"; there "to accept" or "to choose" after test made. A similar thought is expressed in Luke 16:15; Acts 1:24, "knows," Romans 8:27; Revelation 2:23, and often in the Old Testament, "searches." To these may be added Proverbs 21:2, "weighs."

our hearts.—the literal heart, hidden in the body, is the chief organ of physical life, hence the word is used figuratively for the hidden springs of the personal life. Of course there is no actual association between the thoughts, affections, etc., and the physical organ.

The heart is the seat of:

- grief, John 14:1; Romans 9:2; 2 Corinthians 2:4:
- joy, John 16:22; Ephesians 5:19:
- the desires, Matthew 5:28; 2 Peter 2:14:
- the affections, Luke 24:32; Acts 21:13:
- the perceptions, John 12:40; Ephesians 4:18:
- the thoughts, Matthew 9:4; Hebrews 4:12:
- the understanding, Matthew 13:15; Romans 1:21:
- the reasoning powers, Mark 2:6; Luke 24:38:
- the imagination, Luke 1:51:
- conscience, Acts 2:37; 1 John 3:20:
- the intentions, Hebrews 4:12, cp. 1 Peter 4:1:

- purpose, Acts 11:23; 2 Corinthians 9:7:
- the will, Romans 6:17; Colossians 3:15:
- faith, Mark 11:23; Romans 10:10; Hebrews 3:12.

In every part of our being, says the apostle in effect, we "are naked and laid open before the eyes of Him with whom we have to do," Hebrews 4:13.

2:5 For—vv. 3, 4 describe the general character of the labors of the missionaries, v. 5 reverts to their stay at Thessalonica.

neither at any time were we found—see note on 1:5, where the same word is translated "came." "Found" must not be mistaken as = "found out," "detected"; the words of the orig. simply mean "we did not resort to flattering words."

using words of flattery,—mentioned here only in the New Testament

as ye know,—see vv. 1:2, and 1:5.

nor a cloak—*prophasis* = a "pretense," Mark 12:40; Luke 20:47; Philippians 1:18, or "excuse" John 15:22; i.e., something assumed to mislead others as to one's real motives. The word is well illustrated in Acts 27:30, where it is translated "color."||

of [i.e., for] **covetousness,**—*pleonexia,* lit., "the desire to have more" in the New Testament always in a bad sense. Sometimes it is used of material possessions, Luke 12:15; 2 Peter 2:3, and specifically of money, 2 Corinthians 9:5; sometimes of sensuality, Ephesians 4:19; 5:3; Colossians 3:5; 2 Peter 2:14, and sometimes it is used in a general way, here, Mark 7:22, and Romans 1:29, where the particular form of covetousness in view is not indicated by the context. See on "wrong," 4:6.

For a contrast to the ways of the apostle here mentioned, cp. Isaiah 56:11; Jeremiah 6:13, etc.

God is witness;—concerning flattery, which is of the tongue he appealed to his readers; concerning covetousness, which is of the heart, he appealed to God.

2:6 nor seeking glory—*doxa,* i.e., dignity, preeminence, cp. Luke 14:10; John 5:44. By a figure of speech called metonymy, in which one word is used for another, with which it is closely associated, "glory" is here probably = material gifts, honorarium, stipend, cp. Genesis 31:1; Psalm 49:16, LXX; Revelation 21:26, inasmuch as the glory men value is usually expressed in things material. Cp. Luke 12:15.

of [lit., out of] **men,**—as the source of supplies.

neither from you,—as a channel through which supplies might be expected: referring to the Thessalonian converts.

nor from others,—referring to converts elsewhere. During their short stay at Thessalonica the missionaries had received supplies at least twice from the church at Philippi, Philippians 4:16; but the church at Thessalonica must not be allowed to suppose that these gifts had been sent in response to appeals. No appeal had been made save to God, Philippians 4:6. Recollection of this timely succor in which God had shown His care for His servants at Thessalonica, encouraged them to look to Him still at Corinth, for about the time he wrote these words he was in need in that city, as he afterwards told the Corinthian saints, but not until at least three years had elapsed, 2 Corinthians 11:9.

when we might have been—*dunamai*, to be able, i.e., to have the right or the authority, or the opportunity, as in 1 Corinthians 3:1, 11; 7:21; 14:31, *e.g.*

burdensome,—*baros* = a weight; this word, noun, adjective, and verb, occurs frequently in the New Testament, but nowhere is it "honor," as R.V. marg., which must therefore be ignored. The simple meaning of the word, 1 Timothy 5:16, and the context, show that the reference is to temporal things, see v. 9, and 2 Thessalonians 3:8, 9, where a strengthened form of the same word is used. Thus the apostle adds to his repudiation of covetousness, which is the desire for unlawful gain, a declaration that they had foregone even a right and lawful claim. For an instructive parallel cp. Nehemiah 5:1–18, particularly v. 15, marg.

as apostles of Christ.—for a full statement of this right see 1 Corinthians 9:1–18, and cp. 2 Corinthians 11:8; 1 Timothy 5:17, 18.

"Apostle," from the Greek ("missionary" is the corresponding word from the Latin) = a person sent, cp. John 13:16, marg. The word is used of the Lord Jesus to describe His relation to God, Hebrews 3:1, see John 17:3.

The twelve disciples chosen by the Lord for special training were so called, Luke 6:13; 9:1, 10. After the ascension Matthias was chosen by lot to take the place ot Judas, Acts 1:26, and was henceforth numbered with them, 2:14. See also at Galatians 1:19.

Paul, though he had seen the Lord Jesus, 1 Corinthians 9:1; 15:8, had not "companied with" the Twelve "all the time" of His earthly ministry, and hence was not eligible for a place among them, according to Peter's description of the necessary qualifications, Acts 1:22. Paul was commissioned directly, by the Lord Himself after His ascension, to carry the gospel to the Gentiles, or non-Jewish peoples of the earth, see Acts 26:17; Romans 11:13; Galatians 2:7, 8; 1 Timothy 2:7. In proof of his apostleship he appealed to his experience outside Damascus, and to the signs wrought through him among the Corinthians, alike in the spiritual, 1 Corinthians 9:1, and material, 2 Corinthians 12:12, spheres.

The word has also a wider reference in the New Testament. In Acts 14:4, 14 it is used of Barnabas as well as of Paul; and in Romans 16:7 of Andronicus and Junias. In 2 Corinthians 8:23 two unnamed brethren are called "apostles of the churches"; in Philippians 2:15 Epaphroditus is referred to as "your apostle." It is used here of Paul, Silas, and Timothy, to define their relation to Christ.

2:7 But—having denied categorically the sevenfold imputation made upon them by their enemies at Thessalonica, viz., of deception, of sensuality, of fraud, of sycophancy, of flattery, of covetousness, of seeking material advantage, the apostle proceeds to describe what their manner of life there had actually been.

we were gentle—*ēpios,* as in 2 Timothy 2:24; in Greek writers commonly used of the kindness of parents toward children. Cp. the false apostles of 2 Corinthians 11:13, 20.||

in the midst of you,—i.e., "in our intercourse with you," suggesting that no attempt had been made to lord it over the converts, 1 Peter 5:3. Apostles though they were, they had identified themselves with those who accepted their message, cp. 1 Peter 5:1, 2, as helpers of their joy, 2 Corinthians 1:24, and had become "their servants for Jesus' sake," 4:5, and according to His command, Matthew 23:8–12, cp. Luke 22:27.

as when—introducing a simile, i.e., a comparison of things unlike in general, but resembling each other in certain particulars; for further examples of simile see Deuteronomy 32:11; Matthew 23:37.

a nurse—*trophos,* here, as the following words shew = a nursing mother.||
The corresponding verb, *trephō* = to feed, Luke 23:29, and then = to bring up, Luke 4:16.

cherisheth her own children—*thalpō* = to warm; it is used of birds covering their young with their feathers, Deuteronomy 22:6, LXX. See also Ephesians 5:29, where it is used of Christ and the church.||

2:8 even so, being affectionately desirous of you,—*homeiromai,* a word which occurs in LXX only in Job 3:21, "long." Here it is in keeping with the preceding simile, and expresses the strong desire of the apostle for the confirmation and blessing of the converts. See Galatians 4:19, for an allied expression of his interest in, and affection for, those in whose conversion he had been the instrument.||

we were well pleased—denoting not merely pleasure in the action, but free and deliberate choice. The tense here is continuous and hence expresses not merely a generous impulse, but a determination made and adhered to.

to impart unto you,—*metadidōmi*, a modified form of *didōmi*, usually rendered "give." The effect of the prefix, *meta*, is to suggest the idea of sharing as distinguished from giving. Thus Paul speaks of sharing some spiritual gift with the saints at Rome, 1:11, and, later in the same epistle, counsels those to whom ministry in temporal things is committed, to discharge it not as giving but as sharing rather, and that generously, 12:8; see also in Luke 3:11, and Ephesians 4:28.

not the gospel of God only,—see note at v. 4.

but also our own souls,—i.e., our own selves, our lives; not merely to die for them, cp. 1 John 3:16, but to live for them, cp. 2 Corinthians 12:15, and notice marg., "spend and be spent out." Here speaks the pastor, as the evangelist speaks in Philippians 2:17; Colossians 1:24; 2 Timothy 2:10. To this they were constrained by the example of Christ Who had given Himself for them all, missionaries and converts, Galatians 2:20; Ephesians 5:2.

because ye were become very dear to us— = "ye had come to be beloved by us"; the aorist or point tense suggests a result; labors among them, begun under the constraining love of Christ, 2 Corinthians 5:14, had produced in the missionaries deep affection for the converts committed to their care.

"Very dear," *agapētos*, is the same word as that translated "beloved" in Matthew 3:17; Philippians 2:12, *et al.*, cp. 1:4.

2:9 for ye remember,—cp. Paul's remembrance of their labor, 1:3, in each case a labor of love.

brethren,—see note at 1:4.

our labor—see note at 1:3.

and travail:—*mochthos*, see 2 Thessalonians 3:8; 2 Corinthians 11:27, where as here it is subjoined to "labor"; it emphasizes the toil involved in the work.||

working—*ergazomai*, the Greek word covers much the same ground as the English; it is used, e.g., of manual work, Ephesians 4:28; 1 Thessalonians 4:11; of trading, Matthew 25:16; Revelation 18:17; of the conscience, 2 Corinthians 7:10; of preaching and the work of Christ generally, 1 Corinthians 16:10.

An ancient Jewish writer describing the duty of a father toward his son, says he must circumcise him, teach him the law, and teach him a trade. In accordance with this wise custom, which obtained among the Jews, Paul had been taught to make tents of goats' hair cloth, Acts 18:3. Concerning the trade followed by Silas and Timothy there is no available information, but the statement of the text includes them as well as their leader.

night and day,—i.e., not spasmodically, or on occasion merely, but continuously.

that—*pros*, lit., "toward," i.e., with this end in view. In working to maintain themselves they had acted not from motives of independence but of solicitude for the work of the Lord and to cut off occasion from detractors.

we might not burden—*epibareō*, as in 2 Thessalonians 3:8; 2 Corinthians 2:5; see note at v. 6.‖

any of you,—though Jason and others were apparently men of substance, Acts 17:9, and though some of the chief women of the community were also among the converts at Thessalonica, v. 4, it must not be assumed that the church as a whole was wealthy. Probably it did not differ greatly from other churches of saints then and since; indeed, the apostle later appealed to the example of the churches of Macedonia, among which that at Thessalonica is to be reckoned, in proof that poverty and liberality are not incompatible, 2 Corinthians 8:1, 2.

we preached—the gospel of God.—see notes at v. 2.

unto you—in v. 2 Paul refers to the work of the missionaries as evangelists among the as yet unconverted Thessalonians; in v. 8 he refers to their work as pastors, and in v. 9 as teachers, among the converts. The evangelist speaks the gospel of God to the unconverted, the pastor shares it with, the teacher proclaims it to, the saints. Thus the threefold ministry centers in Christ and unfolds the gospel of God concerning His Son, Romans 1:1-3, for this alone glorifies God, saves sinners, confirms, comforts and edifies saints.

2:10 Ye are witnesses, and God *also,*—cp. note at v. 5, where there is a contrast between conduct, which man sees, and motives, which only God can know. Here there is a climax, "ye, and not ye only, God also, knows the truth of the matters we affirm." This is a bold appeal of the missionaries—from the world that knew little of them to the church that knew more, and, finally, to God Who knows all. Cp. 1 Corinthians 4:3, 4, where again the apostle appeals from man's day, i.e., the world, to "you," i.e., the saints, from the saints to his conscience from his conscience to his Lord.

how holily—*hosiōs*, which is not related to *hagios*, see note at 3:13.‖
The adjective, *hosiōs*, is used of God in Revelation 15:4; 16:5; and of the body of the Lord Jesus in Acts 2:27; 13:35, citations from Psalm 16:10, LXX,

and Hebrews 7:26; and of certain promises made to David which could only be fulfilled in the resurrection of the Lord Jesus, Acts 13:34. In 1 Timothy 2:8, Titus 1:8, it is used of the character of Christians.||

The noun, *hosiotēs,* occurs in Luke 1:75; Ephesians 4:24, and in each case "righteousness" is found with it.||

By Greek writers *hosiōs* was used for the careful discharge of one's duties to God, and *dikaios* = righteous, for the careful discharge of one's duties to man. This distinction does not always hold good in the Scriptures, however, for *dikaios* appears in Luke 1:6, "righteous before God," and *hosios* occurs in 2 Samuel 22:26, LXX, "merciful."

In LXX, *hosiōs* frequently represents the Hebrew word *chasid,* which varies in meaning between "holy" and "gracious," or "merciful," cp. Psalm 16:10 with 145:17. The "holy" man, in this sense of the word "holy," is one who walks with due regard to both grace and truth, and who manifests each quality equally in his conduct.

and righteously—*dikaiōs,* formerly "righteous" was spelled "rightwise," and in that form stands self-explained as = straight dealing. In the New Testament, it always has this sense, see Luke 23:41; 1 Corinthians 15:34; Titus 2:12, and here, of men in their ways, 1 Peter 2:23, of God in His ways.||

The uprightness of character and conduct which Paul had maintained when under the law, Philippians 3:6, he now manifested in the power of "the Spirit of life in Christ Jesus," Romans 8:2, 4.

and unblameably—*amemptōs,* as at 5:23, from *a* = not, and *memphomai* = to find fault, as in Mark 7:2; Romans 9:19; Hebrews 8:8.|| The adjective *amemptōs,* appears in Luke 1:6; Philippians 2:15; 3:6; 1 Thessalonians 3:13; Hebrews 8:7.||

The word signifies that no charge could be maintained, whatever charges might be made.

we behaved ourselves toward you,—lit., "became among you," as in 1:5, where see notes.

that believe:—lit., "the believers"; see note at 1:7.

2:11 as ye know how we *dealt with*—the absence of any verb from the orig. (it is supplied in English by the italicized words) is doubtless due to the informal character of the writing. See Introductory Notes, "The Epistle."

each one of you,—the emphasis rests on the word "one"; this is an indirect appeal to the individual converts in support of the general statement immediately preceding.

as a father with his own children,—the simile of the mother nursing her babes shows the tenderness of the missionaries' love; the simile of the father dealing with his children is the complement of this, showing the sterner aspects of the same love. Nonetheless were all brethren, missionaries and converts, see v. 9, Galatians 4:12; Philemon 16, children of one Father, differing only as older and younger members of the same family do. Figures based on the parental relationship are found only in the epistles of this writer to those in whose conversion he had been instrumental, see 1 Corinthians 4:14–21; 2 Corinthians 6:13; Galatians 4:19, and cp. Philemon 10.

exhorting you,—*parakaleō*, lit., "to call to one's side"; a word of frequent occurrence in the New Testament, the uses of which may be classified thus: *a*, to entreat, Matthew 8:5; 2 Corinthians 5:20, but not in these epistles; *b*, to urge one to pursue some course of conduct, here 3:2; 4:1, 10; 5:11, 14; 2 Thessalonians 3:12, and cp. 1 Thessalonians 2:3; in these senses it is prospective, looking to the future and aiming at progress in the Christian life; *c*, to comfort, 3:7; 4:18; 2 Thessalonians 2:17, and cp. v. 16; in this sense it is retrospective, looking to some trial encountered and aiming at submission to the will of God.

and encouraging *you,*—*paramutheomai*, this word does not differ greatly in meaning from the preceding one, and, like it, has different senses. In John 11, 19, 31, = to comfort, to console, with reference to what had happened; here, and in 5:14, = to stimulate to the energetic discharge of the common duties of life.||

Cp. also 1 Corinthians 14:3 and Philippians 2:1, where the corresponding noun occurs.||

and testifying,—*marturomai* = to bear witness, as in Acts 20:26; 26:22; Galatians 5:3; Ephesians 4:17; it is closely related to the word translated "bear witness," *martureō*, in John 21:24, *et al.*||

This word "testify" is added inasmuch as the apostle exhorted them to, and encouraged them in, only those things that he had himself proved in his own experience to be the "good and acceptable and perfect will of God," Romans 12:2.

2:12 to the end that—the purpose the missionaries had before them in all their dealings with the converts, cp. Romans 1:11; 1 Corinthians 10:6.

ye should walk—*peripateō*, a figurative use of the word, signifying the whole round of the activities of the individual life whether of the unregenerate, Ephesians 4:17, or of the believer, 1 Corinthians 7:17; Colossians 4:6. It is applied to the observance of religious ordinances, Acts 21:21; Hebrews 13:9, marg., as well as to moral conduct. The Christian is to walk in newness of life, Romans 6:4, after the spirit, 8:4, in honesty, 13:13, by faith, 2 Corinthians 5:7, in good works, Ephesians 2:10, in love, 5:2, in wisdom, Colossians 4:5, in truth, 2 John 4, after the commandments of the Lord, v. 6. And, negatively, not after the flesh, Romans 8:4, not after the manner of men, 1 Corinthians 3:3, not in craftiness, 2 Corinthians 4:2, not by sight, 5:7, not in vanity of the mind, Ephesians 4:17, not disorderly, 2 Thessalonians 3:6.

A synonym (i.e., a different word with a similar meaning), *stoicheō*, is used in Acts 21:24; Romans 4:12; Galatians 5:25; 6:16; Philippians 3:16. Both words mean "to walk," the difference between them being that whereas the former refers to the general conduct of the individual, the latter refers to his relation with others, and may be paraphrased "keeping step," cp. "walk orderly," Acts 21:24.||

Other synonyms are *orthopodeō*, Galatians 2:14, where see note, and *poreuomai* in 1 Peter 4:3, *et al.*

worthily of God,—*axiōs*, as 3 John 6. Cp. "worthily of the Lord," Colossians 1:10, "of the gospel of Christ," Philippians 1:27, "of the saints," Romans 16:2, and of their calling, Ephesians 4:1.||

Christians are to be holy, for God is holy, 1 Peter 1:15, "to be perfect as their Heavenly Father is perfect," Matthew 5:48, in a word, to be "imitators of God" since they are His "beloved children," Ephesians 5:1. Thus the expression "worthily of God" describes the ideal Christian life, the ambition of every spiritual man.

who calleth you—present continuous tense. God, Who had called them to salvation, 2 Thessalonians 2:13, 14, still called them to the pursuit of holiness, Hebrews 12:14, encouraging them with the assurance of His purpose and His power to accomplish it, 1 Thessalonians 5:24. In harmony with the words of the Lord Jesus in John 6:44, 65, etc., the calling of the saints is always referred to God the Father, cp. Romans 8:29, 30; Galatians 1:15, 16.

into His own kingdom—that Paul had preached the kingdom of God at Thessalonica, and the Lord Jesus as its king, is implied in the accusation made against Jason and his friends before the magistrates of the city, Acts 17:7.

The kingdom of God is (*a*) the sphere of God's rule, Psalms 22:28; 145:13; Daniel 4:25; Luke 1:52; Romans 13:1, 2. Since, however, this earth is the scene of universal rebellion against God, see e.g., Luke 4:5, 6; 1 John 5:19; Revelation 11:15–18, the kingdom of God is (*b*) the sphere in which, at any given time, His rule is acknowledged. God has not relinquished His sovereignty in the face of rebellion, demoniac and human, but has declared His purpose to establish it, Daniel 2:44; 7:14; 1 Corinthians 15:24, 25. Meantime, seeking willing obedience, He gave His law to a nation and appointed kings to administer His kingdom over it, 1 Chronicles 28:5. Israel, however, though declaring still a nominal allegiance shared in the common rebellion, Isaiah 1:24, and, after they had rejected the Son of God, John 1:11, cp. Matthew 21:33–43, were "cast away," Romans 11:15, 20, 25. Henceforth God calls upon men everywhere, without distinction of race or nationality, to submit voluntarily to His rule. Thus the kingdom is said to be "in mystery" now, Mark 4:11, that is, it does not come within the range of the natural powers of observation, Luke 17:20, but is spiritually discerned, John 3:3, cp. 1 Corinthians 2:14. When, hereafter, God asserts His rule universally, then the kingdom will be in glory, that is, it will be manifest to all, cp. Matthew 25:31–34; Philippians 2:9–11; 2 Timothy 4:1, 18.

Thus, speaking generally, references to the kingdom fall into two classes, the first, in which it is viewed as present and involving suffering for those who enter it, 2 Thessalonians 1:5; the second, in which it is viewed as future and is associated with reward, Matthew 25:34, and glory, 13:43. See also Acts 14:22.

The fundamental principle of the kingdom is declared in the words of the Lord spoken in the midst of a company of Pharisees, "the kingdom of God is among you." Luke 17:21, marg., that is, where the king is, there is the kingdom. Thus at the present time and so far as this earth is concerned, where the king is and where His rule is acknowledged, is, first, in the heart of the individual believer, Acts 4:19; Ephesians 3:17; 1 Peter 3:15; and then in the churches of God, 1 Corinthians 12:3, 5, 11; 14:37; cp. Colossians 1:27, where for "in" read "among."

Now, the king and His rule being refused, those who enter the kingdom of God are brought into conflict with all who disown its allegiance as well as with the desire for ease and the dislike of suffering and unpopularity, natural to all. On the other hand, subjects of the kingdom are the objects of the care of God, Matthew 6:33, and of the rejected king, Hebrews 13:5, Who has promised to be with each believer, Matthew 28:20, and wherever two or three of them are gathered together in His name, 18:20.

Entrance into the kingdom of God is by the new birth, Matthew 18:3; John 3:5, for nothing that a man may be by nature, or can attain to by any form of self-culture, avails in the spiritual realm. And as the new nature received in the new birth, is made evident by obedience, it is further said that only such as do the will of God shall enter into His kingdom, Matthew 7:21, where however, the context shows that the reference is to the future, as in 2 Peter 1:10, 11. Cp. also 1 Corinthians 6:9, 10; Galatians 5:21; Ephesians 5:5.

The expression "kingdom of God" occurs four times in Matthew, "Kingdom of the Heavens" usually taking its place. The latter, cp. Daniel 4:26, does not occur elsewhere in the New Testament, but see 2 Timothy 4:18, "His heavenly Kingdom." The expressions cover the same ground, cp. Matthew 19:23 with

v. 24, and again with Mark 10:23, 24; Matthew 19:14 with Mark 10:14; Matthew 13:11 with Luke 8:10. This kingdom is identical with the kingdom of the father, cp. Matthew 26:29 with Mark 14:25; and with the kingdom of the son, cp. Luke 22:30. Thus there is but one kingdom, variously described: of the Son of Man, Matthew 13:41; of Jesus, Revelation 1:9; of Christ Jesus, 2 Timothy 4:1; "of Christ and God," Ephesians 5:5; "of our Lord, and of His Christ," Revelation 11:15; "of our God, and the authority of His Christ," 12:10; "of the Son of His love," Colossians 1:13. Cp. Mark 9:43, 45 with 47, where "kingdom of God" and "life" are interchanged.

Concerning the future, the Lord taught His disciples to pray, "Thy Kingdom come," Matthew 6:10, where the verb is in the point tense precluding the notion of gradual progress and development, and implying a sudden catastrophe as declared in 2 Thessalonians 2:8.

Concerning the present, that a man is of the kingdom of God is not shown in the punctilious observance of ordinances, which are external and material, but in the deeper matters of the heart, which are spiritual and essential, viz., "righteousness, and peace, and joy in the Holy Spirit," Romans 14:17.

and glory.—*doxa,* as at v. 6. These words define the aspect of the kingdom in view here. The path of the believer lies through suffering on behalf of a kingdom refused, Acts 14:22; 2 Thessalonians 1:5, into a kingdom glorious and triumphant. It is the prospect of the latter that sustains him in the former, Romans 8:18; 2 Corinthians 4:17. In the midst of trial he rejoices in hope of the glory of God, Romans 5:2, 3, the earnest and pledge of which is the resurrection, 1 Peter 1:21, and ascension, Hebrews 2:9, of Christ. Cp. also Matthew 4:14, and 2 Thessalonians 2:14.

2:13 And for this cause—referring to what follows, as in John 12:18, and renewing the thanksgiving with which the epistle opened.

we also—i.e., "we as well as you"; "we" is made emphatic by the preceding *kai,* see note at 5:23. It is probable that in the message lately brought by Timothy, 3:6, the converts had expressed thanksgiving to God for their salvation.

thank God without ceasing,—see notes on 1:2, 3.

that,—*hoti,* as at 1:5.

when ye received from us—*paralambanō,* as at 4:1, where see note.

the word of the message,—lit., "word of hearing," as in Hebrews 4:2, and cp. Romans 10:17; Galatians 3:2, where see note; the same word is translated "report," Romans 10:16. See note on 1:6.

even the word **of God,**—emphasizing the divine origin of the message, see notes at 1:5, and 1:8.

ye accepted *it*—*dechomai,* as at 1:6, where see note. There is a slight, though real, difference between the words "received" and "accepted"; the first refers to the ear, the second, adding the idea of appropriation, refers to the heart.

not *as* **the word of men,**—the words in italics may be omitted with advantage. The gospel had been received from men, indeed, but it had been accepted, not as originating with men but with God. The apostle does not state merely that the converts had esteemed the message to be from God, he asserts that it is so. No person or society can by its sanction add weight to the word of God, the authority of which is inherent; cp. Matthew 7:28, 29; Luke 1:37; 4:32, 36; 20:1–8.

but, as it is in truth,—*alēthōs,* see note on 1:9, truth as distinguished from falsehood.

the word of God,—cp. 1 Corinthians 2:13; Galatians 1:11, 12.

which—i.e., "the word," not "Who," for where God is the worker the verb is always in the active voice, see 1 Corinthians 12:6, 11; Galatians 2:3, 5, 8, where see notes, Ephesians 1:11, 20; Philippians 2:13; here it is in the middle voice, hence the relative pronoun is to be translated "which."

also—*kai,* to be read with "worketh," see note at 5:23, marking the contrast between those who merely heard the gospel and those who hearing believed. Many had received the message with the ear, some had accepted it in the heart; in these its claim to be from God was vindicated by its active power in their lives, cp. Hebrews 4:12.

worketh—*energeō,* present continuous tense. In Hebrews 4:12, the Word of God is described as "living," *zaō* (used of God in 1:9) and "active," *energēs,* by it the soul is saved, James 1:21, and the new birth effected, 1 Peter 1:23. By it Christians are sanctified, John 17:17, cp. 1 Timothy 4:5, and edified, Acts 20:32. It bears fruit and increases throughout the world, Colossians 1:6, growing and prevailing mightily, Acts 19:20.

Like the seed, Mark 4:26, 27, the Word of God bears its life and power within itself, hence its manifold activities and its boundless increase. It is compared with fire as against that which is false and with a hammer against that which is strong, Jeremiah 23:29; it is light in the midst of darkness, Psalm 119:105, and it is the sole weapon of attack in the Christian's armory, Ephesians 6:17.

For an analysis of the New Testament use of *energeō* see note at Galatians 3:5.

in you that believe.—see note on 1:7.

2:14 For ye, brethren, became imitators—see notes on 1:4, 6.

of the churches of God—see note on 1:1.

This term is used in the New Testament by Paul only, and only of local companies of Christians, as those at Ephesus, Acts 20:28; at Corinth, 1 Corinthians 1:2; 10:32; 11:22; at Jerusalem, Galatians 1:13; 1 Corinthians 15:9; and, generally, of any such company, 1 Timothy 3:5, 15. "Churches of God" occurs again 1 Corinthians 11:16; 2 Thessalonians 1:4.||

Alternative descriptions of these companies are "churches of Christ," Romans 16:16, and "churches of the saints," 1 Corinthians 14:33. Sometimes an ethnographical description is added, as "of the Gentiles," Romans 16:4; sometimes a local description as "of Asia," 1 Corinthians 16:19; "of Macedonia," 2 Corinthians 8:1; "of Galatia," 1 Corinthians 16:1; "of Judaea," Galatians 1:22; "of [the] Laodiceans," Colossians 4:16; "of [the] Thessalonians," 1:1; 2 Thessalonians 1:1.

"The Church which is His [Christ's] Body," Ephesians 1:22, 23, is not in Scripture called by any of these names; "churches of God," "of Christ," "of the saints" are obviously inapplicable thereto, inasmuch as these phrases are found in the plural, "churches," whereas "the Church which is His Body" is one and indivisible and of this the plural could not be used.

which are in Judaea—lit., "the existing churches," suggesting that as persecution had not brought the work of God to an end in the place of its origin and the home of its fiercest enemies, it would avail as little at Thessalonica. Paul had himself persecuted the church at Jerusalem, 1 Corinthians 15:9, *et al.*, and in it Silas had been a leader, Acts 15:22. Thus the missionaries formed a living link between people differing in nationality, and unknown to each other by face.

in Christ Jesus:—cp. Colossians 3:3; the measure of their realization of the strength of this spiritual bond may be gauged by the character of the fellowship with Judaean Christians shown later by the church at Thessalonica, see 2 Corinthians 8:14. Churches are knit together not by any external bond, as of order, organization, history, or distinctive doctrine but by the vital relation of each to the one Lord of all, on Whom each is directly dependent, and to Whom alone each is directly responsible.

for ye also suffered the same things—sympathy, lit., "fellow-suffering," is a strong bond of unity. Jews and Gentiles in origin, they were now happily united in Christ and in "the fellowship of His sufferings," Philippians 3:10.

of your own countrymen,—see Acts 17:5; the Jews by making a wily appeal to political passions, v. 7, had aroused the Gentiles to attack Paul and his colleagues; thence followed the persecution of the church at Thessalonica, which had not yet subsided.

even as they did of the Jews;—i.e., as the churches of Judaea had suffered at the hands of the Jews, their own countrymen. Cp. the quotation by the Lord, in Matthew 10:35, 36, of Micah 7:6.

2:15 who both killed—_apokteinō,_ see note at 5:10.

the Lord Jesus—that this would be the end of His public testimony the Lord Himself foresaw and declared, Matthew 16:21; 21:33–39. But when His enemies thought to compass His death privately, His popularity deterred them, Matthew 21:46, and, as a public trial and execution according to their own laws were barred by the authority of the Romans, John 18:31, they accused Him before Pilate on a trumped-up political charge, Luke 23:2, and so procured His death, the actual executioners being the Roman soldiery, Matthew 27:27, 31. While this distinction is fully recognized, Luke 24:20; Acts 13:27, 28, e.g., yet, on the principle everywhere acknowledged, that what a man obtains to be done by others he does himself the words of Peter, Acts 3:14, 15, and of Stephen, 7:52, and of Paul, here are also true to fact. And, further, the persecution of the Christians by the Jews of the Dispersion, John 7:35; 1 Peter 1:1, shewed how thoroughly they were imbued by the same fanatical spirit that animated those who dwelt in Judaea.

Since this is a purely historical reference the apostle attaches the title to the personal name, see note on "Lord," 1:1.

This digression, to the end of v. 16, is probably to be accounted for by the apostle's latest experience of the truculent fanaticism of his fellow countrymen, see Acts 18:6.

and the prophets,—not all of them, of course, but this was the characteristic attitude of the Jews toward the messengers of God, see Nehemiah 9:26; 1 Kings 18:4; 19:10; 2 Chronicles 24:20, 21; Jeremiah 2:30; Matthew 23:37.

and drave us out,—_ekdiōkō,_ cp. 5:15, point tense referring to the events recorded in Acts 17:5–9. The word occurs elsewhere in the New Testament in Luke 11:49, where it is translated "persecute"; in LXX it occurs in Deuteronomy 6:19; 1 Chronicles 8:13, _et al._||

and please not God,—_areskō,_ as at v. 4; 4:1, where see notes; present continuous tense. Though to please God was their avowed aim, cp. John 16:2; Romans 10:2, they had only succeeded in making themselves obnoxious to Him, cp. Jeremiah 32:30.

and are contrary to all men;—*enantios*, for the meaning of the word see Acts 27:4, where it is used of the wind, and cp. 26:9.

God had called Israel to dwell apart with Himself, Numbers 23:9, 21, in order that He might bless the rest of mankind through them, Genesis 22:16–18, cp. Jeremiah 4:1, 2. But He had long departed from them, and the spirit of pride and jealousy had taken the place of the spirit of grace and service. Consequently, descendants of Isaac after the flesh though they were, they had become Ishmaelites in spirit, their hand against every man, Genesis 16:12.

2:16 forbidding us to speak—as at Pisidian Antioch, Acts 13:45, 50; at Iconium, 14:1–5; at Lystra, 14:19; at Berea, 17:13; and at Corinth, 18:12, as well as at Thessalonica. The suggestion that God meant to send a messenger to the Gentiles aroused the Jerusalem Jews to jealous fury, 22:22, 23, notwithstanding the repeated testimony of the Scriptures that it was His purpose to bless all nations; see Paul's quotations in Romans 9 and 15. Another form of the same spirit was denounced by the Lord, see Luke 11:52.

to the Gentiles—*ethnos*, from which "heathen" is formed; in the singular it is occasionally used of the Jews, Luke 7:5; John 11:48; Acts 10:22, but ordinarily, and always where it appears in the plural, it refers to non-Jewish nations, civilized or uncivilized.

Another word, *laos* = "the chosen people" Matthew 1:21; Luke 2:10; John 11:50; Acts 4:10. The exceptions are occasions when it is used in the plural, Luke 2:31; Acts 4:25; Romans 15:11. In Acts 4:27, "peoples" = tribes.

that they may be saved;—*sōzō*, see note at 1:10. *Sōzō* = to save *sōtēria*, and *sōtērion* = salvation, *sōtēr* = savior, are words of frequent occurrence in LXX and New Testament; in the latter one or other of them is found in every book save Galatians, Colossians, Philemon, and 2 and 3 John. "Savior" is used in the New Testament exclusively of God, Luke 1:47; Titus 1:3, and of the Lord Jesus, Luke 2:11; Titus 1:4, an important testimony to the essential deity of the latter, cp. Isaiah 43:11; Hosea 13:4, and Titus 2:13; 2 Peter 1:1.

"Salvation," is occasionally used for "Savior," as in Luke 2:30; 3:6; 19:9, 10, cp. Matthew 10:6, and in John 4:22, cp. Isaiah 49:6; 62:11.

God, in Christ, is not only the Savior of Israel, Jeremiah 14:8; Acts 13:23, He is the Savior of the Gentiles also, Acts 13:47, that is, He is "the Savior of the World," John 4:42; 1 John 4:14, cp. John 3:17; 12:47; 1 Timothy 2:3, 4. And while in a wider sense He is the Savior of believers, God is also "the Savior of all men," 1 Timothy 4:10, inasmuch as "He Himself giveth to all life and breath and all things," cp. Matthew 5:45; Acts 14:15–17; 17:25.

In the New Testament, as in LXX, the words are frequently used of material and temporal deliverances from danger and oppression, national, Matthew

24:13; Acts 7:25; Romans 11:26, and personal, Acts 27:20; 2 Timothy 4:18, as from:

- the Flood, Hebrews 11:7;
- the sea, Matthew 8:25; Acts 27:34;
- prison, Philippians 1:19;
- disease, Matthew 9:21;
- deformity, Acts 4:9;
- demoniacal power, Luke 8:36;
- death, Mark 15:30, 31; John 11:12; 12:27;
- and out of death, Luke 8:50; Hebrews 5:7.

But the characteristic use of the words in the Bible is to sum up and describe the spiritual and eternal deliverances which result from the intervention of God on behalf of those who trust Him. Salvation has its origin in the mercy of God, Titus 3:5, and in the grace of God, 2:11, Whose gift it is, Ephesians 2:8. And in the fact that salvation is also traced to the grace of the Lord Jesus, Acts 15:11, lies another testimony to His essential deity.

Faith in the Lord Jesus is the condition on which salvation is obtained, Acts 16:31; Romans 10:8–13. To be saved is to enter into the kingdom of the heavens, or of God, Matthew 19:23–25. It is to obtain the remission, or forgiveness, of sins, Luke 7:50, cp. 1:77. Forgiveness alone is seldom intended; it is indeed the first of the blessings vouchsafed by God to the repentant sinner, cp. Psalms 32:1, 2; 103:1; Acts 2:38; Ephesians 1:7, but to be saved means much more than to be forgiven: it means also to be made whole and to enter upon the enjoyment of peace, Luke 8:48.

Those who are said to be saved in this sense are also said to be redeemed (lutroō), Titus 2:14; 1 Peter 1:18, cp. Hebrews 9:12, justified, Acts 13:38, 39, and sanctified, Hebrews 10:10; 13:12, and to have eternal life, John 5:24, and peace with God, Romans 5:1.

The believer's present experience of the power of God to deliver from the bondage of sin, Romans 6:6, is also included in salvation, and is the primary reference of the word in 2 Corinthians 2:15; Hebrews 7:25; James 1:21, cp. 1 Timothy 4:16, and Philippians 2:12; 1 Peter 1:9; 3:21. Salvation in this sense is intended by the word "sanctification," as in 1 Thessalonians 4:3, where see note; it is the experience of present deliverance from the dominion of sin, Romans 6:14, and is as much the privilege of the believer, and as much the mind of God for him here and now, as it is that he should have present assurance that his sins have been forgiven him.

Salvation is also the object of hope, 1 Thessalonians 5:8, inasmuch as its consummation is reserved until the Lord comes, Romans 5:9, 10; 13:11; 1 Corinthians 3:15; 5:5; Philippians 3:20; Hebrews 9:28; 1 Peter 1:5. In this sense salvation is associated with the redemption *(apolutrōsis)* of the body, Romans 8:23; 1 Corinthians 1:30; Ephesians 1:14; 4:30, and with the impartation to it of that eternal life or immortality, Mark 10:30; John 6:27; 12:25; Romans 6:22; Titus 1:2; 3:7; Jude 21, on which believers enter at the Parousia of the Lord Jesus, 1 Corinthians 15:51–56.

In many passages salvation is used in an inclusive sense covering all the meanings noticed above and summing up all the blessings bestowed by God on men in Christ, through the Holy Spirit, Matthew 1:21; Acts 4:12; Romans 1:16; 2 Corinthians 6:2; Hebrews 5:9; Jude 3.

to fill up their sins—God permits men to go far in wickedness, because He is longsuffering and gives time for repentance as in the days of Noah, 1 Peter 3:20, cp. 2 Peter 3:9; Romans 2:4. On the other hand, God permits the evil things He sees in a man, or in a nation, to grow and develop until they become manifest to other eyes than His own, that thus the righteousness of His judgments, when they do come may be put beyond dispute, see Psalm 89:2, 14. So He dealt with the Amorites, Genesis 15:16 (the language of which the apostle uses here from the LXX), and in due time judgment fell upon them, see Joshua 10. Gabriel ascribed this reason for the delay of the divine retribution, Daniel 8:23; and the Lord warned the leaders of Israel that they were pursuing the same infatuated course that involved their fathers in disaster and exile, Matthew 23:32.

alway:—*pantote,* as at 1:2. Cp. Acts 7:51, where however, a different word, *aei,* is translated "always," referring to a characteristic rebellious condition of heart, as this refers to an uninterrupted succession of rebellious acts.

but the wrath—see Luke 21:23 and note at 1:10.

is come upon them—*phthanō,* point tense, lit., "came," and, of course remains, cp. John 3:36. The verb suggests that what came was not expected, as here and Romans 9:31, or that it came in a manner other than that in which it was expected, Matthew 12:28; Luke 11:20, or that it came before something, or some person, else. See also 2 Corinthians 10:14, see also 2 Corinthians 10:4; Philippians 3:16, and 4:15 below, where see note.||

The Jews were already a scattered people, their land under a foreign yoke and within twenty years of the writing of these words their temple and their city were destroyed. The phrase "come upon" occurs elsewhere only in Matthew 12:28 and Luke 11:20, suggesting a solemn contrast between what might have been had they recognized the time of their visitation, Luke 19:41, 44, and what actually followed on their determined rejection of the Messiah.

to the uttermost.—ct. the same phrase in John 13:1. The reference is to the prophecy of Deuteronomy 28:15–68; but inasmuch as the gifts and the calling of God are not repented of, Romans 11:29, marg., God will not make a full end of Israel, Jeremiah 30:4–11, though still heavier sorrows await the nation before final deliverance comes, Matthew 24:15–28.

2:17 But we, brethren,—resuming his assurance of an affection which had been rather strengthened than cooled by separation, and which stood in marked contrast to the hatred shown by the Jews.

being bereaved of [lit., from] **you**—*aporphanizomai,* cp. John 14:18; James 1:27, where a corresponding noun, *orphanos,* is translated "desolate" and "fatherless." It suits the similes of v. 7 and v. 11, and has a wider significance than the English word "orphan" which is derived from it.

for a short season,—lit., "a season of an hour," combining the words elsewhere used to describe a brief interval of time; for the first, *kairos,* see 5:1, and note there; for the second, *hōra,* cp. Galatians 2:5.

Apparently about five years elapsed before the apostle visited Thessalonica again, but neither of that, nor of any subsequent visit, are any particulars preserved.

in presence,—*prosōpon,* lit., "in face," cp. Matthew 6:17, and later in this verse; here = "in body." The same word is sometimes rendered "person," see Galatians 2:6, and note there.

not in heart,—by metonymy = "thoughts," see note on v. 4. For a similar idea differently expressed see Colossians 2:5; for a different idea expressed in the same words see 2 Corinthians 5:12.

endeavored the more exceedingly—what efforts he made are not recorded, but from these words it is evident that Paul did not acquiesce without protest in his exclusion from the city.

to see your face—i.e., to see you, as at 3:10.

with [*en* = in] **great desire**—*epithumia,* the same word is used by the Lord of the Last Passover, Luke 22:15, and by Paul of his desire to be with Christ, Philippians 1:23. Elsewhere in the New Testament only in a bad sense, as at 4:5.

2:18 because we would fain—*thelō* = to desire, or to design, to do anything.

have come unto you,—once and again;—not only had the apostle desired to see them; twice at least he had resolved to do so, but in each case his purpose had been frustrated. With the phrase "once and again," cp. Philippians 4:16.

I Paul—the three co-workers had parted at Berea, Acts 17:14; Timothy had visited Thessalonica again, ch. 3:6, and probably Silas had accompanied him, Acts 18:5, or had joined him there.

and Satan—a Hebrew word = an adversary, occurs first in Numbers 22:22, 32, where it is used of an angel of Jehovah; see also 1 Samuel 29:4; 2 Samuel 19:22; 1 Kings 5:4; 11:14, 23, 25, where it is used of men, as also in Psalm 38:20; 71:13; 109:4, 6, 20, 29. In eighteen other places the word is transliterated as a proper name, and in one, Zechariah 3:1, it is translated "adversary" and refers to the Devil; see below.

In the New Testament the word occurs thirty-six times, and always with reference to the sinister and mysterious enemy of Christ and His people. That Satan is not merely the personification of the evil influences at work within the heart is evident, among other reasons, because *(a)* Satan tempted, or tried, the Lord Jesus, in whose heart no unholy thought ever could have arisen, cp., e.g., 2 Corinthians 5:21; John 14:30; Hebrews 4:15 (for "without sin" read "apart from sin," as in 9:28; the original is the same); *(b)* the personality of Satan is even more plainly asserted in the New Testament than in the Old Testament If the language of the Old Testament had been intended to be figurative, the fuller light of the New Testament would have made this evident. Indeed, more is learned about Satan from the words of Christ than from any other source.

Satan is also called:

- The Devil, *Diabolos* = an accuser or slanderer, cp. Matthew 4:1 with v. 10. *Diabolos* is used in the plural only in 1 Timothy 3:11; 2 Timothy 3:3; Titus 2:3, and in these places, by metaphor, of human beings, cp. John 6:70. The word *daimōn*, frequently translated "devil" in the Gospels, should always be rendered "demon" as in marg.
- Beelzebub = Old Testament Baalzebub = "lord of flies," 2 Kings 1:2, or Beelzeboul, = "lord of dung," Mark 3:22, 23.
- The Great Dragon, Revelation 12:9.
- The Old Serpent, Revelation 12:9.
- The Tempter, Matthew 4:3; 1 Thessalonians 3:5.
- The Evil One, Matthew 6:13.
- The Enemy, Luke 10:19.
- The Ruler of this world, *kosmos,* John 12:31.
- The Ruler of the authorities of the air, Ephesians 2:2.

- The God of this age, 2 Corinthians 4:4.
- "Belial," lit., "Belier," as marg. = "worthlessness"; see 1 Samuel 2:12, marg.; 2 Corinthians 6:15.

Satan is not, in Scripture, represented as a rival deity, coequal with, or but slightly inferior to, God; but always as a creature of God, subordinate to God, and holding his authority from God, even when he uses it in defiance of the will of God.

Of his history little is known, save that he was originally among the sons of God, Job 1:6, but fell through pride, 1 Timothy 3:6. Nevertheless he still retains, in some real, though limited, Romans 13:1, sense, the rule of the kingdoms of the world, Luke 4:6, cp. 22:53, John 14:30. His destiny is to be learned from Revelation 20:1–10.

hindered us—the position of the names is emphatic, "I, Paul, at least, and hindered us—Satan!" How Satan hindered him is not stated, but probably the bond that Jason and his friends gave to the civil authorities at Thessalonica, Acts 17:9, included an undertaking that Paul would not reenter the city. It may be he refers to his ineffectual efforts to have this bond cancelled in v. 17. In that case he traced the violence of the Jews, who caused the trouble at Thessalonica, to Satan, as the Lord Himself did when they sought to kill Him, John 8:37–44.

Satan is not omnipresent (or ubiquitous), nevertheless he has power to distress the people of God. Thus he can hinder the coming of those who care for them, as in this case and cp. Daniel 10:13; he can raise up false teachers among them, 2 Corinthians 11:13–15, cp. Revelation 2:24; he can turn them aside from the right ways of the Lord, Acts 5:3; 2 Corinthians 2:11; 11:3; Ephesians 6:11; 1 Timothy 5:15; he can afflict their bodies, Job 2:7; Luke 13:16; 2 Corinthians 12:7; and he can arouse the passions of men against them, 1 Peter 5:8; Revelation 2:13.

Satan seeks to have servants of Christ put into his hands for testing, Job 1:6–12; Luke 22:31; he lays snares for them, 1 Timothy 3:7, and by these he succeeds at times in making them his captives, 2 Timothy 2:26 (where read "that they may return to soberness out of the snare of the Devil—having been taken captive alive by him—unto the will of God"). The final triumph of the saints over their adversary is, nevertheless, assured, Romans 16:20.

The power to distinguish between the experience here referred to and that of Acts 16:7, is a spiritual attainment, the way to which lies through obedience to the Word of God, see Romans 12:1, 2; Ephesians 5:10.

2:19 For—introducing his reason for so ardently desiring to be among them again; this is conveyed in the form of a question, asked not to elicit information, but to express his deep feeling more effectively than a mere statement would have done.

what is our hope,—see note at 2 Thessalonians 2:16.

Here the apostle has in mind his hope of reward as a servant. In similar terms he addresses his other Macedonian converts, Philippians 4:1, the firstfruits of his labors in Europe.

Or joy,—*chara,* as at 1:6, and see note on "grace," *charis,* at 1:1; for the corresponding verb see note at 5:16.

or crown—*stephanos,* the victor's crown, the symbol of triumph in the games or other contest; by metonymy = a reward, a prize.

A synonym of *stephanos* is *diadēma* = the symbol of imperial dignity, Revelation 12:3; 13:1; 19:2.||

The metaphor of the crown is found in the Old Testament, see Proverbs 17:6, *stephanos;* the words occur together in Isaiah 62:3, LXX.

[Where "as" or "like" is used, the figure is a simile, Job 31:36, e.g., see note at v. 7. Where neither "as" nor "like" appears the figure is a metaphor.]

of glorying?—*kauchēsis* = exultation, as in Romans 15:17; 2 Corinthians 1:12, *et al.* Here, as in Philippians 2:16, the Judgment Seat of Christ is in Paul's mind; the converts would be to him, then, instead of the chaplet of laurel with which earthly victors were crowned.

Crowns, in the New Testament, are promised to the Christian as rewards for patient endurance or for faithful service. Cp.:

"An incorruptible crown," a general description applicable to all rewards promised to those who stand approved at the Judgment Seat of Christ, 1 Corinthians 9:25.

"The crown of righteousness," describing the character of the award corresponding to the character of the Giver, 2 Timothy 4:8.

"The crown of life," describing the permanent nature of the reward, in contrast to the transient experience of trial in which it is won, and corresponding to the nature of the living God who gives it; James 1:12; Revelation 2:10.

"The crown of unfading glory" (*doxa,* as in v. 20), describing the reward of those who give themselves without ostentation and without hope of gain to the care of the flock in the absence of the Chief Shepherd, 1 Peter 5:4.

"A man is tried by his praise," i.e., the things wherein a man glories afford an index to his character, Proverbs 27:21, see marg., a test which may be applied to the writers of these epistles. The apostle gloried in:

- God, through our Lord Jesus Christ, Romans 5:11; 1 Corinthians 1:31;
- Christ Jesus, Philippians 3:3:

- the Cross, Galatians 6:14:
- hope of the glory of God, Romans 5:2:
- his rapture to the Third Heaven, 2 Corinthians 12:1-6:
- his apostolic authority for edification, 2 Corinthians 10:8:
- his large sphere of gospel service, 2 Corinthians 10:13:
- his ability to waive his claim to temporal support, 2 Corinthians 11:10:
- his converts, here, and 2 Corinthians 1:14:
- the spiritual growth of his converts, 2 Corinthians 7:14:
- their liberality, 2 Corinthians 9:2:
- their patience and faith, 2 Thessalonians 1:4:
- tribulation, Romans 5:3:
- his weaknesses, 2 Corinthians 11:30; 12:5, 9:
- a good conscience, 2 Corinthians 1:12:

With this "glorying" are to be contrasted and the "vaunting," *perpereuomai,* of 1 Corinthians 13:4:|| and the "vaunting" and "vainglory," *alazoneia,* of James 4:6 and 1 John 2:16:|| and the "boastful" persons, *alazōn,* of Romans 1:30; 2 Timothy 3:2.||

Cp. also the "empty glorying," *kenodoxia,* of Galatians 5:26 and Philippians 2:3.

Are not even ye, before—cp. "before our God and Father," 3:13. The language shows how closely the Lord Jesus was associated with God in the mind of the apostle: to be in the presence of the Son is to be in the presence of the Father.

our Lord Jesus—see notes at 1:1. Though Satan had succeeded in hindering Paul from returning to the Thessalonians, he could not prevent the consummation of his hope of seeing them again when the Lord Jesus should catch them all away to Himself in the air, 4:17. It is evident that the apostle expected to recognize them in their changed bodies, Philippians 3:20, 21.

at [lit., in] His coming?—*parousia* occurs in the Apocrypha in 2 Maccabees 8:12; 15:21; Judith 10:18, which may be consulted for the meaning of the word.|| *Parousia,* lit., as marg. "presence." *Parousia,* here rendered "coming," is a noun formed from the verb *pareimi* = to be present, as in Luke 13:1; John 11:28; Acts 10:33, etc., and hence = "a being present with." In a papyrus document (see note at 1:3) it is used of a royal visit to a certain district; in another, a person states that the care of her property demands her "presence" in a certain city. In Philippians 2:12 Paul speaks of his *parousia,* his "presence," at Philippi, in contrast with his *apousia,* his "absence," from that city. Always, wherever it occurs, *parousia* refers to a period of time more or less extended. The usual translation is misleading, because "coming" is more appropriate to other words, such as *erchomai,* Luke 12:45; 19:23; *eleusis,* Acts 7:52;|| *eisodos,* 13:24; the difference being that whereas these words fix the attention on the journey to, and the arrival at, a place, *parousia* fixes it on the stay which follows on the arrival there. It would be preferable therefore to transliterate the word rather than translate it, that is to use "parousia," rather than "coming," wherever the reference is to the Lord Jesus.

Where *parousia* is used of the Lord Jesus it refers to a defined period. Thus in 2 Peter 1:16 it describes, not the daily and general companying of the Lord with His disciples among the people, but that limited period during which He was transfigured before them, Matthew 17:1-8. Where it is used prophetically, *parousia* refers to a period beginning with the descent of the Lord from heaven into the air, 1 Thessalonians 4:16, 17, and ending with His revelation and manifestation to the world; see note on "with us," 2 Thessalonians 1:7.

During the Parousia of the Lord in the air with His people, Paul expected to give account of his stewardship before the Judgment Seat of Christ, 1 Corinthians 4:1-5; 2 Corinthians 5:10; the presence there of the Thessalonian converts and their commendation by the Lord, would mean reward to the evangelists who had been the means of their conversion, and to the pastors and teachers who had labored among them. For a similar thought see 1 John 2:28, and cp. 1 Peter 5:1-4. There, too, all would be abundantly compensated for the afflictions they were enduring.

The Parousia of the Lord Jesus is thus a period with a beginning, a course and a conclusion. The beginning is prominent in 4:15; 5:23; 2 Thessalonians 2:1; 1 Corinthians 15:23; James 5:7, 8; 2 Peter 3:4; the course here and in 3:13, Matthew 24:3, 37, 39; 1 John 2:28; the conclusion in 2 Thessalonians 2:8; Matthew 24:27.

In addition to its use of the Lord in the passages mentioned in the preceding paragraphs, *parousia* occurs of:

- the Lawless One, 2 Thessalonians 2:9:
- the Day of God, 2 Peter 3:12:
- Paul, or his companions, 1 Corinthians 16:17; 2 Corinthians 7:6, 7; 10:10; Philippians 1:26; 2:12.||

2:20 For ye are our glory—*doxa,* as at v. 6; they had been charged with preaching the gospel with an eye to immediate material gain, whereas in fact they looked for reward of a very different kind at the Judgment Seat of Christ.

and our joy.—There had been joy in heaven over the conversion of each individual Thessalonian, Luke 15:10, in this the missionaries had shared. There will be "exceeding joy" when all the redeemed are presented together before God, see Jude 24, and in that joy also they hoped to share.

In all his labors the apostle kept the end in view. His aim was to present every man perfect in Christ; for this he prayed, Philippians 1:8–11, and for this he toiled, Colossians 1:28, 29; the souls won by his preaching continued to be the objects of his care; cp. what is said of the Lord in John 13:1.

1 THESSALONIANS

CHAPTER THREE

Verses 1–13

3:1 Wherefore—i.e., because of his affection for them, and the frustration of his attempts to return to them.

when we could no longer forbear,—*stegō*, which signifies either that that of which it is predicated supports what is placed upon it, or covers what is placed underneath it. The former idea is prominent here and in v. 5 and 1 Corinthians 9:12, while both ideas may be present in 1 Corinthians 13:7. His mingled hope, 2:17, and fear, v. 5, imposed a strain in the mind of the apostle for which he sought relief in the manner described.

we—it is obvious that though he uses the plural form of the verb, Paul here refers to himself alone. Where Silas was when Timothy was dispatched from Athens is not stated, here or in Acts, but both had rejoined him when he wrote, Acts 18:5; they had shared his labors at Thessalonica, and they shared his love for the converts there; hence Paul associates them with himself in these letters, not merely as of courtesy but as of right. Here, making a statement of fact true only of himself he still uses the plural, but immediately defines it, v. 5, by repeating the statement in the singular; see Intro. Note on the style of the Epistle, and cp. 2:17, 18.

thought it good—*eudakeō*, see note on 2:8.

to be left behind at Athens alone; 3:2 and sent Timothy,—see Intro. Note.

our brother and God's minister—*diakonos;* a description of the relationship between servants of Christ among themselves on the one hand, and between each servant and the Lord on the other. It is significant that it is the older man who speaks, cp. Intro. Note.

Diakonos, from *diakō* = to pursue, is used of one who renders service of whatever character to another. From it the English word "deacon" is derived. It occurs in the New Testament of:

- domestic servants, John 2:5, 9:
- the civil ruler, Romans 13:4:
- Christ, Romans 15:8; Galatians 2:17:

- the followers of Christ in relation to their Lord, John 12:26; Ephesians 6:21; Colossians 1:7; 4:7:
- the followers of Christ in relation to one another, Matthew 20:26; 23:11; Mark 9:35; 10:43:
- the servants of Christ in the work of preaching and teaching here, 1 Corinthians 3:5; 2 Corinthians 3:6; 6:4; 11:23; Ephesians 3:7; Colossians 1:23, 25; 1 Timothy 4:6:
- those who serve in the churches, Romans 16:1 (used of a woman here only in the New Testament), Philippians 1:1; 1 Timothy 3:8, 12:
- false apostles, servants of Satan, 2 Corinthians 11:15.

Once *diakonos* is used where, apparently, angels are intended, Matthew 22:13; in v. 3, where men are intended, *doulos* is used.||

Closely associated with *diakonos* is *hupērētēs,* originally an under-rower in a war galley, later a subordinate official who waits on the commands of his superior. Its New Testament use may be studied in typical passages, such as Matthew 5:25; John 18:18, "officer," Luke 1:2; Acts 13:5, "attendant," 26:16; 1 Corinthians 4:1.

Another word, *leitourgos* = one who performs public duties, Romans 13:6; 15:16; Hebrews 1:7; 8:2 (of the Lord), or performs representative service, Philippians 2:25; 1 Thessalonians 3:2.

Doulos, originally a bond servant, or slave, has not, in the New Testament, always and of necessity the idea of bondage, it is in fact the most common and general word for "servant," Matthew 8:9; it is sometimes set in contrast with *diakonos,* 20:26, 27.

Other New Testament synonyms of *diakonos,* are:

- *therapōn,* service of freedom, confidence, dignity (Trench, *Synonyms,* IX.), quoted from Numbers 12:7, LXX; Hebrews 3:5:||
- *misthios,* a hired servant, Luke 15:17, 19:||
- *misthōtos,* a hired servant, Mark 1:20; John 10:12, 13:||
- *oiketes,* a household servant, Luke 16:13; Acts 10:7; Romans 14:4; 1 Peter 2:18:
- *pais,* which is sometimes used of a child, Luke 8:51, 54, e.g., sometimes of a household servant, 12:45, e.g. It is used of Israel, Luke 1:54, of David, v. 69, and of the Lord Jesus, 2:43, "boy," Acts 3:13, *et al.,* "servant."

Speaking generally, the *diakonos* is a servant viewed in relationship to his work; the *doulos,* Matthew 8:9; Luke 2:29; John 18:18; Romans 1:1, and many places, is a servant viewed in relationship to his master, the *huperētēs* is a servant viewed in relationship to his superior; the *leitourgos* is a servant viewed in relationship to public duties.

in the gospel of Christ,—the sphere of the service, cp. Romans 1:9; 2 Corinthians 10:14; Philippians 4:3. See note at 2:2.

to establish you,—the meaning of the verb *stērizō (epistērizō)* in Acts 14:22; 15:32, 41‖ may be learned from its use in Exodus 17:12, LXX, "stayed up"; Luke 9:51, "steadfastly set," 16:26, "fixed."

To the establishment, or confirmation, of his brethren the Lord called Peter, Luke 22:32; and to the confirming of souls, Acts 14:22, of the brethren, 15:32, of churches, 15:41, cp. 16:5, and of the disciples, 18:23, such men as Paul, Barnabas, Silas and Judas devoted much labor; indeed it was with this purpose in view that Paul desired to visit Rome, Romans 1:11, 12. The means used to effect this confirmation was the ministry of the Word, see Acts 15:32; 2 Peter 1:12: neither laying on of hands nor the impartation of the Holy Spirit is mentioned in the New Testament in connection either with *stērizō* or with its synonym, *bebaioō,* 1 Corinthians 1:8; 2 Corinthians 1:21, etc. That the confirmation of the saints is ultimately the work of God, see 3:13; 2 Thessalonians 2:16, 17; 3:3; Romans 16:25; 1 Peter 5:10. Finally, James exhorts Christians to establish, or confirm, themselves, 5:8.‖

and to comfort *you*—*parakaleō,* or, better, "encourage," cp. Acts 15:32, and see note at 2:11.

concerning—*huper,* as in Romans 9:27; 2 Thessalonians 2:1, "touching."

your faith;—*pistis.* The apostle uses this word in different senses, as of:
  a, trust, as in 1:3, 8; 5:8; 2 Thessalonians 3:2, and here:
  b, trustworthiness, as in Romans 3:3; Titus 2:10:
  c, what is believed, as in 3:10; Titus 1:13:
  d, a ground for faith, an assurance, Acts 17:31.

3:3 that no man be moved—*sainō* = to disturb, disquiet. It stands in contrast to the word "establish" in v. 2. This danger, which threatens the converts in every field of missionary activity, is described by the Lord in Mark 4:16, 17.

by [lit., in, or amid] **these afflictions;**—*thlipsis,* see notes at v. 7 and 2 Thessalonians 1:6.

for yourselves know—*oida,* as at 1:4; this knowledge, however, was imparted to them by their teachers, see v. 4. Compare the expression in the Corinthian epistles, "Know ye not . . . ?"

that hereunto we are appointed.—*keimai* = to lie, lit., as in Luke 2:12; for its meaning here cp. Luke 2:34, and Philippians 1:17. It indicates, not an ultimate destiny, but a temporary experience ordained as a means to an end. Though affliction is the common lot of the godly, 2 Timothy 3:12; it is transient, not eternal, cp. 2 Corinthians 4:17, 18; 1 Peter 1:6; knowledge of the will of God in the matter secures the suffering Christian from surprise and dismay. Cp. Luke 9:22–24; John 16:33.

3:4 For verily, when we were with you,—"with" = *pros,* as in 1:8, "toward." The words more frequently rendered "with," *meta,* 3:13, and *sun,* 4:17, denote in company with; *pros* always implies active intercourse with, see Mark 9:16; John 1:1; 2 Corinthians 5:8; Galatians 1:18, etc.

we told you beforehand—continuous tense = "we used to tell you." The margin, "plainly," conveys the sense, for the apostle is not here asserting his prophetic gift, but is reminding his readers that he had not disguised from them the inevitable consequences of accepting the gospel.

that we are to suffer affliction;—*thlibō,* corresponding to the noun in v. 3. It is translated "straitened" in Matthew 7:14; "throng" in Mark 3:9; "pressed" in 2 Corinthians 4:8. Thus the word refers to the sufferings that arise from the pressure of circumstances or from the antagonism of persons.

even as it came to pass, and ye know.—i.e., from experience: see below.

3:5 For this cause—cp. 2:13.

I also, when I could no longer forbear,—see note on v. 1.

sent that I might know your faith,—Timothy's was a mission with a double object, to strengthen the faith of the converts, and to obtain for Paul information concerning their welfare.

The word translated "know," *ginōskō,* occurs here only in these Epistles, and = to get to know, to ascertain. *Oida,* vv. 3, 4, is the perfect tense of a verb, *eidein* = to see (from which "idol" is derived, see note on 1:9, and cp. the English word "idea" = what the mind sees). Hence *oida* suggests fullness of knowledge, rather than progress in knowledge, which is expressed by *ginōskō.* The use of the two verbs is well illustrated in John 8:55, "Ye have not known," i.e., begun to know, *ginōskō,* "Him, but I know Him," i.e., know Him perfectly, *oida;* and in 13:7, "What I do thou knowest not now," i.e., Peter did not yet perceive, *oida,* its significance, "but thou shalt understand," i.e., get to know, *ginōskō,* "hereafter." See Galatians 2:9; 4:8 and note there.

lest by any means—cp. 2 Corinthians 11:3, and Galatians 4:11.

the tempter—as in Matthew 4:3, see note on "Satan," 2:18.

had tempted you,—*peirazō,* the point tense indicates that the apostle feared not merely an assault on their faith, but a successful assault = "that the tempter had succeeded in tempting you." Satan was doubly active, he had hindered the missionaries from continuing the work at Thessalonica; had he succeeded in overthrowing what they had done?

Peirazō, means, first, to attempt to do something, to assay, as in Acts 9:26; 16:7; 24:6; then, to make trial of deliberately, as the Queen of Sheba made trial whether Solomon were as wise as he was reputed to be, 1 Kings 10:1, LXX; and as the Pharisees made trial of the integrity of the Lord Jesus, Matthew 19:3; 22:18, and many places; or unconsciously, but not less really, as those who sinned in the wilderness made trial of the holiness of God, 1 Corinthians 10:9, cp. Hebrews 3:8, 9; as Ananias and his wife made trial whether the Holy Spirit were indeed with the church, Acts 5:9; and as the Jewish believers made trial of the grace of God, Acts 15:10.

A synonym of *peirazō, dokimazō,* is frequently found in the New Testament, see note at 2:4. Both words are used in 2 Corinthians 13:5 in such a way as to show how closely they resemble one another in meaning, and whereas the former is used in Revelation 2:2, the same writer uses the latter in 1 John 4:1, as does Paul in 5:21, three closely allied passages.

But while *dokimazō* is never used of Satan, or in a bad sense, *peirazō* frequently is. Satan tried, *peirazō,* the Lord Jesus, Matthew 4:1; Luke 4:13; Hebrews 2:18; 4:15, and he tries men, as here; he is, indeed, "The Tempter," see note above.

Peirazō, on the other hand, is only once used in the New Testament of God, Hebrews 11:17, cp. Genesis 22:1, where LXX has the same word, and once of the Lord Jesus, John 6:6.

Trial, *peirasmos,* Acts 20:19; Galatians 4:14; 1 Peter 1:6; 2 Peter 2:9; Revelation 3:10, may proceed either from Satan, whose object is to overthrow faith, or from God, whose purpose is to establish it. In any case, God overrules to prevent any trial coming upon any one of His children beyond his strength to bear, 1 Corinthians 10:13, cp. 2 Corinthians 12:7-9.

The children of God are to pray that they may not be carried into trial, i.e., by forces beyond their own control, Matthew 6:13; they are to watch and pray that they enter not into trial, i.e. through their own carelessness or disobedience, Matthew 26:41.

But when trial comes, it is sent, or permitted, that what is genuine, *dokimion,* in faith may produce patience and issue in the perfecting of Christian character, James 1:3, 4; 1 Peter 1:6, 7.||

James 1:13-15 seems to contradict other statements of Scripture in two respects, saying, *a,* that "God cannot be tempted with evil," and, *b,* that "He Himself tempteth no man." But God tempted, or tried, Abraham, Hebrews 11:17, and the Israelites tempted, or tried, God, 1 Corinthians 10:9. Verse 14, however, makes it plain that whereas in these cases the temptation, or trial, came from without, James refers to temptation, or trial, arising within, from uncontrolled appetites and from evil passions, cp. Mark 7:20–23. But though such temptation does not proceed from God, yet does God regard His people while they endure it, and by it tests and approves them; see James 1:2, 12, where *peirasmos* is apparently used in its widest sense of trial from whatever source.

and our labor—as at 1:3.

should be in vain.—see note on 2:1; it was the apprehension of this possibility that had burdened the apostle's mind till he could no longer endure the strain, v. 1. Cp. Galatians 4:19.

3:6 But when Timothy came even now unto us from you,—see Intro. Note.

and brought us glad tidings—*euangelizomai,* from which the English word "evangelize" is derived, is used in LXX of any message calculated to have a cheering effect on those who receive it, 1 Samuel 31:9; 2 Samuel 1:20. In the New Testament, with few exceptions, here and Luke 1:19, e.g., it is used of the good news concerning His Son which God has sent to men, cp. Romans 1:1–3.

of your faith and love,—their faith was expressing itself through love, Galatians 5:6, and see note on 1:3. Cp. the fuller statement in Colossians 1:4, "faith in Christ Jesus . . . love . . . toward all the saints"; see also Philemon 5, and 1 John 3:23. The absence of the third member of the trio, "hope," is significant in view of the section of the epistle beginning at 4:13.

and that ye have good—*agathōs,* see note at 5:21.

remembrance of us—*mneia,* always in connection with prayer; in Philippians 1:3; 2 Timothy 1:3, it is rendered as here, but elsewhere the verb "to make" appears with it and it is rendered "mention," 1:2; Romans 1:9; Ephesians 1:16; Philemon 4.||

always,—*pantote,* i.e., on all occasions of prayer, see notes at 1:2.

longing to see us, even as we also *to see* **you;**—Titus brought a similar message from the Corinthians to Paul while he was in Macedonia, perhaps at Thessalonica or Philippi, and that after he had written his severe first epistle to them, 2 Corinthians 7:7. Writing from Rome, Paul expressed his longing to see again the well-known saints at Philippi, 1:8, a longing in which Epaphroditus, his coworker, shared, 2:26; and writing from Corinth, he expressed his longing to be with the saints in a city he had not yet visited, Romans 1:11; 15:23; cp.

also 2 Timothy 1:4. The only other object of his longing of which the apostle speaks in his Epistles is the glorified body, 2 Corinthians 5:2.

The comparison here and 2:11; 3:12; 4:5, is made by means of a different word, *kathaper,* from the more frequent and less forcible *kathōs,* used in 3:4, *et al.*

3:7 for this cause, brethren,—because of the report brought by Timothy.

we were comforted—see note at 2:22, "exhorting."

over you—an expression beautifully in keeping with the simile of 2:7.

in all our distress—*anankē,* Paul sometimes uses this word of an inward pressure of spirit, as in 1 Corinthians 9:16, "necessity"; sometimes of lack of material things, 2 Corinthians 6:4; 12:10, and here, apparently.

and affliction—as at v. 3, and 2 Thessalonians 1:4; referring to persecution at the hands of men, mobs or rulers, cp. Matthew 13:21; Acts 11:19, "tribulation." Paul had in mind their sufferings at Philippi, ch. 2:2, and again at Thessalonica itself 2:15, and yet again at Berea, Acts 17:13, which, though actually past, still weighed on the apostle's mind, apparently producing something akin to despondency, cp. note on 2:2. Trouble did not threaten at Corinth until after this letter was written, cp. verse 6 with Acts 18:5, 6.

through your faith:—i.e., through the tidings that their faith not only continued, it "was growing exceedingly," 2 Thessalonians 1:3; cp. 1:8; 2 Corinthians 7:4.

3:8 for now we live,—*zaō,* see note at 5:10, i.e., enjoy life; a vivid rhetorical description of the contrast between his state of apprehension when he was in ignorance of their welfare, and the comfort and ease of mind produced by Timothy's good news.

This is the only instance of the figurative use of "live" in the New Testament, but cp. Psalm 119:175; Jeremiah 38:20.

if ye stand fast in the Lord.—*stēkō,* to stand, literally as in Mark 11:25, or figuratively, Romans 14:4; cp. Philippians 4:1; and "in the faith," 1 Corinthians 16:13; in the "apostles' teaching," 2 Thessalonians 2:15; in freedom from legal bondage, Galatians 5:1; "in one spirit," Philippians 1:27. The tense is continuous; the word "if" is not intended to question their stability but to suggest that the apostle's peace of mind depended on their steadfastness: = "while ye are standing fast we are happy."||

3:9 For what thanksgiving—i.e., no thanksgiving within their power would be adequate, cp. 2:13.

can we render again—*antapodidōmi,* see note at 2 Thessalonians 1:6, "recompense." Here only in the New Testament is it used of thanksgiving to God, cp. Psalm 116:12, LXX.

unto God for you, for all the joy wherewith we joy—cp. 2:19, 20. Joy is always associated with life, v. 8, as sorrow is with death; but it is experience of sorrow that enlarges the capacity of the heart for joy.

for your sakes—i.e., on the ground of their steadfastness in the midst of so much trial, and because God had sustained them in the face of so many assaults by the Adversary.

before our God;—the sense of the presence of God is the effect upon the mind of such general promises and assurances as those contained in Psalm 23:4; Isaiah 8:10; 43:2, reinforced by such as were given to Moses, Exodus 4:12; Joshua, 1:5, Jeremiah, 1:8; 15:20, when they were called to special service. A similar message was given to Paul about the time of the writing of this epistle, Acts 18:10. Thus the presence of God is not a prospect merely as in v. 13, but a present purifying and invigorating experience.

3:10 night and day—at 2:9, and 2 Thessalonians 3:8 of work, as here of prayer; see note on "without ceasing," 1:3.

praying—*deomai,* which may be used of requests addressed to men, Acts 21:39, e.g., whereas *proseuchomai,* 5:17 (where see note) 25, 2 Thessalonians 1:11; 3:1, in the New Testament is used only of requests addressed to God. The notion of worship is involved in the latter, but not in the former, which is well translated "beseech" in 2 Corinthians 5:20. For further notes on prayer see at 5:17, 25.

exceedingly—as in 5:13; Ephesians 3:20, a strengthened form of that so translated in 2:17.||

that we may see your face,—as he longed to do, v. 6, as he had strenuously endeavored to do, 2:17, so he prayed that he might be permitted to do.

and may perfect—*katartizō,* the object of the apostle in desiring so earnestly to see the converts was not his own gratification, but their profit, cp. Romans 1:11; 2 Corinthians 12:19.

This word is used of mending nets, Matthew 4:21; Mark 1:19, and is translated "restore" in Galatians 6:1. It does not necessarily imply, however, that that to which it is applied has been damaged, though it may do so, as in these passages; it signifies, rather, right ordering and arrangement, Hebrews 11:3, "framed"; it points out the path of progress, as in Matthew 21:16; Luke 6:40, and cp. 2 Corinthians 13:9; Ephesians 4:12, where corresponding nouns occur.

It indicates the close relationship between character and destiny, Romans 9:22, "fitted." It expresses the pastor's desire for the flock, in prayer, Hebrews 13:21, and in exhortation, 1 Corinthians 1:10; 2 Corinthians 13:11, as well as his conviction of God's purpose for them, 1 Peter 5:10. And it is used of the Incarnation of the Word in Hebrews 10:5, "prepare," quoted from Psalm 40:6, LXX, where it is apparently intended to describe the unique creative act involved in the Virgin Birth, Luke 1:35. Here it means to supply what is necessary, as the succeeding words show.||

Another form of the same word, *exartizō*, hardly to be distinguished from *katartizō* in meaning, occurs in Acts 21:5, "accomplished," 2 Timothy 3:17, "furnished completely."||

Elsewhere a different word, *teleioō*, is rendered "perfect," "make perfect," etc., = to make fit for a purpose, Hebrews 2:10, to bring to maturity, 2 Corinthians 12:9; James 2:22, and cp. the corresponding noun in Matthew 5:48; 1 Corinthians 14:20, "men," i.e., mature, or "of full age," as marg.

that which is lacking—i.e., that which, through the premature interruption of his labors as a teacher among them, he had been unable to impart to them, cp. Colossians 1:24 (where the reference is not to the vicarious suffering of Christ on the Cross, but to those afflictions which He endured on the way thither, and which must still be endured by His servants in order that that sole sufficient death may be made known throughout the world, cp. Matt. 20:23; 2 Cor. 1:5; 2 Tim. 2:10), Philippians 2:30.

in your faith?—"faith" here is to be understood, not of confidence in God, as in v. 2:6, but of the body of Christian doctrine, as in Jude 3; cp. Acts 2:42, "the apostles' teaching." See note at v. 2.

Cp. *parathēkē*, "the deposit," in 1 Timothy 6:20; 2 Timothy 1:12-14.||

The principal things lacking, apparently, concerned their conduct, their hope, and their mutual relationships in the church, for instruction on these points occupies the remainder of the Epistle; the first is dealt with in 4:1-12, the second in 4:13—5:11, the third in 5:12-22.

3:11 Now may our God and Father himself,—in the original "Himself" is in the place of emphasis at the beginning of the sentence, as at 4:16; 5:23; 2 Thessalonians 2:16, where see note.

and our Lord Jesus,—Paul had earnestly and strenuously endeavored to come to them, but in vain. Satan had successfully opposed him. But over all is God, and to God, their Father and his, and to the Lord Jesus, their Lord and his, the apostle made his final appeal, nor does he refer to the subject again throughout the Epistles. God is mightier than Satan, and wiser than His servants, Proverbs 16:9; Jeremiah 10:23, so all is well. We see what was hidden from Paul and his adversary, for out of Satan's success and the apostle's disappointment came these Epistles which have enriched the churches and comforted the saints ever since.

direct—*kateuthunō*, to make straight, as in Luke 1:79; 2 Thessalonians 3:5; ct. "hindered," 2:18.||

This verse is of much importance because of the doctrine of the deity of Christ therein implied. The epistle, it will be remembered, is one of the earliest Christian documents, and as such supplies most valuable testimony to primitive apostolic teaching, see Intro. Notes. From this verse then it is evident the Thessalonians had been taught to think of the Lord Jesus as One with God, for:

a, prayer is addressed to the Lord Jesus conjointly with the Father. It is equally important to notice that while the Lord Jesus is united with the Father in respect of His Godhead, He is distinguished from the Father in respect of His personality:

b, the Lord Jesus is associated with God the Father as controller of the ways of men:

c, the Greek verb translated "direct" is in the singular number notwithstanding that two names form its subject Thus the simple grammatical law, that a verb must agree with its subject in number, is set aside in order that the unique relationship existing between the Persons may be indicated; cp. 2 Thessalonians 2:16, 17:

d, the sentence may be translated thus: But God Himself even our Father and our Lord Jesus, direct our way unto you. Cp. John 5:19.

our way unto you—cp. Romans 1:10; 15:32, and see note at 2:18.

3:12 and—or "but," *de*, i.e., whatever happens, whether I come to you or not.

the Lord—*kurios;* with the possible exceptions of 1:8; 5:2, which are best understood as in the Old Testament, Isaiah 38:4; Joel 2:1, etc., this title, throughout these Epistles, refers to the Lord Jesus, cp. 3:13 with 4:15. Two of the divine titles in Hebrew, Jehovah and Adonai, are represented in LXX by *kurios*, just as they are represented in the English Version by "LORD" and "Lord," respectively. Hence its use for the Lord Jesus, without any addition, is further evidence that the doctrine of the deity of Christ was an essential part of the primitive faith.

make you to increase—*pleonazō* = to extend, to be enlarged; it occurs in the New Testament of:

a, trespasses (*paraptōma*, lit., "a fall to the side"), Romans 5:20:

b, sins (*hamartia*, lit., "a missing of the mark"), Romans 5:20:

c, grace, Romans 6:1; 2 Corinthians 4:15:

d, the Manna, 2 Corinthians 8:15:

e, "fruit" (i.e., the ministry of temporal things, which adds to the credit of the believer's account in heaven; Matt. 6:20), Philippians 4:17:

f, love in manifestation, here, and 2 Thessalonians 1:3, where see note:

g, the elements of Christian character, 2 Peter 1:8.||

and abound—*perisseuō,* to exceed, to go beyond; taken together the words may be understood as = "increase so that you may abound"; they occur together again in 2 Corinthians 4:15; Philippians 4:17, 18.

"You" precedes "Lord" in orig. and has thus an emphatic position in the sentence; the meaning accordingly is: "whatever God's will concerning our movements and service may be, we know this to be His will for you that you should learn how, through love, to be servants one to another"; cp. Galatians 5:13; and for a similar contrast cp. "you" and "us," see Hebrews 13:21.

in love—*agapē,* this is the characteristic word of Christianity, and since the Spirit of revelation has used it to express ideas previously unknown, inquiry into its use, whether in Greek literature or in LXX, throws but little light upon its distinctive meaning in the New Testament Cp., however, Leviticus 19:18; Deuteronomy 6:5.

Agapē and *agapaō,* the corresponding verb, are used in the New Testament, *a,* to describe the attitude of God toward the human race, generally, John 3:16, and to such as believe on the Lord Jesus Christ, particularly, John 14:21, and see note on 1:4; *b,* to convey His will to His children concerning their attitude one toward another, John 13:34, end toward all men, here, 1 Corinthians 16:14; 2 Peter 1:7; and *c,* to express the essential nature of God, 1 John 4:8.

Love can be known only from the actions it prompts. God's love is seen in the gift of His Son, 1 John 4:9, 10. But obviously this is not the love of complacency, or affection, that is, it was not drawn out by any excellency in its objects, Romans 5:8. It was an exercise of the divine will in deliberate choice, made without assignable cause save that which lies in the nature of God Himself, cp. Deuteronomy 7:7, 8.

Love had its perfect expression among men in the Lord Jesus Christ, 2 Corinthians 5:14; Ephesians 2:4; 3:19; 5:2; Christian love is the fruit of His Spirit in the Christian, Galatians 5:22.

Christian love has God for its primary object, and expresses itself first of all in implicit obedience to His commandments, John 14:15, 21, 23; 15:10; 1 John 2:5; 5:3; 2 John 6. Self-will, that is, self-pleasing, is the negation of love to God.

Christian love, whether exercised toward the brethren, or toward men generally, is not an impulse from the feelings, it does not always run with the natural inclinations, nor does it spend itself only upon those for whom some affinity is discovered. Love seeks the welfare of all, Romans 15:2, and works no ill to any, 13:8–10; love seeks opportunity to do good to "all men, and especially toward them that are of the household of the faith," Galatians 6:10. Paul described the way of love in His exhortation to the Philippians not to look each "to his own [interests] but each also to the [interests] of others," and for the reason that it was this mind, i.e., His love, that brought forth Christ for our salvation, 2:4, 5. See further 1 Corinthians 13, and Colossians 3:12–14. Self-seeking is thus the negation of love to man, and every precept addressed to the Christian in the New Testament is either an attack on, or a safeguard against, this most assiduous and subtle enemy, and is also a direction for the strengthening of the new man, Ephesians 4:24. In its essence sin is selfishness, Isaiah 53:6, and love is the opposite of sin as light and life are the opposites of darkness and death; love is unselfishness, for love seeketh not its own, 1 Corinthians 13:5, but it is much more beside.

Christian love must be distinguished from affection, which is more nearly represented in the New Testament by another word, *phileō*. Its noun, *philia*, occurs but once, James 4:4; cp. Matthew 26:48, where *phileō* is translated "to kiss."

On the other hand, *agapaō* and *phileō* are sometimes interchanged, see Genesis 37:3 and 4, and Proverbs 8:17, e.g.; both are used of the love of the Father for the Son, John 3:35, and 5:20, and for the believer, 14:21 and 16:27; both are used of the love of the Lord Jesus for a certain disciple, 13:23, and 20:2; and while *agapaō* appears in Romans 8:28 and all similar passages, *phileō* is used in 1 Corinthians 16:22, and cp. John 16:27, where the Lord uses it of His disciples' love to Himself as well as of God's love for them.

one toward another,—referring to the narrower circle of the believers, cp. the teaching of the Lord Jesus in John 13:34. Love for the children of God is evidence of the new birth, 1 John 3:14; 4:7, 8, 20, 21.

and toward all men,—(the word "men" is not expressed in the original but is implied in the word "all") referring to the wider circle of the human race, cp. the teaching of the Lord Jesus in Luke 6:32–35, and see 5:15, Galatians 6:10; 2 Peter 1:7. The cruelty of their fellow-countrymen, 2:14, might have led the Thessalonian believers to retaliate, where opportunity offered, and where retaliation was impracticable, at least to harbor resentful and bitter thoughts; against this danger the apostle's words suggest the best safeguard. The Christian obligation to love and to serve is not to be limited in its objects to other Christians nor does it in any way depend on the love or hate that others may show. See Matthew 5:44–48.

That love characterized their behavior Timothy had reported, v. 6, and Paul acknowledged, 4:9–10; 2 Thessalonians 1:3. But there is no limit to the heart's capacity for love, nor to the opportunities afforded for its exercise in daily life, hence these repeated exhortations, 4:1, 10; 2 Thessalonians 3:5.

even as we also *do* **toward you;**—the missionaries followed Christ in this, that they set an example in the things they taught, cp. 1 Corinthians 11:1; Philippians 4:9, with Matthew 11:29; John 13:15; see also 1 Peter 5:3.

3:13 to the end—cp. 2:12; love is not an end in itself but a means to an end, and that end is holiness. The exercise of love toward others builds up one's own Christian character, 1 Corinthians 8:1; the object of the gift of Christ in ministry is that each may be taught to speak in truth and to act in love, and that so the whole body may build itself up in that which characterizes its head, Ephesians 4:7, 15, 16.

He may establish—as at 3:2.

your hearts unblameable—as at 2:10.

in holiness—*hagiōsunē,* occurs again in Romans 1:4; 2 Corinthians 7:1. See note at 4:3. In each place character is in view, perfect in the case of the Lord Jesus, growing toward perfection in the case of the Christian. Here the exercise of love is declared to be the means God uses to develop likeness to Christ in His children. The sentence may be paraphrased thus: "The Lord enable you more and more to spend your lives in the interests of others, in order that He may so establish you in Christian character now, that you may be vindicated from every charge that might possibly be brought against you at the Judgment Seat of God"; cp. 1 John 4:16, 17.||

before our God—God is judge of all, Hebrews 12:23, but He has committed "all judgment to the Son," John 5:22, cp. Acts 10:42; 17:31, hence that before which the Christian is to be made manifest is called "the Judgment Seat of Christ," 2 Corinthians 5:10, as well as "the Judgment Seat of God," Romans 14:10.

and Father,—the addition of these words shows that believers will stand before the Judgment Seat as sons of God. The question of relationship is settled from the moment a man believes on the Lord Jesus, Galatians 3:26, the public recognition of service awaits the Parousia of Christ.

at the coming of our Lord Jesus—see note on *parousia,* 2:19.

with—*meta,* see note on 3:4.

all His saints.—i.e., all who are Christ's, cp. 1 Corinthians 15:23, whether of this age or of the last, and of this age alike those who have fallen asleep, and those that are alive, that are left, 4:16, 17, cp. 1 Corinthians 15:52, 54.

Saints, *hagioi,* lit., "holy ones"; save in Philippians 4:21 the word does not occur in the singular, and there "every" is prefixed, cp. Psalm 106:16. In one passage, Jude 14, angels are apparently intended, cp. Daniel 8:13. See note on 2:10. In Hebrews 9:1, 2, 3, 24, the same word, but in the neuter gender, is used for the tabernacle.

The holy person, place, or thing, is holy not because some change has been wrought in or on it, but because he, or it, has been set apart for God. Saints are made such in this life, cp. Acts 9:32, 41; 1 Corinthians 14:33; the designation is common to all believers in the Lord Jesus Christ, Ephesians 1:1, *et al.,* and not merely to persons of exceptional godliness, living or dead.

1 THESSALONIANS

CHAPTER FOUR

Verses 1–18

4:1 Finally—lit., "for the rest," not necessarily implying that the letter is drawing to a close, but marking a transition in the subject matter, cp. Philippians 3:1. Hindered from speaking to them face to face, he must seek by means of paper, ink, and pen, 2 John 12; 3 John 13, to supply what was lacking in their faith, see note on 3:10.

then,—lit., "therefore"; as he had prayed for their establishing in holiness, so now he exhorts them to the same end; for the only way to holiness is along the path of obedience to the revealed will of God.

brethren, we beseech—*erōtaō,* to ask, as an alms, Acts 3:3, or a question, Matthew 21:24; it is used of prayer to God only of the Lord Jesus, John 14:16; 15:20; 16:26; 17:9. This, and 5:12; 2 Thessalonians 2:1; and Philippians 4:3 are the only occurrences of the word in Paul's Epistles, i.e., only in those to Macedonian churches.

and exhort you—as at 2:11.
    The two words occur together here only in the New Testament, and = "we beg you and urge you," and express the writer's sense of the paramount importance of maintaining the Christian character, cp. Philippians 1:27; Titus 3:8, and many other places.

in the Lord Jesus,—in the original the order is "we beseech you, and we exhort in the Lord Jesus"; thus the name of the Lord is directly associated only with the word "exhort." Paul begs on his own account, as one who loved them, but he urges in the name of his Lord and theirs, cp. 2 Thessalonians 3:12. What he laid on the consciences of the saints did not originate with himself but with the Lord, to whose authority, therefore, he appealed. For a good illustration see Matthew 8:9.

that, as ye received of us—*paralambanō,* see note on 2:13, where the reference is to the beginning of the gospel among them; but the missionaries had not only declared the way of salvation to the heathen, they had taught the converts how to live to please God. Now Paul confirms this teaching before he proceeds to supplement it.

how ye ought to walk—*peripateō,* see note at 2:12.

and—*kai* = "even" when used, as here, in an epexegetical, or explanatory, sense, cp. John 1:16; 1 Corinthians 1:30 ("wisdom from God, even righteousness, etc.") 8:12, e.g.

to please God,—*areskō,* as in 2:4, 15, where see notes. In Genesis 5:22, which is apparently in the apostle's mind, the Hebrew has "Enoch walked with God," the LXX has "Enoch pleased God," cp. Micah 6:8. In Hebrews 11:5 the LXX alone is quoted; here the ideas are combined; to walk with God is to please God.

even as ye do walk—cp. v. 10:5, 11; this he adds lest they should be grieved by an apparent assumption on his part that they had failed to heed his former counsels.

——that ye abound more and more.—*perisseuō,* as at 3:12.
There is no finality in practical holiness while the Christian remains on the earth. Life is marked either by growth or by decay. Hence Christians are to be "rooted and grounded in love," Ephesians 3:17, to be "healthy in love," Titus 2:2, marg.; for as they "walk in love" toward one another and toward all men, they walk so as to please God, see Ephesians 5:2; to be contrary to men in this respect is to be displeasing to Him, see 2:15.

4:2 For ye know what charge—*parangelia,* plural, lit., "charges," i.e., commands, strictly used of commands received from a superior and transmitted to others. This word should be compared with, and added to, those used in 2:11 to describe the ministry of the missionaries at Thessalonica. Comparing the use of the same word in Acts 5:28; 16:24, the statement may be thus paraphrased: "you know what responsibility we publicly imposed upon you, namely, that in all the relations of life you should walk in love and holiness with the object of pleasing God." Cp. also 1 Timothy 1:5, 18.||

we gave you through the Lord Jesus.—The words "in the Lord Jesus," v. 1, are an appeal to their relationship to Him as the reason why they should respond to an exhortation. Here the words "through the Lord Jesus" are intended to give the weight of His authority to a command, cp. "I give charge, yea not I, but the Lord," 1 Corinthians 7:10, and cp. Romans 15:30.

4:3 For—the charges delivered to the converts did not originate with the missionaries—they expressed the will of God.

this is the will of God,—lit., "a thing willed," *thēlema,* "by God," cp. 5:18; for the verb see 2:18. The character of a person is expressed in his will; therefore, since God is holy, He can desire only holiness for His children, 1 Peter 1:15, 16. But all men by nature follow the desires, *thēlemata,* of the flesh and of the mind, Ephesians 2:3, and are thus in inveterate opposition to the will of God, Romans 8:8; 1 Corinthians 2:14. Hence the need of all men for a new and spiritual birth, John 3:5, 7, and for that conversion to the state of the child which is the evidence of the new birth, Matthew 18:3; and hence, too, the need for that lifelong discipline in which is learned by experience "what is the good and acceptable and perfect will of God," Romans 12:1, 2; cp. 1 Peter 4:2.

even **your sanctification,**—*hagiasmos,* which is uniformly so translated, is used of:

    a, separation to God, 1 Corinthians 1:30; 2 Thessalonians 2:13; 1 Peter 1:2:

    b, the course of life becoming those who have been separated to God, 4:3, 4, 7; Romans 6:19, 22; 1 Timothy 2:15; Hebrews 12:14.

Synonyms found in the New Testament are:

- *hagiotēs* = sanctity, the abstract quality of holiness, 2 Corinthians 1:12; Hebrews 12:10:
- *hagiōsunē* = the manifestation of the quality of holiness in personal conduct, 3:13 (where see note), Romans 1:4; 2 Corinthians 7:1:||
- *hosiotēs,* which occurs in Luke 1:75; Ephesians 4:24; see note on 2:10.||

These words are all uniformly translated "holiness."

The corresponding verb, *hagiazō,* is rendered "hallowed" in Matthew 6:9; Luke 11:2, and "made holy" in Revelation 22:11, elsewhere always "sanctify." It is used of:

    a, the gold adorning the temple and of the gift laid on the altar, Matthew 23:17, 19:

    b, food, 1 Timothy 4:5:

    c, the unbelieving spouse of a believer, 1 Corinthians 7:14:

    d, the ceremonial cleansing of the Israelites, Hebrews 9:13:

    e, the Father's Name, Luke 11:2:

    f, the consecration of the Son by the Father, John 10:36:

    g, the Lord Jesus devoting Himself to the redemption of His people, John 17:19:

    h, the setting apart of the believer for God, Acts 20:32, cp. Romans 15:16:

    i, the effect on the believer of the death of Christ, Hebrews 10:10, said of God, and 2:11; 13:12, said of the Lord Jesus:

    j, the separation of the believer from the world in his behavior—by the Father through the Word, John 17:17, 19:

    k, the believer who turns away from such things as dishonor God and His gospel, 2 Timothy 2:21:

    l, the acknowledgment of the Lordship of Christ, 1 Peter 3:15.

Since every believer is sanctified in Christ Jesus, 1 Corinthians 1:2, cp. Hebrews 10:10, a common New Testament designation of all believers is "saints," *hagioi*, i.e., "sanctified" or "holy ones," see note on 3:13. Thus sainthood, or sanctification, is not an attainment, it is the state into which God, in grace, calls sinful men, and in which they begin their course as Christians, Colossians 3:12; Hebrews 3:1.

The effect of the death of Christ on the relation of the believer to a righteous God is to justify him, Romans 5:9; the guilt of sin having been put away, the justified sinner stands before the Judgment Seat uncondemned, 5:2.

The effect of the death of Christ on the relation of the believer to a Holy God is to sanctify him, Hebrews 10:10; 13:12; the defilement of sin having been put away, the sanctified sinner enters into the Holiest, 10:19.

Therefore God is said to have made Christ unto us both "righteousness and sanctification," 1 Corinthians 1:30. And as it is evident that there are no degrees of justification, so there are no degrees of sanctification; a thing is set apart for God, or it is not, there is no middle course; a person is either in Christ Jesus, justified and sanctified, or he is out of Christ, in his sins and alienated from God. But while there are no degrees of sanctification, it is evident there can and should be progress therein; hence the believer is urged to "follow after . . . sanctification" and is warned that without it "no man shall see the Lord," Hebrews 12:14.

The words "justified" and "sanctified" are not to be understood as figurative expressions. They represent realities which, when apprehended in the soul, fill the heart with peace and joy, Romans 5:1, 2, and the lips with praise, Hebrews 13:15.

The responsibility rests upon each believer to maintain a holy walk in keeping with his holy calling, 2 Timothy 1:9; 1 Peter 1:15–16, so that whereas formerly his behavior bore witness to his standing in the world in separation from God, now his behavior should bear witness to his standing before God in separation from the world, Romans 6:19, 22.

Sanctification, then, is that relationship with God into which men enter by faith in Christ, Acts 26:18; 1 Corinthians 6:11, and to which their sole title is the death of Christ, Ephesians 5:25, 26; Colossians 1:22; Hebrews 10:10, 29; 13:12.

"Sanctification" is also used in the New Testament of the separation of the believer from evil things and ways. This sanctification is God's will for the believer, here, and His purpose in calling him by the gospel, v. 7; it must be learned from God, v. 4, as He teaches it by His Word, John 17:17, 19, cp. Psalms 17:4; 119:9; and it must be pursued by the believer, earnestly and undeviatingly, 1 Timothy 2:15; Hebrews 12:14. For the holy character, *hagiosunē*, 3:13, is not vicarious, i.e., it cannot be transferred or imputed, it is an individual possession, built up, little by little, as the result of obedience to the Word of God, and of following the example of Christ, Matthew 11:29; John 13:15; Ephesians 4:20; Philippians 2:5, in the power of the Holy Spirit, Romans 8:13; Ephesians 3:16.

For the "sanctification of the Spirit," i.e., the sanctification in which the Holy Spirit is the agent, see note at 2 Thessalonians 2:13.

that ye abstain from fornication;—the apostle in stating the will of God for the sanctification of His people, had in mind those particular temptations to which, from their past history as idolaters, his readers were peculiarly susceptible, and to which, from their present environment, they were still exposed. Since the Gentiles refused to have God in their knowledge, God had given them up to a reprobate mind and to the doing of unseemly things, Romans 1:21, 28, resulting in familiarity with vice and deadness to the claims of moral purity. From such conditions those to whom the apostle wrote had been delivered by the gospel. Now lest, growing careless under the evil influences to which they were daily exposed, they should relapse into Gentile ways, it was necessary that conscience should be aroused and instructed, cp. 1 Corinthians 12:2; Ephesians 4:17–19; 1 Peter 4:3. Apparently Timothy's report had given the apostle some ground for apprehension on this point, 3:10; hence he begins the section of his Epistle in which he seeks to supply the things lacking in their faith, see note at 3:10, by words concerning the self-control which they must exercise in order to be preserved in holiness as regarded themselves, v. 4, and in righteousness as regarded each other, v. 6.

The Council of Apostles and Elders at Jerusalem deemed it needful to insert a warning on the same subject in their circular letter to the churches of the Gentiles, Acts 15:29. Earlier in the journey in the course of which he visited Thessalonica, Paul had himself delivered this letter in several places, Acts 16:4.

4:4 that each one of you know—*oida*, as at 1:4.

how to possess himself—*ktaomai* = to acquire, as money, Matthew 10:9; Luke 18:12, or lands, Acts 1:18, or political liberty, 22:28, or the (gifts of) the Holy Spirit, 8:20. In Luke 21:19, "In your patience ye shall win your souls," it apparently = "acquire mastery over."||

of his own vessel—*skeuos* = a vessel or implement of any kind, in New Testament used frequently in a literal and general sense, as Mark 3:27; 11:16, e.g.; in Acts 27:17 of the sail of a ship. It is also used, metaphorically, of men, Acts 9:15; Romans 9:22, 23; 2 Timothy 2:21. It is used of the body in 1 Samuel 21:5, LXX, and, with the addition of "earthen," in 2 Corinthians 4:7; in 1 Peter 3:7 it is used of a wife.

Under the figure of a vessel the apostle is understood by some to refer to the believer's body, by others, to his wife; New Testament parallels for both usages are available, see above. Similarly, *ktaomai* is appropriate to the soul, and so would not be inappropriate of the body, and it is actually used of a wife in Ruth 4:10, LXX.

If by "vessel" the body is understood, 1 Corinthians 9:27, "I buffet my body and bring it into bondage" may be compared, and "neither present your members unto sin as instruments" in Romans 6:13, since in such passages the body is looked upon as belonging to and as used by the man who dwells within it.

If, however, by "vessel" the wife is understood, then the meaning is that of 1 Corinthians 7:2. The apostle is commending an honorable entry upon the estate of holy matrimony, and he goes on, v. 5, to exhort to an honorable maintenance of that estate.

in sanctification—as in v. 3 = chastity.

and honor,—*timē*, as in 1 Peter 3:7; the use of the same word in these passages has some weight in favor of understanding "vessel" = "wife" here. So also with Hebrews 13:4, where "honorable" is *timios*.

4:5 not in the passion—*pathos* as in Romans 1:26; Colossians 3:5.‖

of lust,—*epithumia*, as at 2:17, where see note. The former, "passion," is described by Trench (*Synonyms of New Testament*, § lxxxvii), as the diseased condition out of which the latter, "lust," springs.

even as—as at 3:6.

the Gentiles—as at 2:16.

which know not God;—*oida* = "to perceive," see note at 1:4. Inasmuch as man was created, and still is, in the image and likeness of God, Genesis 1:27; 9:6; 1 Corinthians 11:7; James 3:9, he possesses the faculty for knowing God, Romans 1:19. Since, however, men had not thought it worthwhile (*dokimazō*, as in 2:4), to continue in the knowledge of God, God had given them over to a reprobate mind, with the consequence that they had become abominable in their works, i.e., in their ways and conduct, Romans 1:28, 29, cp. Ephesians 4:18. Denial of the Creator resulted in the degradation of the creature; idolatry and immorality are closely allied, as Israel had learned, see 1 Corinthians 10:7, 8. The words are quoted from Psalm 79:6, and Jeremiah 10:25, LXX.

4:6 that no man transgress,—*huperbainō*, lit., "to step over," here, of the limits which divide sanctification from sin, chastity from licentiousness.

and wrong—*pleonekteō,* to overreach, as Satan does the saints, 2 Corinthians 2:11, and as Paul and his companions were sometimes charged with doing, 7:2; 12:17, 18. See note on "covetousness" at 2:5.||

Here the reference is to that particular form of covetousness dealt with in the second clause of the Tenth Commandment.

his brother—though there is no other instance in Paul's epistles of the use of this word of mankind in general, it is difficult to suppose that the apostle here limited its meaning to the Christian relationship; cp. Matthew 7:3.

in the matter—in the matter under discussion, which, as the preceding words show, is now narrowed to the sin of adultery.

because—introducing one reason for the admonitions of vv. 3:4.

the Lord is an avenger—*ekdikos* = one who deals justice, whether a ruler among men, Romans 13:4, or God Himself as here, cp. Psalm 94:1. See further at 2 Thessalonians 1:8.||

in all these things,—all that violates chastity, cp. Hebrews 13:4.

as also we forewarned you—see at 3:4.

and testified.—*diamarturomai,* an intensified form of the verb, occurring at 2:11, where see note.

Before he dismisses the subject the apostle reminds his readers that the God who loved them and called them in grace, is nonetheless the God of recompenses, who will surely requite every defection from His laws, Jeremiah 51:56, as well as reward all faithful obedience to them, for not the heathen but the Christian is in view throughout the passage.

4:7 For—introducing another reason for the admonitions given in vv. 3–6; the first is prospective and warns of what God will do: the second is retrospective and reminds of what He has done. The Christian maintains purity of life not merely from fear of the judgment of God, but also because he enters into God's purpose for all His children, viz., that they should be holy because He is holy; see 1 Peter 1:16.

God called us—point tense, referring to a definite act in the past. Ct. 2:12 and 5:24, where see notes, and cp. 2 Thessalonians 2:14.

not for—*epi,* here, = with a view to, as in Galatians 5:13; Ephesians 2:10; 1 Thessalonians 4:7, 8.

uncleanness,—as in 2:3. The effect of the gospel in purity of life presented a marked contrast to the uncleanness that characterized contemporary pagan religions.

but in sanctification.—as at v. 4. The thought is apparently that the Christian is to live his life in a holy atmosphere.

The section v. 3—v. 7 is an instance of chiasm, see note at 5:5, thus: This is the will of God:

a, even your sanctification,

b, that ye abstain from fornication,

c, that each one of you know, etc.

d, not in the passion of lust,

d, even as the Gentiles which know not God;

c, that no man transgress, etc.

b, for God called us not for uncleanness,

a, but in sanctification.

4:8 Therefore—*toigaroun,* as in Hebrews 12:1; it directs attention to the conclusion which follows it in a more forcible way than do simpler and more frequent words.

he that rejecteth,—lit., "the one who sets aside," "the rejecter," referring to the "charges" mentioned in v. 2. The same word is used of the evasion of the Fifth Commandment, Mark 7:9; and of a breach of the law of Moses, Hebrews 10:28; and of the refusal of John's baptism on the part of the scribes and Pharisees, who thus rejected, not the counsel of John but, the counsel of God, Luke 7:30.

rejecteth not man, but God,—when Christ charged His apostles and sent them forth, He told them that as He represented the Father so they represented Him, and, consequently, that such as refused to hear them refused to hear, that is, they rejected, Him and the Father, Luke 10:16, cp. John 12:48, ct. Matthew 10:40. So at Thessalonica; behind the charges given by the missionaries lay the immutable laws of God; behind the missionaries was God Himself. To set at nought these injunctions, therefore, was to reject, not the missionaries, but God whose will they declared; see 2:13 and note; cp. 1 Samuel 8:7; 10:19.

who giveth—lit., "the Giver," the present tense is used because the words describe the distinguishing character of God. For though there be that are called gods, yet to us there is one God, 1 Corinthians 8:5, 6, who is the Father of our Lord Jesus Christ, Ephesians 1:3, and the giver of His Holy Spirit. Cp. Ezekiel 37:14.

His Holy Spirit unto you.—to each believer was this gift given when he believed, John 7:29, cp. Acts 5:32; Romans 8:9, an inalienable possession, John 14:16; Ephesians 1:13, 14; for as he was "born of the Spirit," John 3:8, so by the Spirit he lives, Galatians 5:25, and should walk, Galatians 5:16, 25.

The emphatic word in the sentence is "Holy," in keeping with the subject of the section. The same reason is adduced in the same connection in 1 Corinthians 6:19.

Hence to reject the solemn charges concerning purity which the missionaries laid upon the converts at the first, and which the apostle here reaffirms, would be not only to reject God, but would also involve despite to His Holy Spirit; cp. 1 Corinthians 3:16. Thus there is the double witness; without the Word of God, within His Holy Spirit.

4:9 But—ye have no need that one write unto you:—suggesting a contrast with the subject of the preceding paragraph, concerning which apparently, there was such need.

concerning love of the brethren—*philadelphia*, as in Romans 12:10; Hebrews 13:1; 1 Peter 1:22; 2 Peter 1:7; the name of a city in Revelation 3:7.

The corresponding adjective appears in 1 Peter 3:8, "loving as brethren."||

Love of the brethren is not expressed in words but in deeds, 1 John 3:18; in mutual affection and respect, Romans 12:10; in hospitality to the friendless, and in sympathy with those who suffer, Hebrews 13:1-3; and that not in a bargaining or grudging spirit, "nicely calculating less or more," but with generous warmth, 1 Peter 1:22, cp. Matthew 10:8, "for love's strength stands in love's sacrifice." Where love is, love cannot be hid, but will find a way to prove itself in service, whether of life, 1 John 3:16, or possessions, v. 17.

for ye yourselves are taught of God—*theodidaktoi*, lit., "God-taught persons," cp. *didaktoi theou*, "taught of God," John 6:45.||

As the Lord Jesus had taught His disciples, John 13:34, so the missionaries had taught the converts, to love one another, but, deeper than human language can reach, God Himself spoke to their hearts, 1 John 2:20, 27, directing them into the love of God, cp. 2 Thessalonians 3:5. For love is of God, 1 John 4:7, 8, 12, witness to the Christian of his new birth, 3:14, and evidence to the world of his discipleship, John 13:35. Early testimony to the presence of this fruit of the Spirit, Galatians 5:22, among believers, is on record in the statement of Tertullian (*circa* A.D. 192), "The heathen often exclaimed in wonder, 'see how these Christians love one another,'" and Lucian, himself a heathen, wrote about the same time, "It is incredible to see the fervor with which the people of that religion help each other in their wants. They spare nothing. Their first legislator [i.e., the Lord Jesus] has put it into their heads that they are all brethren."

to love one another;—*agapē*, lit., "into [i.e., with this end in view] the love one of the other"; they had not merely been taught the simple and direct lesson of mutual love, God Himself had become their teacher, with this purpose in view in all His teaching, namely, that they might learn to love others as He Himself had loved them. John 15:12, 13. See note at 3:12.

Doctrine is never set forth in Scripture as an end in itself, but always for the sake of its effect upon the conduct of the believer. A notable example of this principle, which underlies the writer's words here, is contained in Philippians 2:4-11, where the revelation concerning Christ is given in order to illustrate and enforce the lesson that all who follow the Lord Jesus Christ must deny self, Matthew 16:24, and consider others, that is, must learn from this marvelous example what love is and how to practice it.

4:10 for indeed ye do it toward all the brethren which are in all Macedonia—i.e., the exercise of their love was limited only by the opportunities afforded to it. Personal predilection was not permitted to influence them for one or against another. They had not become sectarian, i.e., they did not act with any faction, Philippians 2:3, they showed love toward all, as love delights to do.

The privilege of hospitality as an expression of love is frequently urged, Romans 12:13; 1 Timothy 3:2; Titus 1:8; Hebrews 13:2; 1 Peter 4:9; and Timothy had probably reported how happily the believers at Thessalonica abounded in this grace toward saints from other churches, as the central position of their city would bring them frequent opportunity of doing, see Intro. Notes.

But we exhort you, brethren, that ye abound more and more;—see notes on 3:12, "increase and abound," and 4:1. The Christian may not rest in any measure of attainment, however great, but must always be stretching out after a closer approximation to the standard, which is Christ.

4:11 and that ye study—_philotimeomai_, lit., "to love honor," hence "to be ambitious," "to strive restlessly after" (Lightfoot); see also Romans 15:20; 2 Corinthians 5:9.||

to be quiet,—_hēsuchazō_, = to be at rest, as in Luke 23:56; elsewhere always of silence, 14:4; Acts 11:18; 21:14.||

The ambition of the world lies along the path of emulation and strife toward the goal of personal distinction; this the child of God is taught to eschew, that he may lead a tranquil and quiet life, 1 Timothy 2:2, and that in him Christ may be magnified, Philippians 1:20.

But though he may escape the excitements of social and political life, the Christian is exposed to the more subtle dangers of religious excitement, always a chief hindrance to love of the brethren, for as fever prevents the due discharge of the functions of the body, so does excitement the healthy activities of the spirit.

The paradox—the words may be paraphrased "restlessly strive to be quiet"— is designed to heighten the contrast between the ideals of the world and the laws of Christ.

and to do your own business,—i.e., "attend to your own [affairs]"; the noun is not expressed in the original and the pronoun is plural. The same expression occurs in John 1:11 with reference to the land, which belonged to the Lord in virtue of His descent from Abraham, Genesis 12:7, and to the throne, His in virtue of His descent from David, Jeremiah 23:5, cp. Matthew 1:1; and in John 16:32, the disciples would return to the things with which they had formerly been occupied, cp. John 21:2, 3; Mary became not merely an inmate of John's house, she was treated as a member of his family, 19:27. See also Luke 18:28; Acts 21:6.||

God has not spoken of any place for idlers among His children; to each one his work is appointed, Mark 13:34. But at Thessalonica, apparently, the "trivial round, the common task," was neglected by some on the plea of the superior claims of religion, a vicious idea that has wrought much mischief since, notwithstanding its emphatic and repeated repudiation by the apostle, cp. Titus 3:8, 14.

The life of the Christian cannot be divided as into secular and sacred, cp. Colossians 3:23, 24, the whole is to be lived for God always. Moreover, idlers, neglecting their own, easily become "meddlers in other men's matters," lit., "overseers of others' concerns," 1 Peter 4:15, and not infrequently indolent dependents on other men's bounty as well.

and to work with your hands,—a notion common among converts with the example of an idolatrous priesthood, always idlers, before them, is that the ordinary occupation should be discarded for the preaching of the gospel. This mistaken assumption the apostle emphatically condemned, as he condemned also the other assumption common in every land, and prevalent even among Christians despite the example of the Lord and of His apostle, that there is something derogatory in manual labor. Cp. 1 Corinthians 7:24.

even as we charged you;—as in 2:12; 4:1, where see notes.

4:12 honestly—*euschēmonōs,* = becomingly, decently, as the English word "honest" primarily signifies; see Romans 13:13, where it is used in contrast with the confusion of Gentile social life, and 1 Corinthians 14:40, in contrast with confusion in ministry in the churches of the saints. *Euschēmonōs* is the opposite of *ataktōs,* see 5:14, below.

toward—*pros,* see note at 3:4.

them that are without,—i.e., unbelievers, and as such outside the family of God. The phrase occurs again in Mark 4:11; 1 Corinthians 5:12, 13; Colossians 4:5, and, slightly modified, in 1 Timothy 3:7.||

If unbelievers could know nothing of the spiritual blessings of the gospel, cp. 1 Corinthians 2:14, they could at least appreciate the difference between order and confusion, between idleness and diligence, between sponging and independence. See also 1 Peter 2:12, 15; 3:16. In a word, the good effects of the gospel were to be shown in every relation with all men in daily life, lest the way of the truth should be evil spoken of, cp. 2 Peter 2:2.

and may have need of nothing.—and more than this, that they might thus be able to provide for their own families, 1 Timothy 5:8, and to secure withal the greater blessing attached to giving, Acts 20:35, to such as might be in need, Ephesians 4:28.

These sober words, however, do not seem to have had the effect desired, for in his second letter the apostle returned to the subject and dealt with it more at length, 3:6–15.

The close connection between the commendations of vv. 9:10, and the exhortations of vv. 10:12, is not accounted for by any circumstance concerning the church at Thessalonica with which Scripture makes us acquainted. But the connection itself suggests that the unhealthy symptoms therein implied were, at least to some extent, the indirect consequences of unwise courses pursued by some in the name of love of the brethren. If wealthier brethren by their disbursements relieved the poorer brethren from the necessity of working for daily bread, such evils as these must have resulted. To remedy them the apostle did not exhort the former to refrain from giving, for each form of service is beset by dangers peculiar to it, and spiritual men, learning to trust God in their service, are not to be deterred thereby from the faithful discharge of the particular stewardship committed to them by God. Rather he addressed himself to the poorer brethren, encouraging them to a healthy spirit of independence, which is equally essential if love of the brethren is to continue and to grow.

4:13 But we would not have you ignorant, brethren,—a not infrequent formula in Paul's epistles, used sometimes to introduce personal matters. Romans 1:13; 2 Corinthians 1:8, cp. Colossians 2:1; once to introduce the reason underlying preceding statements, Romans 11:25; once to adduce the dangers and failures of the past to justify a warning for the present, 1 Corinthians 10:1; and once to introduce a new phase of his subject, 1 Corinthians 12:1; here only, to introduce a new subject altogether.||

The language of this paragraph suggests that during the brief interval since the apostle left Thessalonica, one, at least, of the converts there had died. Some apprehension seems to have been felt as to whether the departed saint would participate in the fulfillment of the hope of the Lord's return held out to them in the gospel. Having heard from Timothy of this perplexity, the apostle proceeded to remove the difficulty that had arisen in their minds, cp. note at 3:10.

concerning them that fall asleep;—*koimaomai*, present continuous tense, = "that are lying asleep," or, perhaps, "them that fall asleep from time to time." *Koimaomai* is used in the New Testament, of natural sleep, Matthew 28:13; Luke 22:45; John 11:12; Acts 12:6; and of the death of the body, but only of such as are Christ's; yet never of Christ Himself, though He is said to be "the firstfruits of them that have fallen asleep," 1 Corinthians 15:20. It is used of saints who departed before Christ came, Matthew 27:52; Acts 13:36; of Lazarus, while Christ was yet upon the earth, John 11:11; and of believers since the Ascension, here and vv. 14:15, and Acts 7:60; 1 Corinthians 7:39; 11:30; 15:6, 18, 51; 2 Peter 3:4.||

This metaphorical use of the word sleep is appropriate because of the similarity in appearance between a sleeping body and a dead body; restfulness and peace normally characterize both. The object of the metaphor is to suggest that as the sleeper does not cease to exist while his body sleeps, so the dead person continues to exist despite his absence from the region in which those who remain can communicate with him, and that, as sleep is known to be temporary, so the death of the body will be found to be. Sleep has its waking, death will have its resurrection.

That the body alone is in view in this metaphor is evident, *a*, from the derivation of the word *koimaomai*, from *keimai*, to lie down (cp. *anastasis*, resurrection, from *ana*, "up," and *histēmi*, "to cause to stand"), cp. Isaiah 14:8, where for "laid down," LXX has "fallen asleep"; *b*, from the fact that in the New Testament the word resurrection is used of the body alone; *c*, from Daniel 12:2, where the physically dead are described as "them that sleep [LXX *katheudō*, as at 5:6] in the dust of the earth," language inapplicable to the spiritual part of man; moreover, when the body returns whence it came, Genesis 3:19, the spirit returns to God who gave it, Ecclesiastes 12:7.

When the physical frame of the Christian, "the earthly house of our tabernacle," 2 Corinthians 5:1, is dissolved and returns to the dust, the spiritual part of his highly complex being, the seat of personality, departs to be with Christ, Philippians 1:23. And since that state in which the believer, absent from the body, is at home with the Lord, 2 Corinthians 5:6-9, is described as "very far better" than the present state of joy in communion with God and of happy activity in His service, everywhere reflected in Paul's writings, it is evident that the word "sleep," where applied to the departed Christian, is not intended to convey the idea that the spirit is unconscious.

The "unclothed," or "naked," 2 Corinthians 5:3, 4, state of the believer is not final, for man without the body is not complete. When "this corruptible," the decayed and crumbled body, "shall have put on incorruption," then, but not till then, shall the victory of Christ over death be manifestly complete, 1 Corinthians 15:54-57. See further at 5:23, "body."

The early Christians adopted the word *koimētērion* (which was used by the Greeks of a rest house for strangers) for the place of interment of the bodies of their departed; thence the English word "cemetery" = "the sleeping place," is derived.

A metaphor is a figure of speech in which, on account of some of its qualities, the name of one thing is applied to another, see note on 2:19.

that ye sorrow not,—grief for the loss of friends is common to all, and is not inconsistent with acceptance of the will of God, neither does it deny the hope of the Christian. The Lord Jesus Himself wept in sympathy with the mourners at the grave of Lazarus, John 11:33-35. Paul, too, was apprehensive of the sorrow into which he would have been plunged had the sickness of Epaphroditus resulted in death, Philippians 2:27. The converts at Thessalonica grieved not merely for their own loss, they grieved also for the loss sustained, as the survivors supposed, by those of their number who had fallen asleep. It was to save them from grief on this account that the apostle wrote, showing them that their fears were groundless. His words may be paraphrased thus: "We would have you know the purpose of God for all in Christ, living or dead, in order that you may be saved needless sorrow."

even as—*kathōs*, as in 2:4, see note on 3:6; the phrase is to be understood as in 5:11; Romans 1:13, i.e., it must not be strained to mean "so much as," or "in the same manner as." Since, for the believer, to live is Christ, to die not loss but gain, Philippians 1:21, sorrow on behalf of departed saints is precluded entirely. For our loss we mourn, for their gain we rejoice.

the rest,—a phrase frequently used by the apostle to express a contrast between men: Israelites, Romans 11:7; believers, Romans 1:13; 1 Corinthians 7:12, etc. Here, and 5:6, and Ephesians 2:3 = "them that are without," v. 12, cp. Luke 8:10; Acts 5:13.

which have no hope.—i.e., no hope of resurrection, said of those out of Christ in contrast with those in Christ, for while all the dead shall be raised, John 5:28, 29, the resurrection of unbelievers cannot be described as a hope. See at 1:3 and 2 Thessalonians 2:16, for notes on "hope."

In Ephesians 2:12 the Gentiles are said to have "no hope" in contrast with the Jews, for, though some words recorded in the Old Testament expressly deny hope to all who have departed this life, Job 14:7-12; Ecclesiastes 9:4-10; Isaiah 38:18, 19, e.g., yet the Lord Jesus emphatically condemned the Sadducean doctrine that there is no resurrection as an error due to ignorance of the Scriptures, Mark 12:18-27. For however limited in extent the testimony of the Old Testament to resurrection may be it is still unmistakable, see Psalm 16:9, 10; Proverbs 14:32, e.g., Moreover, the figurative language of Isaiah 26:19; Ezekiel 37:1-14; Hosea 6:2, would be meaningless had those to whom the words were originally addressed been without any knowledge of literal resurrection.* Cp. Acts 23:8; 26:7, 8; Hebrews 6:2.

When challenged by the Sadducees to show that resurrection is taught in the Old Testament, the Lord Jesus, who ordinarily quoted its direct statements, answered them by drawing an inference from Exodus 3:6. God, He said, "is not God of the dead, but of the living" (present continuous tense), and yet He calls Himself the God of Abraham, of Isaac, and of Jacob; therefore these, and all who have departed this life, though they are dead to men, do yet live (present continuous tense) unto God. The necessary implication in these words of the Lord, and the conclusion to which He apparently wished to carry His hearers, is, that since the Patriarchs live as to the spiritual part which has returned to God, their bodies, which had crumbled away long ages before, shall surely be raised from the dead, see Matthew 22:31, 32; Luke 20:37, 38.

The Gentiles were strangers to the covenants and promises of Israel and so were without God and without hope, Ephesians 2:12. The language Paul puts into their mouths, "let us eat and drink, for tomorrow we die," 1 Corinthians 15:32, is abundantly corroborated by their literature. Thus Theocritus, a Greek poet of the 3rd century B.C., writes; "Hopes are among the living, the dead are without hope"; and Moschus, his contemporary, speaking of the plants that perish in the garden: "Alas! alas! . . . these live and spring again in another year, but we . . . when we die, deaf to all sound in the hollow earth, sleep a long, long, endless sleep that knows no waking." The Roman poets of the last century B.C. speak in similar strain; thus Catullus: "Suns may set and rise again

---

*It is necessary to distinguish between revelation and inspiration. The Scriptures are "inspired of God," 2 Timothy 3:16, but that does not give Divine authority to all the utterances recorded therein. For example, the record of the conversation between Eve and the Tempter is inspired, but plainly the conversation itself was not. This is also the case with the letters included by Ezra in his book, 4:11-16 and by Luke in Acts 23:25-30, with the proclamation of Nebuchadnezzar, Daniel 3:4-6, and with the speeches of Acts 19:25-27; 24:2-8; see also John 9:27-34, and cp. Acts 27:10 with vv. 22, 23. The book of Ecclesiastes records the deductions of the wise man as he reflects upon what he had observed and experienced, but apart from the illumination of divine revelation. As the words "under the sun," constantly repeated, indicate, he views everything from the purely human standpoint. So also with the words of Job and of Hezekiah, they drew their conclusion from what they had seen. What lies beyond could only be known as and when God was pleased to reveal it. To conclude from the words of Job, Solomon, or Hezekiah, that those who have departed this life are nonexistent is to incur the rebuke of the Lord Jesus, "Ye do err, not knowing the Scriptures, nor the power of God."

but we, when once our brief light goes down, must sleep an endless night;" and Lucretius: "No one awakes and arises who has once been overtaken by the chilling end of life." These sorrowed with a double sorrow: first for the loss they themselves sustained, then for the loss suffered by the departed. Such was the gloom which Greek and Roman philosophy had failed to pierce, and which the gospel came to dispel.

4:14 For if—i.e., "granted that"; cp. Colossians 2:20; 3:1, for a similar use of the word "if."

we—i.e., all Christians, and so throughout this section of the Epistle, save in the opening words of v. 15, where "we" is used as at 3:1, see note there.

believe—i.e., if we accept the death and resurrection of Jesus of Nazareth as historical fact.

that Jesus—see notes on 1:10, and 2:15. The personal name is appropriate here inasmuch as it reminded them that the deliverer for whom they looked, 1:10, and who had Himself undergone that which they dreaded, viz., death, was Himself man, cp. Hebrews 2:17, 18; 4:15, and that His manhood was unimpaired by His experience of death. It was Jesus who died, and it was Jesus who rose again. Cp. Acts 1:11; 7:56; 9:5; 1 Timothy 2:5; 2 Timothy 2:8; Revelation 22:16. Death had not been final in His case, neither would it be in theirs.

died—*apothnēskō;* the first cardinal point in the gospel of God concerning His Son is that He died, and with few exceptions, such as Romans 4:25, "was delivered up," Ephesians 5:25, "gave Himself up," 1 Peter 3:18, "suffered," the statement of this fact is always made in direct terms.

Death, in Scripture, is used of:

a, the separation of the spiritual from the material part of man, i.e., of the soul from the body, and the consequent cessation of the functions of the latter and its disintegration into dust: Adam's body died at the age of 930 years, Genesis 3:19; 5:5; cp. Acts 5:10. Death, in this sense, is an experience that awaits men, Hebrews 9:27.

b, the separation of man from God, cp. Romans 8:6: Adam died in the day (i.e., when, cp. Ezek. 33:12) he disobeyed God, Genesis 2:17, and all mankind "descended from Adam by ordinary generation" are born in the same state of separation from God. Death, in this sense, describes the present condition of all men, John 5:24, 25; Romans 5:12-21; Ephesians 2:1, 5; 4:18; 1 John 3:14; cp. also Luke 15:24.

Death is the opposite of life. Said of man, life is never = existence; death is never = nonexistence. It is stated explicitly that God created man, i.e., called man into existence, Genesis 1:27, but Scripture nowhere states that man will ever cease to exist.

Life, when used of man, as distinguished from its use with reference to the body, "the earthly house of our tabernacle," 2 Corinthians 5:1, may be defined as conscious existence in communion with God; often the word "eternal" is prefixed, John 3:36; 17:2, and cp. 1 Timothy 6:19.

Conversely, death, when used of man, and not merely of his body, may be defined as conscious existence in separation from God, see refs. under *b* above. All out of Christ are dead, all in Christ live, or have eternal life, John 6:47; Colossians 3:4. But all, whether living or dead, equally exist and are equally conscious of existence; cp. Luke 16:19–31.

If death were = nonexistence, the statement that "Jesus died" would convey an idea repugnant to the plain teaching of Scripture, and obviously untrue.

Death, in whichever of the above-mentioned senses it is used, is always, in Scripture, viewed as the penal consequence of sin, and since sinners alone are subject to death, it was as the bearer of sin that the Lord Jesus submitted thereto on the Cross, Romans 5:12; 1 Peter 2:24, and while the physical death of the Lord Jesus was of the essence of His sacrifice it was not the whole. The darkness symbolized, and His cry expressed, the fact that He was left alone in the universe, He was "forsaken," cp. Matthew 27:45, 46. Hence it is that the word of consolation, "sleep," is never used of Him. See further at Galatians 2:20.

Here, however, since not expiation of sin but the resurrection of the saints is in view, attention is concentrated on the simple historical fact of the physical death of the Lord Jesus, see John 19:30. See further at 5:10.

and rose again,—*anistēmi,* the second cardinal point in the gospel of God concerning His Son is, that it was not possible that He should continue to be held by death, Acts 2:24, cp. Romans 1:4; 1 Corinthians 15:4; see notes at 1:10. When He had made purification of sins, He [arose from among the dead and] sat down on the right hand of the Majesty on high, Hebrews 1:3.

This is the only place in which the apostle Paul speaks of the resurrection of the Lord Jesus as His own act (2 Cor. 5:15, is lit., "was raised") ordinarily he speaks of it as the act of God, 1:10, never as the act of the Holy Spirit. So also of the saints, who are said to rise, v. 16, and to be raised, 1 Corinthians 15:52. In both cases resurrection is the effect of the direct exercise of the power of God, 1 Corinthians 6:14; Ephesians 1:20. Cp. John 10:18; Romans 14:9.

When used in its literal sense resurrection always refers to the body, see 1 Corinthians 15:42–44, and cp. Luke 23:52–55; 24:3, with 24:6 and Mark 16:6.

This is the earliest recorded reference to the resurrection in the New Testament; its purpose is to comfort sorrowing hearts. The second is in 1 Corinthians 15, where the purpose is to correct erroneous teaching.

even so——also—when the ellipsis is supplied the phrase runs, "if we believe, as we do, that Jesus died and rose again, even so we believe also—." The same gospel that carried the assurance of the death and resurrection of the Lord, carried also the assurance of the resurrection of all who believe on Him, His resurrection being the pledge of theirs, 1 Corinthians 6:14; 15:16, 20.

them——that are fallen asleep—point tense, lit., "fell asleep," or, as the words may with equal propriety be translated, "were put to sleep." In v. 13, where the tense is continuous, the statement is general; here the apostle refers specifically to those at Thessalonica, tidings of whose departure had just reached him, though of course what he was about to say is equally true of all believers.

in Jesus—the margin, "through," is correct; the preposition *dia* is not elsewhere translated "in," and cannot bear that meaning. Moreover, while the phrase "in Christ" is frequently used by the apostle to express the intimacy of the relation between the believer and the risen Lord, believers are never said to be "in Jesus"; see notes on 1:1.

Where, in Paul's Epistles, the titles "Lord" and "Christ" are omitted, and the personal name "Jesus" appears alone, the purpose of the writer is, apparently, to call particular attention to His humanity, cp. Romans 8:11, or to His earthly life, cp. Ephesians 4:21.

As a matter of grammar the words "through Jesus" may be taken either with what precedes or with what follows. If they are to be connected with "sleep" then the meaning is either:

a, "those who were put to sleep through Jesus," i.e., who died as the result of persecution for His Name's sake, cp. 2:14, 15; 3:3-5; or

b, what was death to men without the hope of resurrection, had come to be sleep for those who trust Him, death, "through Jesus" having been robbed of its victory and of its sting, 1 Corinthians 15:55. If however, the words are to be connected with "bring," then the meaning is—

c, "those who fell asleep will God, through Jesus, bring with Him," i.e., with Jesus.

These interpretations are probably to be preferred in the order *c, b, a.* Which was actually in the writer's mind it is apparently impossible to determine.

will God bring—*agō,* with slight exception used in the New Testament of persons and implying cooperation on their part, hence it is frequently rendered "lead," Mark 13:11, e.g. It is used of the Lord Jesus in the past, Luke 4:1, and in the future, Hebrews 1:6 (where the verb is compounded with *eis* = "into") and it is used of believers now, Romans 2:4; 8:14; Galatians 5:18, and in the future, John 10:16; Hebrews 2:10. "Sweet word, it is spoken of living persons" (Bengel).

In the original the sentence runs: "God them-that-fell-asleep through Jesus will-bring with Him," the word "God" occupying the place of emphasis.

with Him.—i.e., with the Lord Jesus in the manifested glory of His Kingdom, cp. Matthew 25:31; Colossians 3:4; Hebrews 1:6; 2 Thessalonians 1:10. For this they had suffered, 2:12; 2 Thessalonians 1:5, and the possibility that they might yet be deprived of their share in it through death had filled the converts with dismay.

4:15 For—the apostle now proceeds to give his authority for this statement, and to show how the dead in Christ shall share in the Parousia of the Lord Jesus, for, obviously, if they are to be with Him in that, it follows that they will be with Him also when the glory of His kingdom is subsequently revealed, cp. Hebrews 1:6.

this we say unto you—cp. Galatians 3:17; Ephesians 4:17.

by—*en* = in virtue of, or on the authority of.

the—the article is absent from the original; here it is required in English, however, and "the" seems a more appropriate supplement than "a" would be; there is no indefinite article in the Greek language.

word of the Lord,—see notes on 1:6, 8. Nothing recorded in the Gospels can be identified as the source of what follows; Matthew 24:31 most resembles it, but the difference is very great. Neither is there ground for supposing that the apostle quotes here, as in Acts 20:35, some words of the Lord not recorded by the evangelists. He is apparently transmitting a revelation given directly to himself as in Acts 18:9, cp. also Galatians 1:12; Ephesians 3:3, and intended, the phraseology seems to suggest, to meet this perplexity that had arisen at Thessalonica.

that we that are alive,—lit., "we, the living." When the Lord Jesus returns believers will be, as they are now, and indeed as they were even then at Thessalonica, divided into two classes, the living and the dead. But the time of that return has not been revealed, it is among the secret things concerning which God has kept His own counsel, Deuteronomy 29:29; Matthew 24:36; Mark 13:32; Acts 1:7. Consequently, in speaking of the return of the Lord Jesus, the apostle sometimes associates himself with the one class, looking forward to resurrection, as in 2 Corinthians 4:14, sometimes with the other, looking forward to change, as in 1 Corinthians 15:51, 52, and here.

The second epistle to the Corinthians, in which he associates himself with "them that are lying asleep," was written at no greater interval than three or four years after that to the Thessalonians, in which he associates himself with the living at the Parousia. It contains a passage, 5:1-10, expressing his own attitude toward the alternative possibilities, death and the coming of the Lord, and here also he uses "we." In vv. 2-4 he expresses his longing for that which cannot take place until the Lord comes; in v. 6 he asserts that he is of good courage in the face of death, and in v. 8 he repeats the assertion, adding that he is "willing rather to be absent from the body and to be at home with the Lord," i.e., to die. Longing for the Parousia of Christ, which is certain to come, yet not afraid of death, which may possibly come first, is, then, the characteristic attitude of each generation of Christians.

In the epistle to the Philippians, written perhaps seven years later still, while he describes his own attitude toward death, 1:21-24, in language akin to that used to the Corinthians, and suggests that it is no very remote contingency,2:17, he yet uses "we" and "our" in describing the characteristic attitude of Christians to the coming of the Lord. His advancing years and the threatening nature of his circumstances, while they brought before his mind increasingly the possibility that he might die before the Parousia, did not prevent his saying, "Heaven, from whence also we wait for a Savior," Philippians 3:20.

And in the pastoral epistles, latest of all, whereas he uses language only explicable on the hypothesis that he anticipated his speedy execution, he still speaks of the reward awaiting those who have loved the appearing of Christ, 2 Timothy 4:6-8, and of the grace of God, "instructing us—to the intent that we should live—looking for the blessed hope," Titus 2:11-13. Indeed, before he closes the epistle in which he says "I am already being offered," he urges Timothy to come to him "before winter," a season presumably still some distance off, and to bring with him Mark as well as some articles of which he anticipated he would be in need. As always, so now, when there seemed to be no escape from death the apostle stood ready either for suffering or for service as the will of the Lord might appoint, not knowing whether it might not be His will even yet to deliver His servant and to entrust him with further service.

It seems clear, therefore, that no conclusion can be drawn from the apostle's language as to his personal expectations. He shared in what should be the attitude of each generation of Christians, the desire for, and the expectation of, the Parousia of the Lord Jesus, but there is no reason to suppose that he knew more on the subject than he taught, cp. 1 Corinthians 13:12, and see note on "should afterwards" at Galatians 3:23.

Neither can any development in his doctrine, by way of adjustment or correction, be traced in his epistles, read chronologically; much less is there any evidence that the later are intended to correct the earlier. Indeed, these words to the Thessalonians claim to be a revelation from the Lord Himself and, while they might be expanded or explained by later revelation, they could not be set aside, much less could they be attributed to a mistaken apprehension on the part of the apostle.

The apostle throughout his life, as his epistles reflect it, maintains the same attitude toward the great alternatives. There is neither contradiction nor inconsistency. His example and his words alike teach us to be prepared to meet death with unflinching courage, but, above all things, to look for the Parousia of the Lord.

The use of "we" and "us" in Psalm 66:6; Hosea 12:4; Romans 13:11, 13, may be compared.

that are left—*perileipō*, lit., "those who are left over," this word, which occurs again in v. 17, is intended to define what the apostle meant by "the living." These were not necessarily the then living, though there was a reasonable hope that the Lord might come again during the lifetime of those who would read the letter, but those who will be upon the earth when the Parousia takes place. And, being himself still alive, it was natural for him to include himself with those, whoever they might be, who must, when the Parousia does take place, be described in these terms.

The word "left" may also have been intended to suggest that those who had fallen asleep had not died by accident, nor through the malice of Satan; they had been taken away by the Lord, just as his readers themselves had been left among the living by the Lord. Cp. Job 1:21.

And, after all, was the disadvantage theirs who had been taken? Was it not rather theirs who had been left? Cp. "to die is gain—to depart and be with Christ—is very far better," Philippians 1:21-23.

unto the coming of the Lord,—see note at 2:19.

shall in no wise precede—*phthanō*, translated "is come" in 2:16, where see note. Here = "shall in no wise obtain any advantage over." The negative is strongly emphatic and is intended to reassure the bereaved concerning their departed friends.

them that are fallen asleep.—see note at v. 13.

4:16 For—"because," as in 2:14, etc., introducing the more detailed positive statement on which the negative assurance of v. 15 is based.

The Lord—see note on 3:12.

himself—this word stands in the position of emphasis, as in 3:11; 5:23; attention is thus fixed on Him in whom will be centered all the power and all the glory of the occasion, and who is yet the very One who died, v. 14. If He lost nothing by death, neither shall they who fell asleep trusting Him.

shall descend from—*apo;* in 1:10 *ek,* "out of," occurs. *Apo* is appropriately used of the visible heavens, cp. 2 Thessalonians 1:7, *ek* of the invisible, cp. 2 Corinthians 5:2. And correspondingly *apo* is used from the heavenly point of view, i.e., of the Lord, who sends or comes, cp. Romans 1:18; 1 Peter 1:12, while *ek* is used from the earthly point of view, i.e., of believers who receive or expect, cp. Acts 2:2; Philippians 3:20; 2 Peter 1:18.

heaven,—singular, = the sky, the limit of vision upward; cp. Luke 2:15; Acts 1:11; 1 Peter 3:22. See 1:10, and note there.

with—*en,* denoting the circumstances attending the descent of the Lord from heaven; cp. the same use of the word in 2 Thessalonians 1:8; 2:9, 10.

a shout,—*keleusma* = a word of command, military or other, occurs in LXX only in Proverbs 30:27, which reads: "The locusts have no king, yet at the word of command they march in rank."||

This shout is not said to be the voice of the Lord, John 5:28, but simply that it peals forth as the Lord descends. To whom it is addressed is not stated; it may be the signal to the attendant hosts of heaven. It can hardly be intended for the saints; only the voice of the Son of God can awaken them sleeping, or change them living.

with [en] the voice of the archangel,—i.e., the voice in which the shout is uttered is that of an archangel. This title is not found in the Old Testament, and in the New Testament elsewhere only Jude 9, where it is used of Michael, who in Daniel is called "one of the chief princes," and "the great prince" (LXX "the great angel") 10:13, 21; 12:1, cp. also Revelation 12:7. There is no article in the original before either word, so that the quality of the voice, its majesty and authority, is intended; but there is nothing to indicate that any particular angelic chief was in the writer's mind. Whether there are other beings of this exalted rank in the heavenly hosts Scripture does not say, though the description "one of the chief princes" suggests that this may be the case; cp. also Romans 8:38; Ephesians 1:21; Colossians 1:16, where the word translated "principalities" is *archē,* the same word that forms the prefix in archangel.

and—or "even," "that is to say"; what follows is explanatory of what precedes, cp. note on 1:5. The sound of a trumpet is called its voice, Matthew 24:31; 1 Corinthians 14:7, 8, and a loud clear voice is described under the similitude of a trumpet, Revelation 1:10; 4:1.

with [en] the trump of God:—again the article is absent in the original, = a trumpet such as is used in God's service, cp. "songs of God," 1 Chronicles 16:42, "harps of God," Revelation 15:2, and see also Zechariah 9:14. This is apparently the "last trump" of 1 Corinthians 15:52, and with its sound the word of the Lord in John 5:28 begins to come to pass.

If, as seems probable, the subject of this threefold description is one great signal from heaven, then the words may be paraphrased: "with a shout in the archangel's voice, even with the voice of the trump of God."

and the dead in Christ—cp. John 11:11, 12, "Lazarus is fallen asleep. . . . Now Jesus had spoken of his death"; so here "dead in Christ" is an alternative description of "them that fall asleep," v. 13, for not even death can disturb the vital union expressed by the words "in Christ," see notes on 1:1 and v. 14, and cp. Romans 8:38.

The word here translated "dead," *nekros*, occurs about one hundred and thirty times in the New Testament, and is used, adjective or noun, of:

a, the death of the body, cp. James 2:26, by far its most frequent sense:

b, the actual spiritual condition of unsaved men, Matthew 8:22; John 5:25; Ephesians 2:1, 5; 5:14; Philippians 3:11; Colossians 2:13, cp. Luke 15:24:

c, the ideal spiritual condition of believers in relation to sin, Romans 6:11:

d, believers in declension, inasmuch as in that state they are inactive and barren, Revelation 3:1:

e, sin, which apart from law cannot produce a sense of guilt, Romans 7:8:

f, the body of the believer, in contrast to his spirit, Romans 8:10:

g, the works of the law, inasmuch as, however good in themselves, Romans 7:13, they cannot produce life, Hebrews 6:1; 9:14:

h, the faith that does not produce works, James 2:17, 26, cp. v. 20.

shall rise first—so far from being placed at any disadvantage, they shall be raised before the living are changed. There is no reference here to the resurrection of the unsaved. According to the word of the Lord they also shall be raised, see John 5:29, but, apparently, not until after a considerable interval has elapsed, see Revelation 20:5. The word "hour," in John 5:29, is to be taken, as in John 4:23; 5:35; Philemon 15, to mean a more or less extended period.

4:17 then—*epeita*, marking the order of events, but not necessarily indicating any interval. That there will not be any interval between the raising of the dead in Christ and the change of the living saints is plain from the following words and from 1 Corinthians 15:52.

we that are alive, that are left,—see notes on v. 15.

shall——be caught up—*harpazō*, the same verb is used of Paul, "whether in the body, or apart from the body——God knoweth," 2 Corinthians 12:2, 4; of Philip, certainly "in the body," Acts 8:39; and of the "man-child," Revelation 12:5. It conveys the idea of force suddenly exercised, and is well rendered "snatch," see John 10:12, 28, 29; Jude 23; cp. also its use in Matthew 11:12; 13:19, and in John 6:15; Acts 23:10. Hence the word "rapture" = "the act of conveying a person from one place to another" (Oxford Dict.), is frequently used to describe the event here foretold.

There is nothing in these words to indicate that any change will pass on the bodies, whether of the dead in Christ, or of the living believers. Elsewhere, however, it is stated concerning the dead in Christ that they shall be raised in incorruptible bodies, i.e., bodies not liable to the decay which sooner or later reduces to its elements every living organism of which mankind has any experience. This change is described in a series of contrasts in 1 Corinthians 15:42–44, and further in vv. 52–54.

And concerning the living believers it is stated that, inasmuch as in its present natural condition the body cannot enter upon its heavenly inheritance, their bodies shall be changed, "in a moment, in the twinkling of an eye" and without passing through the experience of death; for "this mortal [body] must put on immortality," 1 Corinthians 15:50–53, "what is mortal" (i.e., the body) must be "swallowed up of life," 2 Corinthians 5:4.

Thus "the natural body" of the dead in Christ will be raised, and that of the living will be changed into "the spiritual body"; "the image of the earthly" will give place to "the image of the heavenly"; the body of humiliation will be fashioned anew, and so be conformed to the glorious body of the risen Lord, 1 Corinthians 15:47–49; Philippians 3:20, 21. Some slight conception of what that body is may be formed from the accounts of the Transfiguration, Matthew 17:2; Mark 9:3; Luke 9:29, cp. 2 Peter 1:16–17, and from the vision of John in Revelation 1:14–17.

The change in the bodies of the saints, while it is ascribed to the working of the power of the risen Lord, Philippians 3:21, is also said to follow as the inevitable consequence of the presence of the Holy Spirit in the believer, Romans 8:10, 11. See further at 5:23.

together with them—this mighty work accomplished, then shall, all together and immediately, at the same time and in the same company, be caught away to the Parousia of the Lord.

in the clouds,—lit., "in," or "amid clouds." That the clouds of heaven are intended seems probable from a comparison with Acts 1:9, where the cloud is associated with the ascension of Christ, as here with the ascension of His people, and from Revelation 11:12.

to meet the Lord—*apantēsis,* lit., "into a meeting with"; the word occurs several times in LXX, 1 Samuel 13:10; 2 Chronicles 15:2; 19:2, etc., and in the New Testament again in Matthew 25:1, 6; Acts 28:15. It occurs in a papyrus manuscript of the 2nd century B.C., and in another of the 3rd century A.D., for the reception of a newly appointed magistrate, or other dignitary, by the residents in his district on his arrival there. Almost invariably the word suggests that those who go out to meet him intend to return to their starting place with the person met. So it is, evidently, in all the occurrences noted above, and this meaning seems equally appropriate here. Paul is reassuring the converts that their departed will not miss the promised glory of the kingdom, for God will bring them with Christ when He comes to reign; see note on "with Him," v. 14. But how, if their bodies are lying asleep in the dust of the earth? They will be raised by His quickening voice, and will be caught away to meet Him in the air, and, in due course, will return with Him to the earth from whence they set out; see Matthew 25:31; Colossians 3:4.||

in [*eis,* into] the air:—of the seven occurrences of this word in the New Testament five certainly refer to the atmosphere, viz, Acts 22:23; 1 Corinthians 9:26; 14:9; Revelation 9:2; 16:17; it does not seem necessary, therefore, to depart from this meaning here or in Ephesians 2:2. Like the words "heaven" and "cloud," the word "air" attracts the attention upward without particularly defining the place of the meeting.

The immediate purpose of the apostle having been accomplished, he does not proceed further with the subject; hence his silence here as to any later development is not to be understood as signifying that the Parousia is the final state.

and so—thus, in this way, cp. note on "for," v. 15.

shall we ever be with the Lord.—thus will be accomplished the promise of the Lord, "I come again, and will receive you unto Myself that where I am, there ye may be also," John 14:3.

4:18 Wherefore comfort one another with [*en*] these words.—for in these words alone is the cure for the sorrow that had come upon the converts, and that awaits every child of God, save such as are themselves early called away. See v. 13, and, for "comfort," cp. note at 2:11.

In striking contrast to these words is a papyrus letter of the 2nd century A.D., written by a woman to her bereaved friends. It runs: "Irene to Taonnophris and Philon, greeting! I was as much grieved and shed as many tears over Eumoiros as I shed for Didymas. I did everything that was fitting [this refers apparently to certain rites customary at such times] and so did my whole family. . . . But still there is nothing one can do in the face of such trouble. So I leave you to comfort yourselves. Farewell."

1 THESSALONIANS

CHAPTER FIVE

Verses 1–28

5:1 But—having thus reassured his readers concerning the share of the departed in the glory of Christ by explaining to them that all in Christ, living and dead, will be received into the presence of the Lord before that glory is revealed to the world at all, the apostle proceeds to describe the effect of that revelation upon the world, vv. 2, 3, and to instruct and exhort them as to their own conduct in the meantime, vv. 4–11.

The change of subject is marked, for whereas 4:13–17 is concerned with salvation, 5:1–3 is concerned with judgment. In 4:13–17 the language of the apostle closely follows that of the Lord recorded in John 14:1–3; where the first and second personal pronouns are used, "I come again and will receive you unto Myself" with which compare "the Lord Himself shall descend . . . we . . . shall be caught up . . . to meet the Lord in the air." But in 5:3 the language corresponds with that of the Lord recorded, for example, in Matthew 16:27; 24:31; Mark 13:26; Luke 9:26, where, as always in the Synoptists, the third personal pronoun only is used, "the Son of Man," "they," "them," with which compare "When they are saying, Peace and safety, then sudden destruction cometh upon them."

The brief statement of 5:3 is expanded in 2 Thessalonians 1:7–9, where the glorious accompaniments of the Second Advent are mentioned, in this respect also following closely the words spoken by the Lord and recorded in the Synoptists, such as "The Son of man shall come in the glory of His Father with His angels; and then shall He render to every man according to his deeds"; "they shall see the Son of Man coming . . . with power and great glory." But in 4:13–17 there is nothing of this; there we read that "the Lord Himself shall descend from Heaven." The voice to be heard by His people is His voice, and no other; the sheep of the Good Shepherd, living and dead, shall hear and obey.

The apostle, then, here develops and supplements the words of the Lord Jesus, according to His promise that the Spirit would "teach them all things," and "guide them into all the truth" (John 14:26; 16:13) and maintains the same fundamental distinction the Lord Himself had made between the relation of His Coming to His own and to the world.

concerning the times and the seasons,—these words, *chronos* and *kairos*, are synonyms, and while they have much in common and are used interchangeably on occasion, when they are used together they supplement each the other and hence are to be distinguished in meaning. In the New Testament they appear together again only in Acts 1:7, and in LXX only in Daniel 2:21; Ecclesiastes 3:1; in the latter place, however, the words are both in the singular.

Broadly speaking, *chronos*, "time," *(a)* implies duration, Revelation 10:6, whether longer, Acts 1:21; 13:18, or shorter, Luke 4:5; 18:4, or *(b)* refers to the date of an occurrence, whether in the past, Matthew 2:7; Luke 8:29, or in the future, Acts 3:21; 7:17. *Kairos*, "season," refers to the characteristics of a period, as of harvest, Matthew 13:20; Acts 14:17; Galatians 6:9; of the fulfillment of prophecy, Luke 1:20; Acts 3:19; 1 Peter 1:11; of punishment, Matthew 8:29; of discharging duties, Luke 12:42; of opportunity for doing anything, good, Matthew 26:18; Galatians 6:10; Ephesians 5:16, or evil, Revelation 12:12; of a time suitable for a purpose, Luke 4:13, lit., "until a season," as for the preaching of salvation, 2 Corinthians 6:2. In 2 Timothy 4:6, and a few other passages, the distinction between the two words is not so sharply defined.

Here, "times" refers to the length of the interval before the Parousia takes place, and to the length of time it will occupy; "seasons" refers to the characteristics of the periods before, during, and after the Parousia. An ancient writer expresses the distinction thus: "times" has to do with quantity, "seasons" with quality.

brethren, ye have no need that aught be written unto you.—cp. 4:9, and see note; there, however, the emphasis is on "you," for in the matter of brotherly love his readers were themselves taught of God. Here "written" is the emphatic word, for the missionaries had already instructed their converts on the subject by word of mouth, 2 Thessalonians 2:5. Hence the reference to the judgments awaiting the world is limited to the few words contained in vv. 2, 3.

That the Lord would come in glory and for judgment was common knowledge even in pre-Christian times, cp. Daniel 7:10; Jude 14:15, e.g. That He would deliver His own so that they should "never stand in the dock" (as the words of John 5:24 may be paraphrased) He had as plainly declared. But how that deliverance would be accomplished was not made known until Paul received the revelation recorded in 4:13–17.

5:2 For yourselves know—as at 3:3.

perfectly—*akribōs* = "accurately." Luke uses the same word of his investigations into the history of the Lord Jesus, 1:3; Matthew to describe Herod's instructions to the Wise Men from the East as to their inquiries at Bethlehem, 2:8 (cp. vv. 7 and 16, where the corresponding verb occurs). It is used also of the way in which Apollos, Aquila and Priscilla were accustomed to teach, Acts 18:25, 26. Here its use implies that Paul and his companions were also careful ministers of the Word. In Ephesians 5:15 it is used of the believer's walk. Thus the word suggests a threefold lesson on the need of accuracy and carefulness in:

a, the study of the Scriptures,

b, the teaching of the Scriptures,

c, obedience to what is learned from the Scriptures.

Taken with those that follow, these words seem to imply a paradox, as though the apostle intended his readers to understand "you know perfectly that nothing more can be known about its date than that it will come when least expected."

The circumstances under which the Day of the Lord will be ushered in were described by the prophets of Israel, Joel 2:1–11, e.g.; by the Lord Himself, Matthew 24:29–31, e.g.; and by the apostles, 2 Thessalonians 2:1–12, e.g.; but since "the time of the end," Daniel 8:17, is among "the secret things that belong unto Jehovah our God," Deuteronomy 29:29, speculation and calculation are alike in vain. And not merely so, for attempts to fix future dates can only be made in disobedience to the word of the Lord, Who said, "of that day and hour knoweth no one, not even the angels of heaven, neither the Son, but the Father only," Matthew 24:36, and, after His resurrection, "it is not for you to know times or seasons, which the Father hath set within His own authority," Acts 1:7.

that the day—*hēmera*, a word which occurs frequently and in a variety of meanings in both the Old Testament and the New Testament It is used of—

a, the period of natural light, Genesis 1:5; Proverbs 4:18; Mark 4:35:

b, the same, but figuratively, for a period of opportunity for service, John 9:4; Romans 13:13:

c, one period of alternate light and darkness, Genesis 1:5; Mark 1:13:

d, a period of undefined length marked by certain characteristics, such as "the day of small things," Zechariah 4:10; of perplexity and distress, Isaiah 17:11; Obadiah 12–14; of prosperity and of adversity, Ecclesiastes 7:14; of trial or testing, Psalm 95:8; of salvation, Isaiah 49:8; 2 Corinthians 6:2, cp. Luke 19:42; of evil, Ephesians 6:13; of wrath and revelation of the judgments of God, Romans 2:5:

e, an appointed time, Ecclesiastes 8:6; Ephesians 4:30:

f, a notable defeat in battle, etc., Isaiah 9:4; Psalm 137:7; Ezekiel 30:9; Hosea 1:11:

g, by metonymy = "when," "at the time when,"

    1. of the past, Genesis 2:4; Numbers 3:13; Deuteronomy 4:10;

    2. of the future, Genesis 2:17; Ruth 4:5; Matthew 24:50; Luke 1:20:

h, a judgment or doom, Job 18:20; Psalm 37:13; Jeremiah 50:27; Ezekiel 21:25.

of the Lord—*kurios* = Jehovah, cp. note on 3:12. The phrase "day of the Lord" occurs again in the New Testament only in 2 Thessalonians 2:2; Acts 2:20; 2 Peter 3:10; cp. Revelation 6:17. In the Old Testament it is found between thirty and forty times, viz., in Isaiah, Jeremiah, Ezekiel, Obadiah, Joel, Amos, Zephaniah, Zechariah, Malachi.

The day of the Lord is first mentioned by Amos, 5:18, and Isaiah, 2:12, who were contemporary prophets. Their language, however, shows that the term was in current use for the victories won by Judah over their foes, because the strength in which they overcame was Jehovah's and because their enemies were His enemies also; therefore, the day of their victory was emphatically the "day of the Lord," see also Jeremiah 46:10; Ezekiel 13:5; 30:3. And in all their distresses, to whatever cause due, they hoped to see this day of the Lord repeated. But the prophets warned them that to such as fostered pride in their hearts and dealt unrighteously with their fellows, the day of the Lord would prove a day of darkness and sorrow, not of light and joy, cp. Isaiah 33:14; Zephaniah 1:12.

Days of the Lord, in which He gave them victory over their enemies, became fewer in number as time passed, until at last Judah was carried into exile, *circa* 588 B.C., whither Israel had preceded them by more than one hundred and thirty years, i.e., *circa* 721 B.C. But notwithstanding this disaster and humiliation at the hands of their enemies "a great and terrible day of the lord" was still to come, Joel 2:31; Malachi 4:5. That day, still future, will see Jehovah's final triumph in the complete overthrow of Gentile power, Isaiah 13:9–11; 34:8; Daniel 2:34, 44; Obadiah 15, and the consequent deliverance of His ancient people and the establishment of His "King upon His holy hill of Zion," Psalm 2:6, cp. 110:1. And, though it is not recorded that the Lord Jesus did Himself use the expression, it is evident that He had the day of the Lord in mind when He spoke of the future of the nation, Matthew 24:30; 25:31, cp. 16:27, Luke 21:34.

Unlike the descent of the Lord Jesus into the air to call away His people, of which the concluding paragraph of ch. 4 treats, and concerning which nothing is said about signs, it is stated that certain developments must take place among men before the day of the Lord comes, see Daniel 8:23–25; 11:36, cp. 2 Thessalonians 2:2, 3, and that its imminence will be marked by certain signs, Mark

13:14–27; Acts 2:17–21. This was, therefore, a matter of common knowledge among converts everywhere, but, apparently, the revelation concerning the rapture of the saints was published in this letter for the first time. Nothing previously revealed was altered by it, but what the Lord Himself had said was thus supplemented according to His own promise, John 16:12, 13, and that in a way that cast light on His words "I come again, and will receive you unto Myself that where I am, there ye may be also," 14:3; words which, however, were not put on record by John until long after Paul had written this Epistle.

Other expressions, "day of vengeance of our God," Isaiah 61:2, "the day that the Son of Man is revealed," Luke 17:30, cp. Romans 2:16; Acts 17:31; Revelation 6:17, "My day," John 8:56, are to be understood of the day of the Lord, and the subsequent developments of God's purposes in relation to the human race; see also "the day of God," 2 Peter 3:12.

The grammatical form of the words "the Lord's Day" (*kuriakē*, an adjective formed from *kurios*, lord), in Revelation 1:10 is exactly paralleled in 1 Corinthians 4:3, where "man's judgment," marg. "man's day" (*anthrōpinos*, an adjective formed from *anthrōpos*, man), is used of the present period of man's rebellion against God; it is probable, therefore, that "the Lord's Day" = "the Day of the Lord" which is to bring man's day of rebellion to an end.

The undernoted expressions are more probably to be referred to the period called in this epistle and elsewhere "the Parousia," during which the Lord will be present with His people in the air:—

- the day of Christ, Philippians 1:10; 2:16:
- the day of Jesus Christ, Philippians 1:6:
- the day of the Lord Jesus, 1 Corinthians 5:5; 2 Corinthians 1:14:
- the day of our Lord Jesus Christ, 1 Corinthians 1:8.

In each of these places the thought and the language are similar to that of 2:19; 3:13, where see notes. See further in this connection 1 Corinthians 3:13; 2 Timothy 1:12, 18; 4:8, etc.

so cometh as a thief in the night—the order in the original is, "[the] day of [the] Lord as [a] thief in [the] night so comes," hence the word "night" is not to be read with "day of the Lord" but with "thief," that is, there is no reference to the time of the coming, only to the manner of it. To avoid ambiguity the phrase may be paraphrased, "so comes as a thief in the night comes." The use of the present tense instead of the future emphasizes the certainty of the coming, see note at 1:10.

This simile was used of Himself by the Lord Jesus in one of His parables, Matthew 24:43, 44, and in the Epistle to Sardis, Revelation 3:3, cp. 16:15. In 2 Peter 3:10 it is used, as here, of the day of the Lord. The unexpectedness of the coming of the thief, and the unpreparedness of those to whom he comes, are the essential elements in the figure; cp. the entirely different figure used in Matthew 25:1–13.

5:3 When they are saying,—i.e., people generally, those who do not acknowledge the claims of the Lord Jesus, cp. "the rest," 4:13.

Peace—*eirēnē*, occurs in each of the books of the New Testament, save 1 John, and save in Acts 7:26 ("one") is always thus translated. It describes:

a, harmonious relationships between men, Matthew 10:34; Romans 14:19; cp. v. 13 below:

b, between nations, Luke 14:32; Acts 12:20; Revelation 6:4:

c, friendliness, Acts 15:33; 1 Corinthians 16:11; Hebrews 11:31:

d, freedom from molestation, Luke 11:21; 19:42; Acts 16:36:

e, order, in the State, Acts 24:2, in the churches, 1 Corinthians 14:33:

f, the harmonized relationships between God and man, accomplished through the gospel, Acts 10:36; Ephesians 2:17:

g, the sense of rest and contentment consequent thereon, Matthew 10:13; Mark 5:34; Luke 1:79; 2:29; John 14:27; Romans 1:7; 3:17; 8:6; in certain passages this idea is not distinguishable from the last, Romans 5:1.

See further on v. 23.

and safety,—*asphaleia*, security from disturbance, mental, Luke 1:4, or physical, Acts 5:23.||

Men by nature are at enmity with God, Romans 8:7, sons of disobedience inwrought by a spirit antagonistic to God, Ephesians 2:2, 3, knowing neither the fear of God nor the way of peace, Romans 3:18–21. Read in the light of the Scriptures the tendencies of the age are certainly in the direction indicated by the words of the Psalmist "all his thoughts are, There is no God," Psalm 10:4. Psalm 53 is another vivid prophecy of the moral characteristics of the world, as Psalm 2:1–3 is of the political, at the period immediately preceding the day of the Lord.

Since that period is consistently described as a time of calamity upon the Jewish nation, and since the Gentile powers, "all nations," will then be actually gathered against Jerusalem, Zechariah 14:1–5, cp. Jeremiah 30:4–11; Matthew 24:6, 7, it is evident that the words "peace and safety" cannot refer to the international conditions then obtaining, but are intended to describe the sense of security from divine interposition that will possess the hearts of men up to the very moment at which God breaks the long silence and once again intervenes directly in human affairs, cp. Psalm 50:1–6. So was it in the days of Noah and in the days of Lot, so is it now, and so shall it continue to be until the end of the age, Luke 17:26–30; cp. also the incident recorded in Acts 12:21–23. Pride, and the love of gain, and the sense of security, harden the heart and cause men to ask derisively, "Where is the promise of His Parousia?" Against this error of the wicked (plural) Peter warns his readers to be ever on their guard, 2 Peter 3:3-4; 10:17, cp. 2 Thessalonians 2:10, 11.

then sudden—*aiphnidios,* elsewhere only in Luke 21:34; here it has the place of emphasis at the beginning of the sentence as "destruction" has at its close, lit., "then sudden upon them cometh destruction," cp. Isaiah 48:3, "I have declared. . . . I showed . . . suddenly I did."||

destruction—*olethros* = ruin, occurs in the New Testament only in writings of Paul. In 1 Corinthians 5:5 it is used of the discipline of an erring believer with a view to his spiritual profit; in 1 Timothy 6:9 of the consequences of the indulgence of the flesh (perhaps referring to physical and temporal, while the accompanying word "perdition," *apōleia,* see at 2 Thess. 2:3, refers to spiritual and eternal disaster); here and in 2 Thessalonians 1:9, of the effect upon men of the calamities which are to accompany the revelation of the Lord Jesus at the opening of the day of the Lord.||

This word, like its synonyms, also translated "destroy," "destruction," means, not the destruction of being, but of well being, not annihilation, the putting an end to the existence of a person or thing, but its ruin so far as the purpose of its existence is concerned.

Olothreutēs in 1 Corinthians 10:10, and *olothreuōn* in Hebrews 11:28, forms of the same word, are translated "the destroyer," cp. Exodus 12:23.||

A strengthened form, *exolethreuo,* is found in Acts 3:23, a question from Leviticus 23:29, LXX.||

cometh upon them,—*ephistēmi,* lit., "to stand over," as in Luke 4:39, see also Acts 17:5, where the same word is rendered "assaulting." The word suggests some amount of violence, as when an armed man stands over an unprepared enemy.

as travail upon a woman with child;—just as the figure of the thief suggests the unexpected character of the catastrophe, so this suggests its inevitableness. The words are strongly reminiscent of those of the Lord Jesus recorded in Luke 21:34, cp. Jeremiah 13:21.

and they shall in no wise escape.—*ekpheugō* = to flee away, as Sceva's sons fled from the demoniac, Acts 19:16; cp. 16:27, and 2 Corinthians 11:33. In its other occurrences in the New Testament, viz., Luke 21:36; Romans 2:3; Hebrews 2:3; 12:25, the word, as here, refers to the judgments of God; cp. Psalm 139:7-12.||

5:4 But ye, brethren,—the personal pronoun has the place of emphasis assigned to it twice in this verse, the better to mark the completeness of the contrast between the destiny of Christians and that of the unbelieving world, cp. Ephesians 4:20.

are not in darkness,—*skotos,* sometimes *skotia* = absence of light:

   a, physical, Matthew 27:45; John 6:17; Acts 13:11; 2 Corinthians 4:6:

   b, intellectual, Romans 2:19 (cp. the verb in Rom. 1:21); Ephesians 4:18:

   c, moral, Matthew 6:23; Romans 13:12; 1 John 1:6:

   d, spiritual, Luke 1:79; Acts 26:18.

It is also used of:—

   e, ignorance of the purposes of God, consequent upon estrangement from Him, here and v. 5:

   f, the world in its present condition, John 1:5; 12:35. Ephesians 6:12, which reflects the character of the powers that dominate it, Luke 22:53; Colossians 1:13:

   g, the place of punishment, Matthew 8:12; 2 Peter 2:17:

   h, privacy generally, whether what is done or said therein be good or ill, Matthew 10:27; Luke 12:3; 1 Corinthians 4:5.

With the exception of such passages as fall under *h* "darkness" is always used in a bad sense. Moreover, the different forms of darkness are so closely allied, being either cause and effect, or else concurrent effects of the same cause, that they cannot always be distinguished. 1 John 1:5; 2:8, e.g., are passages which, since both spiritual and moral darkness are intended in them, it would be impossible to allot to either *c* or *d*.

Here the metaphor of darkness is in harmony with the simile of the thief in the night. Ignorance of the purposes of God is darkness that can be dissipated only by revelation from God, and, through His apostles, this divine enlightenment had been given to the believers at Thessalonica.

that—*hina* = so that, with the result that. The word usually expresses the purpose in view, as in 2:16, cp. John 5:34, but it is also used for result, as in Galatians 5:17, and this meaning seems to give the best sense here also.

that day—i.e., the Day of the Lord, mentioned just before.

should overtake you as a thief:—see note on v. 3.

5:5 for—introducing the ground for the assertion that the day of the Lord will not overtake believers when it comes upon the world.

ye are all—"all," standing at the beginning of the phrase in the original, is emphatic, = all believers as believers, a law to which there is no exception.

sons—*huios*, save Matthew 21:5, and a few passages in which the "Children, lit., Sons, of Israel," Matthew 27:9, e.g., are mentioned, is always so translated. Primarily the word signifies the relation of offspring to parent, John 9:18-20; Galatians 4:30, but it is often used metaphorically of prominent moral characteristics, as:

a, sons of God, Matthew 5:9, 45; Luke 6:35:

b, sons of the light, Luke 16:8; John 12:36:

c, sons of the day, here:

d, sons of peace, Luke 10:6:

e, sons of this world, Luke 16:8:

f, sons of disobedience, Ephesians 2:2:

g, sons of the Evil One, Matthew 13:38, cp. "of the Devil," Acts 13:10:

h, sons of perdition, 2 Thessalonians 2:3, where see note, John 17:12.

It is also used to describe characteristics other than moral, as:

i, sons of the resurrection, Luke 20:36:

j, sons of the kingdom, Matthew 8:12; 13:38:

k sons of the bridechamber, Mark 2:19:

l, sons of exhortation, Acts 4:36:

m, sons of thunder, Boanerges, Mark 3:17.

Teknon, children, a synonym of *huios*, is used in the same way as:

a, children of God, John 1:12:

b, children of Light, Ephesians 5:8:

c, children of obedience, 1 Peter 1:14:

d, children of the promise, Romans 9:8; Galatians 4:28:

e, children of the Devil, 1 John 3:10:

f, children of wrath, Ephesians 2:3:

g, children of cursing, 2 Peter 2:14.

Both words are frequently used to describe the relationship between believers and God in virtue of the New Birth, John 3:5; 1 Peter 1:23; the difference being that whereas the word "children" makes the idea of the new nature prominent, Romans 8:16, 21, "sons" emphasizes the dignity of the new position, Romans 8:14, 19. See further at Galatians 3:26.

of light,—*phōs*, which covers the same wide area as the English word. Primarily light is a luminous emanation, probably of force, from certain bodies, which enables the eye to discern form and color. Light requires an organ adapted for its reception, Matthew 6:22. Where the eye is absent, or where it has become impaired from any cause light is useless. Man, naturally, is incapable of receiving spiritual light inasmuch as he lacks the capacity for spiritual things, 1 Corinthians 2:14. Hence believers are celled "sons of light," not merely because they have received a revelation from God, but because in the new birth, they have received the spiritual capacity for it.

Apart from natural phenomena, light is used in Scripture of:

a, the glory of God's dwelling place, 1 Timothy 6:16:

b, the nature of God, 1 John 1:5:

c, the impartiality of God, James 1:17:

d, the favor of God, Psalm 4:6; of the King, Proverbs 16:15; of an influential man, Job 29:24:

e, God, as the illuminator of His people, Isaiah 60:19, 20:

f, the Lord Jesus as the illuminator of men, John 8:12; Acts 13:47:

g, the illuminating power of the Scriptures, Psalm 119:105; and of the judgments and commandments of God, Isaiah 51:4; Proverbs 6:23, cp. Psalm 43:3:

h, the guidance of God, Job 29:3; Psalm 112:4; Isaiah 50:10; and, ironically, of the guidance of man, Romans 2:19:

i, salvation, 1 Peter 2:9:

j, righteousness, Romans 13:12; 2 Corinthians 11:14, 15; 1 John 2:9, 10:

k, witness for God, Matthew 5:14, 16:

l, prosperity and general well-being, Esther 8:16; Job 18:18; Isaiah 58:8–10.

and sons of the day:—lit., "sons of day," extending the idea suggested by the word "light." There does not seem to be any reference to the day of the Lord here.

we—for a similar transition from "ye" to "we" see ch. 4, v. 4 with v. 7. The underlying thought seems to be: "that which characterizes you is common to all believers, we are not of night, nor of darkness." Through the remaining verses of this section the writer uses the first personal pronoun.

are not of the night,—lit., "not of night"; of = belonging to, cp. "of the Way," Acts 9:2, "of shrinking back," and "of faith," Hebrews 10:39, marg. The word *nux,* night, is used of:

a, the period of the absence of light, Genesis 1:5; Matthew 2:14:

b, the period of man's alienation from God, Romans 13:12, and here:

c, a period during which prophecy is silent, Micah 3:6:

d, death, John 9:4.

Thus the same period is called "day," 1 Corinthians 4:3, or "night," as it is looked at from the point of view of unregenerate man, or from that of God.

nor of darkness;—the order, "light . . . day . . . night . . . darkness," in which the first word corresponds with the fourth and the second with the third, constitutes a figure of speech known as "chiasm," from a Greek word signifying a placing crosswise, like the letter X, in Greek pronounced *chi.* It occurs frequently in Scripture, cp. Isaiah 55:8–9; Matthew 12:22; John 10:14, 15; Romans

10:9, 10; 3 John 11. "Sometimes the figure is extended to more than two or three double statements; cp. Romans 2:6-11, in which section seven pairs of corresponding lines are found. Cp. also Numbers 15:35, 36; Isaiah 60:1-3, and see analysis of 1:2-5.

5:6 so then let us not—Paul frequently associated himself with his readers in his exhortations, Romans 13:12, 13; Galatians 5:25, 26, e.g.; cp. Lamentations 3:40-41; Hosea 6:1-3, but ct. the Lord Jesus, Who never thus identified Himself with those whom He addressed, whether the multitude or His disciples, see Matthew 17:27.

sleep,—*katheudō*, occurs over twenty times in the New Testament, but in Paul's Epistle, apart from this section, only in Ephesians 5:14. Only once is it used of death, viz., of Jairus' daughter, Matthew 9:24 and parallel passages. Four times it denotes worldly indifference to things spiritual on the part of believers, here and v. 10, Mark 13:36; Ephesians 5:14; elsewhere always of natural sleep, as in v. 7.

Beside the word translated "sleep" in 4:13, where see note, *hupnos* is also used, but never for death, and only once metaphorically for a slumbrous condition of soul, Romans 13:11.

The metaphor of sleep arises naturally out of that of night, cp. v. 7, and implies a state of spiritual insensibility on the part of a believer, in which state he is conformed rather to the world than to Christ, cp. Romans 12:2. In Romans 13:11; Ephesians 5:14, believers are exhorted to awake out of such a state; here they are warned against falling into it.

as do the rest,—see note on 4:13.

but let us watch—*gregoreō*, which is used of mental alertness, the condition of the mind opposite to that which characterizes it in sleep, Matthew 26:40. Hence it is used of the intentness of the mind bent on getting instruction, Proverbs 8:34, LXX, looking for answer to prayer, Colossians 4:2, and for the return of the Lord, Mark 13:35-37; it is also used of vigilance in carrying out a purpose, Jeremiah 1:12, LXX, and of vigilance against a foe, such as Satan, 1 Peter 5:8, and against evil teachers, Acts 20:31; and of vigilance against spiritual dangers in general, here and v. 10, 1 Corinthians 16:13; Revelation 3:2, 3.

and be sober.—*nēphō* = freedom from the influence of intoxicants, but in the New Testament it is used only in a metaphorical sense, = freedom from credulity, and from excitability. As "watch" denotes alertness, so "sober" denotes stability; as the former is in contrast to the lethargy of sleep, so the latter is in contrast to the excitement of drunkenness, cp. Ephesians 5:18. *Nēphō* occurs again in v. 8, and in 2 Timothy 4:5; 1 Peter 1:13; 4:7; 5:8.||

A modified form, *eknēphō,* is translated "awake up" in 1 Corinthians 15:34, and another, *ananēphō,* appears in 2 Timothy 2:26, for which see note on "hindered us" at 2:18.

The corresponding adjective, *nēphalios,* is used to describe one of the qualities that should mark bishops ("bishop" is derived from the Greek word *episkopos,* lit., "overseer"), 1 Timothy 3:2, and the wives of such as take the lead among the saints, 1 Timothy 3:11; they are to be neither credulous nor excitable. Aged men are exhorted in a similar sense, Titus 2:2; it is to be observed that the Christian sobriety of maturer years is the result of self-control and the study of the Scriptures in youth.

5:7 For they that sleep sleep in the night;—in this statement of the ordinary fact of human experience the metaphorical language of the preceding verses is explained. As sleep is natural in the night, so indifference to God characterizes man in his unregenerate state. But for regenerate man to be spiritually asleep is to seem to be of the night, not of the day, of the world, not of Christ.

and they that be drunken are drunken in the night.—cp. Acts 2:15, and the warnings in Luke 21:34; Romans 13:12, 13, against indulgence in strong drink and its concomitant evils.

5:8 But let us, since we are of the day, be sober,—here again the personal pronoun is emphatic, to present more forcibly the difference that actually exists between believers and the world, and the contrast that should mark their conduct; lit., "we, but, of the day being, let-us-be-sober."

putting on—*enduō* = to clothe oneself with, which beside its frequent use for literal garments, Acts 12:21, e.g., is also used of the incorruptible body, wherein the dead in Christ shall be raised, and of the immortal body, which is to swallow up the mortal body of those who are alive at the Parousia, 1 Corinthians 15:53; 2 Corinthians 5:3.

It is the word used by the Lord Jesus to express the relationship between the promised Holy Spirit and those who were to receive Him, Luke 24:49.

At conversion the believer is said to have "put on the new man," Ephesians 4:24; Colossians 3:10, cp. Galatians 3:27; and "therefore," he is exhorted to "put on a heart of compassion, kindness, humility, meekness, longsuffering, . . . and love," Colossians 3:12, 14. Such is to be the ordinary apparel of the Christian, in this character he is to appear daily in the world.

The believer, however, is "enrolled—as a soldier," 2 Timothy 2:4, and as such has suitable armor provided for him, and with this he is exhorted to clothe himself Romans 13:12; Ephesians 6:11, and here.

The whole is summed up in Romans 13:14, for the man who "puts on the Lord Jesus Christ" stands both in the Christian's dress and in the Christian's panoply.

The difference in the tenses of the verbs is suggestive, for whereas that of "be sober" is continuous, that of "putting on" is momentary. Believers are to continue in sobriety, but to exhort them to continue putting armor on would be to assume that on occasion they might lay it aside; this the Christian may never do. Hence the "point" tense, signifying "put your armor on, and keep it on."

the breastplate,—*thōrax*, a piece of armor which protects the body between the neck and the waist; of the four occurrences of the word in the New Testament two are literal, Revelation 9:9, 17, two figurative, here and Ephesians 6:14.||

Paul draws some of his most striking illustrations from military life. Thus he speaks of:

- the believer as a soldier, 1 Corinthians 9:7; Philippians 2:25; 2 Timothy 2:3, 4; Philemon 2:
- his armor, here, Romans 13:12; 2 Corinthians 6:7; Ephesians 6:11–17:
- his weapons, 2 Corinthians 10:4; Ephesians 6:17; cp. 1 Peter 4:1:
- his warfare, 1 Timothy 1:18:
- order in the ranks, 1 Corinthians 14:40; Colossians 2:5:
- a captain's shout, 4:16:
- the members of the believer's body as God's weapons, Romans 6:13, marg.:

Cp. with these Isaiah 59:17.

The main difference between this passage and that in Ephesians, in which more detail is given, is that, whereas in the later epistle the believer is represented as actively engaged in conflict and his foes are specified, v. 12, here he is represented as on the defensive only.

of faith and love;—in Ephesians 6:14, as in Isaiah 59:17, the breastplate is righteousness. Faith is the proper attitude of the believer toward the Lord Jesus, love his proper attitude toward the saints, cp. Colossians 1:4, and Philemon 5. Faith and love are related as cause and effect, see notes on 1:3, and 3:6.

and for a helmet—*perikephalaia*, the piece of armor which gives protection to the head, as in Ephesians 6:17. It does not seem that the apostle was necessarily thinking of the heart as the seat of the affections, see note on 2:4, nor of the head as the seat of the intellect, since the word is not so used elsewhere in Scripture. Figurative language must not be pressed beyond its immediate purpose.||

the hope—this epistle, and particularly this section of it, is characteristically the Epistle of hope. See notes on 1:3; 2:19. Until the Lord comes the believer will be surrounded by the enervating influences of a world bent on ease and pleasure, hence his eye is directed to the future in order to encourage him to resist the spirit of the age in which he lives. At Ephesians 6:17 "hope" is omitted, since there the believer is represented as engaged in conflict, and salvation as a present experience.

of salvation.—see notes at 2:16.

5:9 For—introducing a further reason why the believer should put on this armor, and particularly why he should take hope as a helmet.

God appointed—*tithēmi,* primarily = to put, to place; it is used of material things, Matthew 5:15; 1 Corinthians 16:2; and of immaterial things, as one's life, John 10:18, cp. also Acts 1:7; 19:21; 1 Corinthians 3:10; 2 Corinthians 5:19. Then it means to appoint to service, general, John 15:16; 1 Timothy 1:12, or particular, Acts 20:28; or to a position, Hebrews 1:2; or to punishment, Matthew 24:51; 1 Peter 2:8, cp. 2 Peter 2:6. In all these cases He who appoints is God, "Who cannot lie," Titus 1:2, but "abideth faithful; for He cannot deny Himself," 2 Timothy 2:13, Whose "gifts and calling are not repented of," Romans 11:29, marg.

Amid the darkness of this age, and in face of the attacks of his adversaries, now subtle, now fierce, the believer is encouraged in a hope that "putteth not to shame," Romans 5:5, by the assurance of the sovereign purpose of God.

us—all such as trust in the Lord Jesus Christ as He is presented in the gospel; see note on v. 5.

not unto wrath,—the outpouring of the wrath of God causes the "sudden destruction" of v. 3, cp. 2 Thessalonians 1:7-9; see note at 1:10. Here "not" is emphatic by position.

but unto the obtaining—*peripoiēsis* = the act of acquiring anything, as e.g., salvation in its completeness, here, 2 Thessalonians 2:14; Hebrews 10:39, cp. Luke 17:33, where the corresponding verb appears. It is also used of the thing to be acquired, Ephesians 1:14; 1 Peter 2:9, "own possession," cp. Acts 20:28, where the verb is translated "purchased"; cp. Isaiah 43:21, "a people whom I have acquired to tell forth My praise," and Malachi 3:17, "they shall be Mine for a possession," LXX. The verb occurs again only at 1 Timothy 3:13, where, probably, the reference is to the higher service hereafter which is the reward of faithful service here, cp. Luke 19:16, 17.||

Those who obtain this salvation and glory do so according to the appointment and calling of God, indeed, cp. 1:4, but only on condition of willing response to that appointment and call.

of salvation—as at 2:16. Here the apostle is speaking of the consummation of salvation in the deliverance of the believer from the wrath of God.

through—= "by means of," see note on "in Jesus," 4:14.

our Lord Jesus Christ,—see notes on 1:1.

5:10 who died for us,—see note on 4:14; this is probably the oldest written statement of the fundamental doctrine of the Christian faith, that the Lord Jesus died on behalf of men.

It would, however, be wrong to assume that because there is only one reference to this doctrine in the epistle, therefore it had little place in the apostle's preaching at this early date. On the contrary, when he wrote he was preaching at Corinth "Jesus Christ and Him crucified," 1 Corinthians 2:2. Moreover, the way the converts' knowledge of it is taken for granted throughout is convincing evidence that at Thessalonica, as at Corinth, the very words in which the missionaries preached the gospel were "that Christ died for our sins according to the Scriptures," 15:1–3.

By metonymy, "blood" is sometimes put for "death," inasmuch as, blood being essential to life, Leviticus 17:11, when the blood is shed life is given up, that is, death takes place. The fundamental principle on which God deals with sinners is expressed in the words "apart from shedding of blood," i.e., unless a death takes place, "there is no remission" of sins, Hebrews 9:22.

But whereas the essential of the type lay in the fact that blood was shed, the essential of the antitype lies in this, that the blood shed was the blood of Christ. Hence, in connection with the Jewish sacrifices, "the blood" is mentioned without reference to the victim from which it flowed, but in connection with the great antitypical sacrifice of the New Testament the words "the blood" never stand alone; the One Who shed the blood is invariably specified, for it is the Person that gives value to the work; the saving efficacy of the death depends entirely upon the fact that He Who died was the Son of God.

The following expressions are found in the New Testament (the pronouns refer to the Lord Jesus):

- "the new covenant in My blood," Luke 22:20:
- "a propitiation . . . by His blood," Romans 3:25:
- "justified by His blood," Romans 5:9:

- "redemption through His blood," Ephesians 1:7:
- "made nigh in [by] the blood of Christ," Ephesians 2:13:
- "peace through the blood of His Cross," Colossians 1:20:
- "[He] through His own blood entered into the Holy Place," Hebrews 9.12:
- "[we] enter into the Holy Place by the blood of Jesus," Hebrews 10:19:
- "the blood of the Eternal Covenant," Hebrews 13:20:
- "elect unto sprinkling of the blood of Jesus Christ," 1 Peter 1:1,2:
- "the blood of Jesus His [God's] Son cleanseth us," 1 John 1:7:
- "unto Him that . . . loosed us from our sins by His blood," Revelation 1:5;
- "thou didst purchase unto God with Thy blood—men," Revelation 5:9:
- "they made [their robes] white in the blood of the Lamb," Revelation 7:14.

Cp. also, "the Church of God which He purchased with His own blood," Acts 20:28.

Where the simple fact of the death of the Lord Jesus, or the responsibility of man for it, or the circumstances of violence and shame which attended it, are in view, the following words are used:

- *anaireō,* to take away, i.e., life; to murder, Acts 2:23:
- *apokteinō,* to kill, Acts 3:15:
- *diacheirizomai,* to lay (violent) hands on, Acts 5:30:
- *kremannumi,* to hang, suspend, 5:30:
- *prospēgnumi,* to fasten, i.e., to the cross, Acts 2:23:
- *sphazō,* to slay, Revelation 5:6:
- *stauroō,* to fasten to a stake, to crucify, Acts 2:36:
- *thuō,* to kill, 1 Corinthians 5:7.

Where the voluntary nature of the act is in view the following expressions are used, and in each case either the purpose of the death, Romans 14:9, or the fact that He died "for" others, is stated:

- He died, 2 Corinthians 5:15:
- He tasted death, Hebrews 2:9:
- He suffered, 1 Peter 2:21:
- He became a curse, Galatians 3:13:
- He offered Himself, Hebrews 9:14:
- He offered His body, Hebrews 10:10:
- He laid down His life, 1 John 3:16, cp. John 10:18:
- He gave His life a ransom, Matthew 20:28:
- He gave Himself, Galatians 1:4:
- He gave Himself a ransom, 1 Timothy 2:6:
- He gave Himself up, Galatians 2:20.

Four prepositions are used in the New Testament to describe the relation of the death of the Lord Jesus to men, and are usually translated "for"; they are:

- *dia* (with an accusative case), on account of, 1 Corinthians 8:11; cp. Romans 4:25; 1 John 2:12.||
- *peri*, concerning, Matthew 26:28 (and here, in some editions of the text, on the authority of certain ancient MSS., including the "Vatican"); this is the word used with "sacrifice," see Hebrews 5:3, cp. 1 John 2:2:
- *huper*, in the interest of, on behalf of, 2 Corinthians 5:14, and here:
- *anti*, the equivalent of instead of, Matthew 20:28, cp. 1 Timothy 2:6.

Of these words the second and third approach one another so nearly in meaning that they are often interchangeable, cp. e.g., the following: 2 Thessalonians 3:1, *peri*, with Romans 10:1, *huper*, and Matthew 26:28, *peri*, with Mark 14:24, Luke 22:20, *huper*.

Both words appear in 1 Peter 3:18, "for, *peri*, sins," "for, *huper*, the unrighteous"; the latter, as in Philemon 13, approaching the meaning of *anti*, in the place of; see note at v. 15. In some other passages *huper* may be understood in the vicarious, or substitutionary, sense, John 10:11, 15; Romans 8:32, e.g.; but it cannot always be so taken, cp. 2 Corinthians 5:15, *for* while it may properly be said that "Christ died in place *of us*," it may not be said that "Christ rose again in place of us."

Peri is used in the following passages:

- for many, Matthew 26:28:
- for us, here:
- for our sins, 1 John 2:2; 4:10:
- for sins, 1 Peter 3:18:
- for sin, Romans 8:3

Huper is used in the following passages:

- for the people, i.e., the Jewish nation, John 11:50, 51:
- for the ungodly, Romans 5:6:
- for the unrighteous, 1 Peter 3:18:
- for many, Mark 14:24:
- for every man, Hebrews 2:9:
- for all, 2 Corinthians 5:14, 15; 1 Timothy 2:6:
- for the life of the world, John 6:51:
- for the sheep, John 10:11:
- for us, Galatians 3:13, for us all, Romans 8:32:
- for it (the church), Ephesians 5:25:

- for you, 1 Corinthians 11:24, him, Romans 14:15, me, Galatians 2:20:
- for their sakes, 2 Corinthians 5:15:
- for our sins, 1 Corinthians 15:3, Galatians 1:4:
- for sins, Hebrews 10:12.

Where the death of the Lord Jesus is traced to the purpose of God, the following expressions are found:

- "Whom God set forth" ("purposed," marg., cp. Eph. 1:9), Romans 3:25:
- "He . . . spared not His own Son, but delivered Him up," Romans 8:32 (cp. Acts 2:23, Rom. 4:25):
- "He made [Him] *to be* sin on our behalf," 2 Corinthians 5:21.

In Matthew 26:31 the Lord Jesus Himself modified the words of Zechariah 13:7 in such a way as to ascribe His experience on the Cross to the direct act of God Himself, "I will smite the Shepherd"; cp. Isaiah 53:6, "Jehovah hath laid on Him the iniquity of us all," and v. 10, "it pleased Jehovah to bruise Him."

It is noteworthy that the omission of these words "Who died for us" would not impair the general sense of the passage; they are evidently introduced in order to make clear that salvation in its consummation as in its inception, Ephesians 2:5; 1 Peter 1:13, is by grace alone. The death of Christ is the sole ground on which any believer will be caught away to the Parousia of the Lord.

that,—*hina*, as in v. 4, but here denoting purpose, = in order that.

whether we wake—*grēgoreō*, translated "watch" in marg., as in v. 6, and each of the twenty-one other places in which it occurs in the New Testament

Or sleep,—*katheudō*, as in v. 6, where see note. It is obviously impossible to understand the words of natural wakefulness and natural sleep. And inasmuch as *grēgoreō is* not used elsewhere in the metaphorical sense of "to be alive," and as *katheudō* means "to be dead" in only one place out of two-and-twenty occurrences in the New Testament, and never elsewhere in Paul's Epistles (see notes on v. 6), there does not seem to be sufficient justification for departing from the usual meaning of the words, i.e., vigilance and expectancy as contrasted with laxity and indifference.

The subjects of the rapture are described in 4:17 without qualification or limitation further than this, that they belong to Christ, 1 Corinthians 15:23. The spiritual condition and attainment of believers vary widely, but every believer has spiritual life, see note on 1:7, however meager his spiritual attainment may be, however low his spiritual condition may fall. That the lax and indifferent will suffer loss is elsewhere plainly taught by Paul, see 1 Corinthians 3:15; 9:27; 2 Corinthians 5:10, e.g., but in this place he does not deal with that aspect of the subject. He does, however, put beyond question that the rapture of believers at the Parousia will not depend on their condition or attainment but solely on the death of the Lord Jesus for them. Reward is always according to works, Revelation 22:12, cp. Romans 2:6; 4:4, whereas salvation is always by grace and by grace alone, Titus 2:11, cp. Romans 11:6, and Deuteronomy 9:4, 5, "Speak not thou . . . saying, For my righteousness Jehovah hath brought me in to possess this land . . . Not for thy righteousness, or for the uprightness of thine heart, . . . but . . . that He may establish the word which Jehovah sware."

we should live—*zaō,* which is used in the New Testament of:

a, God, Matthew 16:16; John 6:57; Romans 14:11:

b, the Son in Incarnation, John 6:57:

c, the Son in Resurrection, John 14:19; Acts 1:3; Romans 6:10; 2 Corinthians 13:4; Hebrews 7:8:

d, spiritual life, John 6:57; Romans 1:17; 8:13*b;* Galatians 2:19, 20; Hebrews 12:9:

e, the present state of departed saints, Luke 20:38; 1 Peter 4:6:

f, the hope of resurrection, 1 Peter 1:3:

g, the resurrection of believers, here and John 5:25; Revelation 20:4, and of unbelievers, v. 5, cp. v. 13:

h, the way of access to God through the Lord Jesus Christ, Hebrews 10:20:

i, the manifestation of divine power in support of divine authority, 2 Corinthians 13:4*b,* cp. 12:10, and 1 Corinthians 5:5:

j, bread, figurative of the Lord Jesus, John 6:51:

k, a stone, figurative of the Lord Jesus, 1 Peter 2:4:

l, water, figurative of the Holy Spirit, John 4:10; 7:38:

m, a sacrifice, figurative of the believer, Romans 12:1:

n, stones, figurative of the believer, 1 Peter 2:5:

o, the oracles, *logion,* Acts 7:38, and word, logos Hebrews 4:12; 1 Peter 1:23, of God:

p, the physical life of men, 4:15, and Matthew 27:63; Acts 25:24; Romans 14:9; Philippians 1:21, 22; 1 Peter 4:5:

q, the maintenance of physical life, Matthew 4:4; 1 Corinthians 9:14:

r, the duration of physical life, Hebrews 2:15:

s, the enjoyment of physical life, 3:8, above:

t, the recovery of physical life from the power of disease, Mark 5:23; John 4:50:

u, the recovery of physical life from the power of death, Matthew 9:18; Acts 9:41; Revelation 20:5:

v, the course, conduct, and character of men,

    1. good, Acts 26:5; 2 Timothy 3:12; Titus 2:12:

    2. evil, Luke 15:13; Romans 6:2; 8:13*a;* 2 Corinthians 5:15*b;* Colossians 3:7:

    3. undefined, Romans 7:9; 14:7; Galatians 2:14:

w, restoration after alienation, Luke 15:32.

Another word, composed of *sun*, "with," and *zaō, i.e., suzaō*, "to live together with," may be included with *zaō* in the above analysis as follows:

g. ——Romans 6:8; 2 Timothy 2:11:

s. ——2 Corinthians 7:3.||

A third word is composed of *ana*, again, and *zaō, anazaō*, = "to live again," "to revive," Luke 15:24, cp. *w.* in list above, and Romans 7:9 = "to manifest activity again."

Here "to live" means to experience that change, 1 Corinthians 15:51, which is to be the portion of all in Christ who are left alive upon the earth at the Parousia of the Lord Jesus, cp. John 11:25, and which corresponds to the resurrection of the dead in Christ which will immediately precede it, 1 Corinthians 15:52–54.

together with Him—according to 4:17 the raised and changed saints are to be with the Lord; here the thought is carried further, alike by the use of "live," and by the addition of "together." In the new birth believers are made partakers of eternal life, John 3, cp. v. 7 with v. 9, and then with v. 14; and this life is not only imparted through Christ, 1 John 4:9, it is also maintained in Him, 1 John 5:11, and rests upon Him, John 6:57. But as yet this "eternal life," which is the essence of sonship, is not revealed, Romans 8:19, cp. 1 John 3:2, as it will be when Christ, Who is our life, shall be manifested in glory, Colossians 3:4. Thus not the impartation of new life, but its complete ascendancy and victory, is to be the experience of the believer at that day. Here and now the believer has eternal life, John 5:24, e.g., then he shall have immortality as well, 1 Corinthians 15:53, 54.

The parallel is noteworthy:

- He died for us,
- We shall live with Him.

5:11 Wherefore—introducing the conclusion of this section of the epistle, 5:1–11, an exhortation similar to that of 4:18 at the close of the previous section. That is concerned with loss calling for comfort, this with duties and dangers calling for vigilance and activity; hence the more comprehensive exhortation here.

exhort one another,—see note at 2:11.

and build——up,—*oikodomeō*, a word of frequent occurrence in the New Testament, both in a literal sense, Matthew 7:24; Luke 4:29, and in a figurative, Acts 20:32; Galatians 2:18. The corresponding noun, *oikodomē*, building, edification, is used in a similar way, literally, Matthew 24:1, figuratively, Romans 14:19.

The word expresses the strengthening effect of teaching, 1 Corinthians 14:3, and example, 10:23, upon oneself and upon others, 14:4, whether for good, 2 Corinthians 10:8, or for evil, 1 Corinthians 8:10, "emboldened." From the familiar spectacle of building operations it transfers to the spiritual realm the idea of assured progress as the result of patient labor.

The word is used of national life, Matthew 21:42, and of church life, Acts 9:31, as well as of the individual, Romans 15:2. It is used of the "Church which is His Body" in Matthew 16:18; Ephesians 4:12, cp. 1 Peter 2:5, and of the local church in 1 Corinthians 3:9; 14:5, 12; Ephesians 2:21.

Once it describes the resurrection body, 2 Corinthians 5:1.

God is said to be the builder, in 1 Corinthians 3:9; Christ in Matthew 16:18; Paul in Romans 15:20, cp. 1 Corinthians 3:10; 2 Corinthians 10:8; 13:10; the "gifts" of the ascended Lord are the builders in Ephesians 4:12, cp. 1 Corinthians 14:12; individual believers, here; and in Ephesians 4:16 the church is said to build itself up in love.

Building up is effected by:

- love, 1 Corinthians 8:1, cp. Ephesians 4:16:
- prophesying, 1 Corinthians 14:3, 4:
- exhortation, here, cp. Hebrews 10:25.

each other—lit., "one the one"; this phrase is more emphatic than the usual word *allēlōn*, 4:18, et al.; it is evident that in the primitive church the care of the saints was not delegated either to an individual official, or to the more gifted among the brethren, cp. Hebrews 3:13, and see Jeremiah 31:34; Malachi 3:16.

And further, the words imply that believers took advantage of occasions of private intercourse for conversation on such subjects as that with which these sections deal.

The spirit of the world, expressed in Cain's question, "am I my brother's keeper?" Genesis 4:9, is diametrically opposed to the spirit of Christ expressed in His words, John 13:34, 35, in His example, 1 Peter 2:21–23, and in the teaching of His apostles, 1 Corinthians 12:25; Philippians 2:4; 1 John 3:16, e.g. In this new spirit each believer sought the welfare of his fellow, not on stated occasions, but as opportunity offered, and not in any formal way but as from the heart, thus realizing the intimate relations that exist between those who are members of one body, Romans 12:5, and giving effectual expression to the unity of all in Christ.

even as also ye do.—see note at 4:1.

5:12 But—lest the preceding words should be misunderstood to imply that churches can be maintained without leaders, the apostle proceeds to urge their recognition; this forms an introduction to the general instructions upon church life which follow.

we beseech you, brethren,—addressing the church apart from its leaders, concerning whom the apostle was about to speak.

to know—*oida,* i.e., to recognize and acknowledge, to appreciate and value; a purely spiritual exercise possible only to spiritual persons. Nonspiritual persons cannot recognize, and would not acknowledge, spiritual workers or their work, 1 Corinthians 2:14. Moreover, the principle of Matthew 10:40, 41 applies here, he who recognizes and acknowledges a God-sent worker, receives his Master and shall share his reward.

In 1 Corinthians 16:15, and cp. 2:12, the same word is used. In 16:18, *epiginōskō* appears, because in v. 15 reference is made to an obvious fact, viz., that Stephanas and his house had given themselves to service among the saints; whereas in v. 18 the personal character of Stephanas and others is in view. These men would not lead the saints into evil courses nor into division as some were doing, hence they were men whose acquaintance was worth cultivating, men worth getting to know, on the reverse of the principle stated earlier in the same epistle, 15:33.

them that labor among you,—lit., "those who are laboring," as at 1:3. The word *kopiaō,* which is sufficiently wide to include the labors of godly women, Romans 16:6, 12, is applicable alike to:

a, physical toil, Matthew 6:28; 1 Corinthians 4:12:

b, the weariness resulting therefrom, John 4:6:

c, the burden of religious observances, Matthew 11:28:

d, labors in the gospel, Galatians 4:11:

e, labors among the saints, Colossians 1:29; 1 Timothy 5:17; Revelation 2:3.

Cp. Philippians 4:3, where a different word, *sunathleō* = "strive," as in 1:27, is used.||

and are over you—*proistēmi,* lit., "to stand before," and hence = "to lead," "to care for," "to attend to"; it is translated "rule," with reference to the family in 1 Timothy 3:4, 5, 12, and with reference to the church in Romans 12:8; 1 Timothy 5:17. It occurs again in Titus 3:8, 14, where it is translated "maintain."||

Those who "rule" are called "elders" in 1 Timothy 5:17, and "elders" are also called "bishops" in Titus 1:7, cp. v. 5, and Acts 20:17, with v. 28. Although we do not find these titles in any Epistle of Paul earlier than that to the Philippians, yet there were elders in Jerusalem quite a number of years before that was written, Acts 11:30, and on his first missionary journey Paul and Barnabas had appointed elders in every church, 14:23. The word "elder," *presbuteros,* had long been in use among the Jews, Exodus 17:5, LXX, and *episkopos*, "bishop," among the Gentiles; hence the latter term only came into use with the multiplication and growth of the churches of the Gentiles, it is first found in connection with that at Ephesus, Acts 20:28.

Another word, *hēgoumenos*, is used for the same persons in Hebrews 13:7, 17, 24, = the guides. Still another term is "shepherds," *poimēn*, Ephesians 4:11, and cp. 1 Peter 5:2.

in the Lord,—these words serve a double purpose, *(a)* they limit the scope of the authority of the elders to the spiritual concerns of the saints, and show that there was no intention to deny or to limit the authority over Christians of civic or political rulers in the things that lie within their proper spheres. And, *(b)* they show that the authority of the elders is not based upon human appointment or election, but upon the relation of all to the Lord.

and admonish you;—*noutheteō*, lit., "to put into the mind," "training by word"; hence it is used, *(a)* of instruction, *(b)* of warning. It is thus distinguished from *paideuō* = to correct by discipline, "training by act," Hebrews 12:6, cp. Ephesians 6:4.

The difference between "admonish" and "teach" seems to be that whereas the former has mainly in view the things that are wrong and call for warning, the latter has to do chiefly with the impartation of positive truth, cp. Colossians 3:16 (they were to let the word of Christ dwell richly in them so that they might be able, [1] to teach and admonish one another, and, [2] to abound in the praises of God; see Nestle's punctuation of the Gk. Text), and 2 Thessalonians 3:15.

Admonition differs from remonstrance in that the former is warning based on instruction; the latter may be little more than expostulation. For example, though Eli remonstrated with his sons, 1 Samuel 2:24, he failed to admonish them, 3:13, LXX. Pastors and teachers in the churches are thus themselves admonished, i.e., instructed and warned, by the Scriptures, 1 Corinthians 10:11, so to minister the Word of God to the saints that, naming the Name of the Lord, they shall depart from unrighteousness, 2 Timothy 2:19.

That the three expressions "labor," "are over," "admonish" refer to the same persons is shown by the presence of the definite article before the first term only, thus, lit., "the [ones] laboring . . . and being over . . . and admonishing."

5:13 and to esteem them—*hēgeomai* = to think, to consider, cp. 2 Thessalonians 3:15; Philippians 2:3, 6.

exceeding highly—see note on "exceedingly," 3:10.

in love—the meaning is more evident if the words are read: "esteem them in love exceeding highly," i.e., love is to govern the attitude of the saints toward their leaders. However much it may be needed, admonition will provoke resentment and rebellion where the heart is not submissive to the word of the Lord. Believers, therefore, are to put themselves in thought in the place of the elders, and to think and act in the spirit of Matthew 7:12.

for their work's sake.—thus not personal affinity, neither the holding of office, but actual service rendered to the Lord in labors among His people, is the ground on which believers are to hold their leaders in loving regard. Cp. 1 Corinthians 16:10, 11; Philippians 2:29, 30; Hebrews 13:17.

Be at peace—_eirēneuō,_ as in Mark 9:50, where it is addressed by the Lord to the disciples in gentle rebuke of their ambitions for leadership, see vv. 33–37; in 2 Corinthians 13:11, where it is rendered "live in peace," a general exhortation to believers under all circumstances, cp. Colossians 3:15; and in Romans 12:18, where the command is somewhat modified by the addition of the words "if it be possible, as much as in you lieth," a limitation made necessary, perhaps, by the presence of the inclusive words "all men," but not intended to excuse any evasion of the plain obligation imposed by the command itself, cp. Hebrews 12:14 and Psalm 34:14.||

among yourselves.—the connection between this and the preceding exhortations is readily discernible. As at Corinth, 1 Corinthians 1:11, 12, so everywhere, there is a natural tendency "to be puffed up for one leader against another," 4:6, a course which inevitably issues in jealousy and strife, 3:3, 4. While, then, they were to acknowledge and to love their leaders in the Lord, they were to be on their guard against rivalries and party making, things that do not make for peace, Romans 14:19, but do most surely destroy it; cp. Philippians 2:3.

5:14 And [lit., but] **we exhort you, brethren,**—here the apostle addresses himself more directly to those of whom he had just spoken, the laborers among, and leaders of, the flock. And yet not exclusively to them, for even the earlier of the exhortations that follow are in measure applicable to all, and before the end of the verse is reached he is evidently addressing all. There is no hard and fast line drawn between the elders and the people. The artificial and unscriptural distinction between "clergy" end "laity" belongs to a period later than the apostolic age.

admonish—as in v. 12.

the disorderly,—_ataktos,_ occurs here only in the New Testament, the corresponding verb in 2 Thessalonians 3:7 only, the adverb in 3:6, 11 only. It is a military term, cp. note on 5:8, = not to keep rank, to be insubordinate, ct.

eutaktos = ordered (bands), Proverbs 30:27, LXX. An insubordinate spirit manifests itself in different ways, of which two, idleness and officiousness, are specified, 2 Thessalonians 3:11, and a third, excitability, is suggested by the word "quietness" in v. 12. This disorderliness was, probably, the failure of the more energetic among the converts. But refusal to submit to rule is evidence of weakness, not of strength. Moreover, it involves disobedience to the direct command of God, that believers are to "be in subjection. . . . to every one that helpeth in the work and laboreth," 1 Corinthians 16:16.

Discipline is necessary to order, *taxis*, with which *ataktos* is connected, lit., "rank keeping," and order in the church is the evidence of the submission of all to the Holy Spirit, 1 Corinthians 14:40, cp. 2 Timothy 1:7. Without rulers no church is properly constituted, cp. Acts 20:17; Philippians 1:1, et al., without godly rule no church can prosper, and without godly submission to rule no church can maintain effectual fellowship or be efficient in service. Hence the elders are urged not to shirk the responsibility of admonishing those who fail in this respect, lest godly order, Colossians 2:5, should be vainly sacrificed in the interests of false peace.

On the other hand, admonition can only be effective when it expresses the judgment, and commands the consciences, of the saints generally. Authority is not sufficient, self-will may usurp authority, and admonition so given could only work mischief. Admonition in the power of the Holy Spirit, and with the fellowship of the church, will minister to the profit of all concerned.

encourage—as in 2:11; after the pattern of the Chief Shepherd, cp. e.g., Isaiah 42:3; Matthew 14:27; Mark 5:36; Luke 5:8–10; John 16:33. See also Isaiah 35:3, 4.

the fainthearted,—*oligopsuchos,* lit., "smallsouled," i.e., the despondent; in LXX it is used, in a good sense, in Isaiah 57:15, "Who giveth endurance to the fainthearted" (for "to revive the spirit of the humble"), and, in a bad sense, in Proverbs 18:14, "who can endure a fainthearted man?"||

The "fainthearted" lack the energy and boldness in which the "disorderly" superabound. They require constraint as the others require restraint. Sensitiveness to criticism, 2:3–6, dread of persecution, 3:3, a sense of failure to follow the Lord, 1:6, apprehensiveness concerning the future, 4:13, are among the causes that produce faintness of heart.

support—*antechomai* = "to hold on by," "keep close to." From some, whose character and ways are described, those responsible for the care of the saints must turn away, 2 Timothy 3:1–5; but from the weak the strong may never turn away, rather must they bear with and care for them in the spirit and after the example of Christ, cp. Mark 6:34; Hebrews 2:17, 18; see also Romans 15:1; Jude 22, 23.

the weak,—*asthenēs,* lit., "strengthless"; some believers are weak through lack of knowledge of the will of God, some through lack of courage to trust God; some, who are timorous or overscrupulous, hesitate to use their liberty in Christ, some, through lack of stability or purpose, are easily carried away; some lack courage to face, or will to endure; persecution or criticism; some are unable to control the appetites of the body or the impulses of the mind. These, and all such as these, are to be the peculiar objects of the shepherd's care, since, more than the rest, they need the sympathy and help of those who are of maturer Christian experience. For characteristic examples of such care see Genesis 33:13, 14; Luke 10:34, 35; John 13:1–17.

be longsuffering—*makrothumeō,* lit., "be long-tempered"; compare "short-tempered." The corresponding noun, "longsuffering," is frequently found with *hupomone* "patience," as at 2 Corinthians 6:4, 6; 2 Timothy 3:10, e.g. Longsuffering is that quality of self-restraint in the fact of provocation which does not hastily retaliate nor promptly punish; it is the opposite of anger and is associated with mercy, and is used of God, Exodus 34:6, LXX; Romans 2:4; 1 Peter 3:20. Patience is the quality that does not surrender to circumstances or succumb under trial; it is the opposite of despondency and is associated with hope, 1:3; it is not used of God.

But while the words are to be thus broadly distinguished, "longsuffering" may also express the idea of "patience," cp. Hebrews 6:12, 15; James 5:7, 10, e.g., where *makrothumia* is so translated; here it is used in its widest sense. See further at 2 Thessalonians 1:4.

Resistance, active or passive, to admonition, exhortation or instruction, imposes a strain upon those who seek the welfare of the saints, hence the need for this further word. Longsuffering characterizes all labor that has love for its motive, 1 Corinthians 13:4.

toward—*pros,* see note on "with," 3:4.

all.—i.e., all the believers, whatever their character. It is always a temptation to show less forbearance with the weak than with the masterful, hence this inclusive word.

5:15 See that none—the apostle now includes all the believers in his address. The word "see" suggests the need for attention lest any should be unexpectedly overtaken by this temptation, or unconsciously drawn into it, cp. Hebrews 12:15. What is enjoined, however, is not watchfulness over others but watchfulness each over himself, cp. 1 Timothy 4:16. See also Exodus 23:4; Proverbs 25:21, 22.

render—*apodidōmi*, lit., "to give back" = to pay, to recompense.

unto anyone—in the widest sense, whether believer or unbeliever.

evil for evil;—*kakos*, that which causes injury, or works mischief of any kind; the recurrence of these words in Romans 12:17; 1 Peter 3:9, suggests that this may have been a saying of the Lord current in apostolic days though not recorded in the Gospels; see Acts 20:35 for another instance. It does not go so far as the words recorded in Matthew 5:38, 39, cp. 1 Peter 2:23. See further at v. 22, below.

At this point the teaching of Christ comes into direct conflict with one of the strongest impulses of fallen human nature, for no vice is more certainly regarded as a virtue among men than is retaliation; nevertheless, "he that studieth revenge keepeth his own wounds green" (Bacon), and exhibits the spirit of the world, not the mind of Christ. It is, however, the obvious duty of every man to recompense in kind all the good he receives from his fellows, Luke 6:32, 33. It is his privilege to return good for evil, Romans 12:21; 1 Peter 3:9, but retaliation in any form is explicitly forbidden to him, Deuteronomy 32:35. Cp. Lamech, Genesis 4:23, 24. The preposition, *anti*, translated "for," is the preposition of equivalence, denoting a price paid, or a balance made, as on the scales, cp. its use in Matthew 5:38; Mark 10:45; John 1:16. See note at v. 10, above.

but alway—a rule to which there is not any exception, and for defection from which no excuse can be valid.

follow after—*diōkō* = "to pursue earnestly," whether with a good purpose, as Philippians 3:12, 14 ("press on") and here, or an evil, as Philippians 3:6. Thus the word has in it not merely the idea of the direction in which the believer is to move, but also of the earnestness with which he should pursue the object set before him.

that which is good,—*agathos*, lit., "the good," i.e., whatever, being useful and helpful, would benefit those to whom it is done; see further at v. 21.

The apostle elsewhere particularizes, in connection with the same word "follow":

- hospitality, Romans 12:13:
- things that make for peace, Romans 14:19, cp. Hebrews 12:14; 1 Peter 3:11:
- things that make for edification, Romans 14:19:
- love, 1 Corinthians 14:1:

- righteousness, godliness, faith, patience, meekness, 1 Timothy 6:11; 2 Timothy 2:22.

one toward another,—i.e., among yourselves.

and toward all—i.e., toward "them that are without," 4:12. Thus God's ideal for His children is that contact with them should leave every man the better, and no man the worse, in soul, body, or circumstances, cp. Galatians 6:10.

5:16 Rejoice—*chairō*, translated "joy" in 3:9 (where see note), "All hail," in Matthew 28:9, "greeting," in Acts 15:23, and "farewell," in 2 Corinthians 13:11, the underlying thought in each case being joy.

alway;—*pantote*, as in 2:16, where see note; *aei*, there referred to, occurs with "rejoice" in 2 Corinthians 6:10. Cp. also Psalm 34:1, and Philippians 4:4. Christian joy is the fruit of the Holy Spirit, 1:6; Galatians 5:22, cp. Acts 13:52; Colossians 1:11, and, particularly, Luke 10:21. It is, consequently, independent of circumstances; indeed the believer is even exhorted to count it an occasion for much rejoicing when he falls into a complication of trials, James 1:2, since he knows that adversity is the school in which the mind of God is learned, Psalm 119:71, and that God works all things together for good with those who love Him, Romans 8:28, marg.

The grounds of Christian joy are found in:

- the Lord, Philippians 3:1; 4:4:
- His incarnation, Luke 2:10:
- His power, Luke 13:17, cp. Acts 8:8:
- His Resurrection, Matthew 28:8; Luke 24:52:
- His presence with the Father, John 14:28, cp. 1 John 2:1:
- His presence with believers, John 16:22; 20:20:
- His ultimate triumph, John 8:56:
- the believer's salvation, 2 Corinthians 8:2, cp. Romans 15:13; Philippians 1:25:
- his enrollment in Heaven, Luke 10:20, cp. Philippians 4:3:
- his liberty in Christ, Acts 15:31, cp. Galatians 5:1:
- his hope of the Glory of God, Romans 5:2, cp. Revelation 19:7:
- his prospect of reward, Matthew 5:12; Luke 6:23.

Occasions of Christian joy are various, such as:

- hearing the gospel, Acts 13:48:
- receiving the Lord, Luke 19:6; Acts 8:39:
- suffering with Him, Acts 5:41, cp. Hebrews 10:34; 1 Peter 4:13:
- the preaching of the gospel, Philippians 1:18:

- suffering therein, Philippians 2:17; Colossians 1:24:
- the conversion of sinners, Luke 15:7; Acts 15:3:
- the gospel harvest, John 4:36:
- the manifestation of grace, Acts 11:23:
- the godly walk of believers, Romans 16:19; 2 Corinthians 7:4; 3 John 3:4:
- their godly submission to admonition, 2 Corinthians 7:9:
- their godly order in assembly, Colossians 2:5:
- meeting with believers, Romans 15:32; 1 Corinthians 16:17; Philippians 2:28, 29; 2 Timothy 1:4; 2 John 12:
- receiving tokens of love and fellowship, Philippians 4:10:
- the rejoicing of others, Romans 12:15; 2 Corinthians 7:13:
- learning of the well-being of others, 2 Corinthians 7:16:
- learning of the kindness of believers one to the other, Philemon 7:
- honor done to others, 1 Corinthians 12:26:
- the triumph of truth, 1 Corinthians 13:6.

5:17 pray—*proseuchomai*, see note at 3:10. Prayer is a comprehensive term covering every form of reverent address to God, whether individual, 2 Kings 4:33; Nehemiah 2:4; Matthew 6:6, or united, Matthew 18:19; Acts 1:14; 16:25. Its main elements are thanksgiving, in which the supply of past need is acknowledged, and supplication, in which present need is declared, Ephesians 1:16, 17; Philippians 1:3, 4. With thanksgiving are associated the praises of God, the declaration of His excellence, alike in what He is, Psalms 8:1:9; 22:3; 104:1; Isaiah 6:3; Revelation 4:8, and in what He has done, 1 Kings 8:23, 24; Psalms 104:2–30; Acts 4:24; Revelation 4:11; 5:9–13, and of His self-sufficiency, Romans 11:33–36, and wisdom, 16:25–27, and power, Jude 24. With supplication, which is concerned with one's own need, is associated intercession, which is concerned with the needs of others, for all men are equally dependent upon God, Matthew 5:45; Acts 14:17; 17:24–29; 1 Timothy 4:10, even though they refuse Him acknowledgment, Romans 1:21. Therefore it becomes those who have learned to pray for themselves to make intercession for others, for the saints, Ephesians 6:18; Colossians 1:3, and for men generally, 1 Timothy 2:1, in behalf of their needs temporal and spiritual.

Prayer, dealing with God, and ministry of the word, dealing with men, are the two chief divisions of spiritual work, Acts 6:4.

In the days of His flesh the Lord Jesus prayed to His Father, Mark 1:25; Luke 6:12, for others, Luke 22:32; John 14:16; ch. 17, and for Himself, Luke 22:41–44; Hebrews 5:7; in the presence of God He still prays, Romans 8:34; Hebrews 7:25; cp. Psalm 2:8.

Prayer is properly addressed to God the Father, Matthew 6:6; John 16:23; Ephesians 1:3, 17; 3:14, and the Son, Acts 7:59; 2 Corinthians 12:8; but in no instance in the New Testament is prayer addressed to the Holy Spirit distinctively, for whereas the Father is in heaven, Matthew 6:9, and the Son is at His right hand, Romans 8:34, the Holy Spirit is in and with the believers, John 14:16, 17.

Prayer is to be offered in the Name of the Lord Jesus, John 14:13, that is, the prayer must accord with His character, and must be presented in the same spirit of dependence and submission that marked Him, Matthew 11:26; Luke 22:42.

The Holy Spirit, being the sole interpreter of the needs of the human heart, makes His intercession therein; and inasmuch as prayer is impossible to man apart from His help, Romans 8:26, believers are exhorted to pray "at all seasons in the Spirit," Ephesians 6:18, cp. Jude 20, and James 5:16, the last clause of which should probably be read "the inwrought [i.e., by the Holy Spirit] supplication of a righteous man availeth much" (or "greatly prevails," _ischuō_, as in Acts 19:16, 20).

Nonetheless on this account is the understanding to be engaged in prayer, 1 Corinthians 14:15, and the will, Colossians 4:12; Acts 12:5 (where "earnestly" is, lit., "stretched out") and so in Luke 22:44.

Faith is essential to prayer, Matthew 21:22; Mark 11:24; James 1:5–8, for faith is the recognition of, and the committal of ourselves and our matters to, the faithfulness of God.

The accompaniments of prayer are sometimes fasting, Acts 13:3; 14:23, and sometimes singing, 16:25; and as the acknowledgment of God's bounty toward the believer reminds him of the needs of others, Mark 14:7, cp. 2 Corinthians 9:7, prayer is also associated with almsgiving, Matthew 6:2, 5; Acts 10:2, 4, 31.

The believer is also to watch against the dangers from which he prays to be delivered, Matthew 26:41; 1 Peter 4:7; and, generally, he is to watch for the due answers to his prayers, Colossians 4:2.

Prayer is not limited to place, but the believer is not in a right place if he cannot continue to pray there. The Lord who commended His disciples to an inner chamber with a closed door for prayer, Matthew 6:6, Himself had none, 8:20, and knew that the bulk of His followers would not have such a convenience available; it is probable, then, that He had in view the inner chamber of the heart, into which the believer may retire and pray to God deliberately as Nehemiah did, 2:4, on the instant of need and without interrupting his duties even for a moment. Daniel prayed in his chamber, 6:10, and by the riverside, 10:4; Paul and Silas in their prison cell, Acts 16:25; the Lord Himself on the hillside, Mark 6:46.

Where the Jews were numerous, as at Thessalonica, they had usually a synagogue, Acts 17:1; where they were few, as at Philippi, they had merely a _proseuchē_, or "place of prayer," of much smaller dimensions, and commonly built by a river for the sake of the water necessary to the preliminary ablutions prescribed by rabbinic tradition, Acts 16:13, 16. There is no indication in the New Testament that any building was erected by, or secured for the use of, any of the apostolic churches.

No particular attitude of body is prescribed as essential during prayer, but it is recorded that David sat, 1 Chronicles 17:16, Solomon stood, 2 Chronicles 6:12, cp. Mark 11:25, Daniel kneeled, 6:10, cp. Acts 9:40; 20:36; 21:5, and that David and the elders of Israel, at a time of much distress, prostrated themselves, 1 Chronicles 21:16, cp. Matthew 26:39, and see also Revelation 7:11.

without ceasing;—*adialeiptōs*, as at 1:2, where see note. Since the dependence of the creature upon the Creator is complete and constant, the believer is to have recourse to prayer at all seasons and upon all matters. But prayer is the exercise of the renewed man, Acts 9:11, and, like every other spiritual activity, calls for diligence and watchfulness, lest its power be forgotten, or its occasions let slip; for the maintenance of the spiritual life depends upon intercourse with God.

This exhortation to incessant prayer is necessary on account of the many hindrances to prayer inherent in the nature and in the environment of the believer, such as:

- lethargy of soul, Isaiah 43:22; 64:7:
- self-confidence, Hosea 7:7–10; James 4:2:
- family discord, 1 Peter 3:7:

these prevent prayer.

- Formality, and desire for a religious reputation, Isaiah 29:13; Matthew 6:5:
- inattention, or disobedience, to the law, i.e., the word of the Lord, Proverbs 28:9:
- sin, the desire, Psalm 66:18:
- sin, the act, Isaiah 59:2, cp. Psalm 65:2, 3; John 9:31; James 5:16:
- covetousness, Job 27:8, 9:
- unjust dealing, and oppression of the needy, Isaiah 1:10–17:
- selfishness, James 4:3:
- a wavering, or doubting, mind, James 1:5–8, cp. Matthew 21:21, 22:

these prevent answers to prayer.

The people of God "continue steadfastly," Romans 12:12, they "do not cease," Colossians 1:9, to pray; they are found praying:

- in the morning, Psalm 5:3; 88:13; Acts 2:1, 15:
- at noon, Psalm 55:17; Daniel 6:10; Acts 10:9:
- in the evening, Psalm 55:17; Acts 3:1; 10:30:

- at midnight, Psalm 119:62; Acts 16:25:
- in the night, Psalm 42:8:
- before dawn, Psalm 119:147:
- day and night, Psalm 88:1; Luke 18:7:
- "night and day," 1 Timothy 5:5:
- "at all seasons," lit., "in every season," Ephesians 6:18:
- "always," here, and Luke 18:1; Colossians 4:12.

See also at 3:10, and v. 25, below.

5:18 in everything—i.e., under all circumstances, even in persecution, 3:3, and bereavement, 4:13. Cp. Cornelius, "who . . . prayed to God alway," lit., "through every circumstance," Acts 10:2.

give thanks—*eucharisteō,* as in 1:2; 2:13; 2 Thessalonians 1:3; 2:13. Failure in thanksgiving for bounties enjoyed is evidence of the alienation of man from God, Romans 1:21, cp. Luke 6:35; thanksgiving under circumstances of adversity and sorrow was characteristic of the Lord Jesus. When the people of certain cities rejected Him, Matthew 11:20–24, He "answered and said, I thank [*examologeomai*] Thee, O Father . . . yea, Father, for so it was well-pleasing in Thy sight," vv. 25:26; and when He was about to break the loaf, the symbol of His imminent death, He "gave thanks," *eucharisteō,* Luke 22:19, cp. v. 42. Thus His thanksgiving arose not out of congenial circumstances, but out of His knowledge that in His adversities also the will of His Father was being accomplished, cp. v. 42, and John 4:34.

This exhortation recurs with added emphasis in Ephesians 5:20, where the "name" of the Lord Jesus suggests His character and so His example, while the title given to God, Father, suggests His compassion, Psalm 103:13, and His care, Matthew 6:8; thus faith is encouraged to "abound in thanksgiving," Colossians 2:7; 3:15, 17, and he who can say "Amen" to the will of God in his heart will be able to say "Hallelujah" also. Thanksgiving is the expression of joy Godward, and, like joy, is the fruit of the Holy Spirit in the heart of the believer, cp. Luke 10:21, with Galatians 5:22, and Ephesians 5:18–20.

for this—the commands immediately preceding these words are so closely associated in form and idea, that it seems best to understand what follows to refer to all three and not merely to the last of them.

is the will of God—*thelēma* (as in 4:3, where see note, cp. also 2:18 and note) = "the gracious design," rather than "the determined resolve," of God. To do the will of God, then, is to yield ourselves to the accomplishment of His designs for us by obeying Him in all that He has revealed to faith, cp. Romans 1:17; Hebrews 11:3. But since neither the desire, nor the power, to do the will of God, dwells naturally in the believer, God works in Him "both to will and to work of His good pleasure," Philippians 2:13, cp. Hebrews 13:21 and 1 Corinthians 12:6. This, however, does not relieve the believer of his responsibility, for he is to "understand what the will of the Lord is," Ephesians 5:17, and understanding it, he is to do it from the heart, 6:6.

Concerning those that do the will of God it is said that:

- they shall get to know (*ginōskō,* see note on 1:4) the verity of the teaching, John 7:17:
- they shall be brought into intimate relationship with the Lord Jesus, Matthew 12:50:
- they shall enter into the kingdom of heaven, Matthew 7:21, cp. 2 Peter 1:10, 11:
- they shall abide forever, 1 John 2:17.

in Christ Jesus—i.e., "expressed in Christ Jesus," as the order of the name and title implies, see note at 1:1. His circumstances made Him "a man of sorrows," Isaiah 53:3; His submission to God made His heart glad even in the face of death, Psalm 16:7–11. He not only taught His disciples to rejoice, Matthew 5:12; Luke 10:20, and to pray, 11:1–13, and to give thanks, John 6:11–23, He was Himself the perfect example to them in these things, cp. Acts 1:1. His conduct, John 6:38; Hebrews 10:9, and His message, John 17:8, 14, together, were the revelation of the will of God to the world.

And in these things also the apostle could say that he was an imitator of Christ, 1 Corinthians 11:1, for see, as to rejoicing, 2 Corinthians 6:10; 7:4, and as to prayer, Philippians 1:9, and as to thanksgiving, 2 Corinthians 2:14, *et al.*

to you-ward.—*eis,* lit., "into you," the preposition expresses not merely the fact that God desires these things in His children, but also that what is thus taught may be made effectual in them by His power, cp. Philippians 2:12, 13, and 2 Corinthians 1:19, 22.

5:19 Quench not—*sbennumi,* in its other New Testament occurrences, refers to fire, literal, Matthew 12:20; 25:8; Hebrews 11:34, or metaphorical, Mark 9:48; Ephesians 6:16. Thus the figure latent in the verb here is that of Matthew 3:11; Acts 2:3, and as fire is always extinguished from without itself the meaning seems to be "do not prevent or obstruct the manifestations of the Holy Spirit's power in others."

Here the tense is present continuous, hence the meaning is "desist from quenching" rather than "do not begin to quench."

In Ephesians 4:30, the words "grieve not the Spirit" refer to His presence in the believer, and to quench the Spirit in another would surely be to grieve

Him in oneself. Where the unregenerate are in view the word is "resist not," Acts 7:51, implying the action of the Holy Spirit upon the man from without.

With this injunction may be compared that in 4:8, which is aimed against any refusal to obey Him as this is against any refusal to listen to Him.

the Spirit;—i.e., the Holy Spirit, see note at 1:5; here the article is present.

The general precepts of vv. 19–22 were intended to remind the believers of their responsibilities when they came together, cp. 1 Corinthians 11:17, 18. From 1 Corinthians 7:17 and 14:31–34 it may be assumed that in the apostolic age all "churches of the saints" followed the general lines indicated in Acts 20:7; Romans 12:3–8; 1 Corinthians 11:17—14:40; Ephesians 4:7–16; 1 Peter 4:10, 11.

It was characteristic of these churches:

- that they came together weekly to break bread, Acts 20:7;
- and for mutual edification, Hebrews 10:25;
- which was secured through a variety of ministry, v. 11, 1 Corinthians 12:4–10;
- appointed by God, 1 Corinthians 12:18, 28–30; Ephesians 4:8;
- and made effectual by the Holy Spirit, 1 Corinthians 12:11;
- that there were in them men who were qualified for, and called to, the ministry of the Word, Ephesians 4:11–14;
- and that such alone were to take part therein, 1 Corinthians 14:29;
- that those who ministered did not because of the energizing of the Holy Spirit lose the responsibility of self-control, 1 Corinthians 14:32;
- on the contrary, they were to use the gift, or to refrain, as the occasion required, 1 Corinthians 14:26–30;
- they were to use it diligently and wisely, Romans 12:6–8;
- with a due sense of the dignity of the ministry and of the insufficiency of the minister, 1 Peter 4:10, 11;
- and they were to submit to the judgment of others on their ministry, 1 Corinthians 14:29.

The peace, order, and edification of the saints were evidence of the ministry of the Spirit among them, 1 Corinthians 14:26, 32, 33, 40, but if; through ignorance of His ways, or through failure to recognize, or refusal to submit to, them, or through impatience with the ignorance or self-will of others, the Spirit were quenched, these happy results would be absent. For there was always the danger that the impulses of the flesh might usurp the place of the energy of the Spirit in the assembly, and the endeavor to restrain this evil by natural means would have the effect of hindering His ministry also. Apparently then, this injunction was intended to warn believers against the substitution of a mechanical order for the restraints of the Spirit.

5:20 despise not—*exoutheneō*, = to set down as of no account, as in Luke 18:9, *et al.*

prophesyings;—*prophēteia*, as in Romans 12:6; 1 Corinthians 12:10, *et al.*

Though much of the Old Testament prophecy was purely predictive, see Micah 5:2, e.g., and cp. John 11:51, prophecy is not necessarily, nor even primarily, = foretelling. It is the declaration of that which cannot be known by natural means, Matthew 26:68, it is the forthtelling of the will of God, whether with reference to the past, the present, or the future, see Genesis 20:7; Deuteronomy 18:18; Revelation 10:11; 11:3. The relation between Aaron and Moses illustrates the relation between the prophet and God, Exodus 4:16; 7:1.

In such passages as 1 Corinthians 12:28; Ephesians 2:20, the "prophets" are placed after the "apostles," since not the prophets of Israel are intended, but the "gifts" of the ascended Lord, Ephesians 4:8, 11, and cp. Acts 13:1; Romans 16:26. Of these nothing is said in the Epistles concerning prediction of future events, but cp. Acts 11:27, 28; 21:10, 11; the purpose of their ministry was to edify, to comfort, and to encourage the believers, 1 Corinthians 14:3, while its effect upon unbelievers was to show that the secrets of a man's heart are known to God, to convict of sin, and to constrain to worship, vv. 24, 25.

With the completion of the canon of Scripture prophecy apparently passed away, 1 Corinthians 13:8, 9. In his measure the teacher has taken the place of the prophet, cp. the significant change in 2 Peter 2:1. The difference is that, whereas the message of the prophet was a direct revelation of the mind of God for the occasion, the message of the teacher is gathered from the completed revelation contained in the Scriptures.

Instructions given to the prophet of apostolic days serve as a general guide to the teacher now. Building up the saints is to be his sole aim, 1 Corinthians 14:5, 12, 26; Ephesians 4:12; to this end his words must be distinctly spoken, and his language must be suited to his hearers, 1 Corinthians 14:7, 9, 11, 16; he must avoid confusion of every kind, since confusion is of the flesh, not of the Spirit, vv. 32, 33. Teachers are to defer one to another, v. 30, nor is any teacher to be judge of the profit, or otherwise, of his own utterances, v. 29. Acceptance of these divine regulations is evidence of spirituality, vv. 37, 38.

In the early churches there was evidently a tendency among the less stable believers to depreciate prophesyings and to exalt "tongues," which had a greater show of the miraculous, see 1 Corinthians 14:1–19. On the other hand, the more sober-minded may have been suspicious of professed revelations; the Lord Himself had warned His disciples of the danger, Matthew 7:15; 24:11, and Paul's own experience at Paphos, Acts 13:6, was probably known at Thessalonica. "Deceivers," 2 John 7, cp. 2 Corinthians 6:8, and "false prophets," 1 John 4:1, cp. Revelation 2:20, early began to trouble the churches, and, apparently, the apostle himself had reason shortly afterwards to suspect that this evil influence was at work there also, 2 Thessalonians 2:2.

5:21 prove—*dokimazō,* as in 2:4, where, and at 3:5, see notes.

all things;—the adjective, which is plural, alone appears in orig., = all spiritual gifts, 1 Corinthians 12:1, including prophecy. The marg. inserts "but" on good authority, and is probably correct.

From the scope of this injunction not even the utterances of an apostle were exempt, Acts 17:11; 2 Timothy 2:7, cp. Isaiah 8:20, for the duty and the right, the responsibility and the privilege, of the individual believer to judge for himself 1 Corinthians 10:15; Galatians 1:8, 9, and to act upon his judgment, Romans 14:4, 5, are an essential feature of Christianity.

While "discerning" or "proving" is itself a "spiritual gift," 1 Corinthians 12:10, all spiritual persons are responsible to form judgments on spiritual things, see note at v. 11, and for this provision is made in the "anointing from the Holy One" which is given to the children in the family of God, 1 John 2:18, 20, 27, cp. 2 Timothy 2:7. Spiritual perception, however, like spiritual power, depends on the walk of the believer, the slothful and evildoers are blind, only the godly have discernment in the truth, Proverbs 28:5; Daniel 9:13; 2 Peter 1:9. Moreover, the desire to be impressed, to have the feelings wrought upon, rather than to be instructed in the ways of the Lord, is a common snare to the saints, 2 Timothy 3:6, 7; 4:3, 4.

The completed Scriptures, i.e., the Old Testament and New Testament, became later the sole and sufficient standard by which all teaching, oral or written, could be tested, but long before that time, believers and churches had multiplied widely. During the intervening period, in the case of revelations for the testing of which the Old Testament was not available, such as that referred to in Colossians 1:26, e.g., believers were encouraged by the promised guidance of the Holy Spirit, John 16:13, to compare utterances claiming to be spiritual, 1 Corinthians 2:13, and so to test the prophecy and the spirit that prompted it, 1 Corinthians 14:29; 1 John 4:6; Revelation 2:2.

In early days a saying, "be ye tried money changers" = "accustom yourselves to distinguish between the true and false," cp. Philippians 1:10, marg., was commonly connected with these words; cp. 1 Kings 3:9; Jeremiah 15:19; Hebrews 5:14. By some ancient writers it was credited to the apostle Paul, by others to the Lord Himself but it does not occur in the New Testament.

hold fast that which is good;—lit., "the good," i.e., that "prophesying," or "tongue," which being tested commends itself to the spiritual mind as having its origin in God, or that teaching which accords with His revealed will.

"Good" here is *kalos* = that which is intrinsically good, as *agathos* (see v. 15, and note there) = that which is good or beneficial in its effect. The words occur together at Luke 8:15, an "honest," *kalos,* heart, one that takes its true place before God, cp. Psalm 32:2, 5, "without guile," since sin is acknowledged; a "good," *agathos,* heart, one that works no ill to a neighbor, cp. Psalm 15. They occur together again at Romans 7:18, "in me—dwelleth no good thing," *agathos,* nothing capable of accomplishing good, consequently the power "to do that which is good," *kalos* = wholly admirable, is absent.

While the difference between the words may be thus generally stated, they are not always readily distinguishable, cp. Romans 2:7, *agathos,* with Galatians 6:9, *kalos,* e.g. Here, however, they are appropriately used, for in v. 15 the good that is to be done to others is intended, but in v. 22 the quality of the teaching in itself was in the writer's mind.

The hearer of the Word of God is to "hold it fast," Luke 8:11, 15; the believer is to "hold fast":

- the gospel, 1 Corinthians 15:2:
- the traditions, i.e., the oral teachings of the apostles before they were committed to writing, 1 Corinthians 11:2:
- the boldness and glorying of the hope, Hebrews 3:6:
- the beginning of the confidence, i.e., of the substance, of the gospel, Hebrews 3:14:
- the confession of the hope, Hebrews 10:23.

These are all summed up here in the single term to *kalos,* "the good."

5:22 abstain from—but if, on being tested, the tongue, prophesying or teaching, was not approved, the saints were to turn away therefrom, cp. 2 Timothy 3:5. This word, *apechomai,* occurs in Job 1:1; 2:3, LXX, which may have been in the mind of the apostle, and in the New Testament again in 4:3, above, Acts 15:20, 29; 1 Timothy 4:3; 1 Peter 2:11. In each of these passages it refers to evil practices, moral and ceremonial, which suggests, with the change in the form of the expressions noted below, that this injunction is more comprehensive than that which precedes it, and is not to be understood of evil teaching only, but of evil practices as well.||

every form—*eidos,* lit., "that which can be seen," see note on "idol," 1:9.

Eidos is used of the Holy Spirit in His descent upon the Lord Jesus, Luke 3:22; and of the appearance of the Lord Jesus Himself, 9:29, Who declared that the Father's "appearance," *eidos* had never been seen by human eyes, John 5:37. It is translated "sight," in 2 Corinthians 5:7, the Christian is guided in his behavior not by what he can behold naturally, but by what he knows to be true though unseen.

of evil.—*ponēros,* cp. v. 15, where the Greek word is *kakos.* These have much in common, the former occurs of thoughts in Matthew 15:19, the latter in Mark 7:21; and so of speech in Matthew 5:11, and 1 Peter 3:10; of actions in 2 Timothy 4:18, and v. 15 above; of men in Matthew 18:32 and 24:48. They are not always interchangeable, however, for *kakos* (which is put first where the two occur together as in 1 Cor. 5:8; Rev. 16:2) = "base," bad in character, while *ponēros* = "malignant," bad in influence and effect. Thus *kakos* is the word of wider, *ponēros* the word of stronger, meaning. *Ponēros* alone is used of Satan, Matthew 5:37, *et al.,* and of demons, Luke 7:21, et al.

The expression "form of evil" may be understood in three ways:

a, of that which seems evil but is not really so; it would thus = "let not your good be evil spoken of," Romans 14:16, cp. 2 Corinthians 8:21. But the evil-disposed will see evil in anything, Titus 1:15, as in the case of the Lord Jesus, e.g., see Luke 7:34, et al.; therefore this meaning may be dismissed:

b, of that which seems evil because it is evil, the meaning intended by marg. "appearance"; the saints were to shun evil in whatever form it showed itself. This interpretation gives an adequate sense to the words:

c, of every sort or kind of evil, a meaning common in contemporary Greek writings (the papyri, e.g., see notes on 1:3 and 4:18), and intended in the text, cp. 2 Timothy 2:19. This gives the best sense.

A contrast is apparently intended between the simplicity of that which is of God, "the good," and the complexity of that which is of the world, the flesh, and the Devil, "every form of evil." Sound teaching, Titus 1:13; 2:1, and holy living, 2 Peter 3:11, are intimately associated, as the apostle's words "holding faith and a good conscience," 1 Timothy 1:19, cp. 3:9, suggest. To give heed to that which cannot be approved when tested by the Scriptures, the sole repository of apostolic teaching, Acts 2:42; 2 Timothy 3:15, 16, is to submit to influences that must ultimately lower the tone of spiritual life and affect for evil the conduct of the believer.

5:23 And—*de,* lit., "but," as in v. 14; 3:11; 4:9, *et al.;* however earnestly and wisely he might instruct and exhort them, however patiently and diligently they might endeavor to keep the word of the Lord, Revelation 3:10, the saints must become a prey to the Evil One apart from the keeping power of God, John 17:15, cp. Jude 1. God, moreover, must Himself be their inward energizer if they were to purpose and to act according to His desire for them, Philippians 2:13. This thought leads to a prayer for their welfare, a prayer brief but intense and comprehensive.

the God of peace—a title recurring Romans 15:33; 2 Corinthians 13:11; 2 Thessalonians 3:16; and Isaiah 9:6; it was probably suggested to the apostle's mind in contrast with the disorders against which he had just warned them.

Other titles of God similarly constructed are:

- the God of glory, Acts 7:2:
- the God of patience, Romans 15:5:
- the God of hope, Romans 15:13:
- the God of all comfort, 2 Corinthians 1:3, cp. Romans 15:4:
- the God of love, 2 Corinthians 13:11:
- the God of all grace, 1 Peter 5:10.

That is to say, God is the source of all these blessings.

himself—this pronoun occupies the place of emphasis in the sentence, as in 3:11; 4:16, where see notes; the contrast suggested by "but" is thus emphasized.

sanctify you—*hagiazō*, see notes at 3:13; 4:3; aorist or "point" tense; what is meant, however, is not an act begun and accomplished in a moment, but a "process seen in perspective," and so contemplated as a complete act. This is the case also with the word "keep," *tēreo*, in 1 Timothy 6:14, where a momentary act is out of the question. These passages are complementary one to the other, here the divine side is presented, there the human, the action in each terminating only with the coming of the Lord, cp. Philippians 1:6.

Since those addressed were already saints, i.e., "sanctified ones" (see note on "saints," 3:13, and 2 Thess. 2:13), the apostle must be understood here to desire for them the continuous and complete realization of this calling, that by His power they might be enabled to live consistently with the fact that every part of their complex being belonged to God, cp. Ephesians 5:25–27.

wholly;—*holotelēs*, lit., "whole-complete," such colloquial expressions as "through and through," "all round," suitably represent it. Thus not an increasing degree of sanctification is intended, but, as the succeeding words explain, that the sanctification of each believer might extend to the whole man in every part.

and—*kai*, introducing an explanation of the preceding words and so = "that is to say."

may your spirit—*pneuma* = the wind, and hence that which is invisible and powerful; this compound idea characterizes the word in its New Testament usage, which may be analyzed approximately as under:

a, the wind, John 3:8 (where marg. is, perhaps, to be preferred), Hebrews 1:7, cp. Amos 4:13, LXX:

b, the breath, 2 Thessalonians 2:8; Revelation 11:11; 13:15, cp. Job 12:10, LXX:

c, the immaterial, invisible part of man, Luke 8:55; Acts 7:59; 1 Corinthians 5:5; James 2:26, cp. Ecclesiastes 12:7, LXX:

d, the disembodied (or "unclothed," or "naked," 2 Cor. 5:3, 4) man, Luke 24:37, 39; Hebrews 12:23; 1 Peter 4:6:

e, the resurrection body, 1 Corinthians 15:45; 1 Timothy 3:16; 1 Peter 3:18.

f, the sentient element in man, that by which he perceives, reflects, feels, desires, Matthew 5:3; 26:41; Mark 2:8; Luke 1:47, 80; John 19:30; Acts 17:16; 20:22; 1 Corinthians 2:11; 5:3, 4; 14:14, 15; 2 Corinthians 7:1, cp. Genesis 26:35; Isaiah 26:9; Ezekiel 13:3; Daniel 7:15:

g, purpose, aim, 2 Corinthians 12:18; Philippians 1:27; Ephesians 4:23; Revelation 19:10, cp. Ezra 1:5; Psalm 78:8; Daniel 5:12:

h, the equivalent of the personal pronoun, used for emphasis and effect:— 1st person, 1 Corinthians 16:18, cp. Genesis 6:3; 2nd person, 2 Timothy 4:22; Philemon 25, cp. Psalm 139:7; 3rd person, 2 Corinthians 7:13, cp. Isaiah 40:13:

i, character, Luke 1:17; Romans 1:4, cp. Numbers 14:24:

j, moral qualities and activities:—bad, as of bondage, i.e., servility, as of a slave, Romans 8:15, cp. Isaiah 61:3; stupor, Romans 11:8, cp. Isaiah 29:10; timidity, 2 Timothy 1:7, cp. Joshua 5:1; good, as of adoption, i.e., liberty as of a son, Romans 8:15, cp. Psalm 51:12; meekness, 1 Corinthians 4:21, as Proverbs 16:18; faith, 2 Corinthians 4:13; quietness, 1 Peter 3:4, ct. Proverbs 14:29:

k, the Holy Spirit, Matthew 4:1; Luke 4:18, see John 4:24, and note at 1:5, cp. Genesis 1:2; Isaiah 61:1:

l, the "inward man" (an expression used only of the believer, Rom. 7:22; 2 Cor. 4:16; Eph. 3:16), the new life, Romans 8:4-6; 10:16; Hebrews 12:9, cp. Psalm 51:10:

m, unclean spirits, demons, Matthew 8:16; Luke 4:33; 1 Peter 3:19 (?), cp. 1 Samuel 18:10:

n, angels, Hebrews 1:14, cp. Acts 12:15:

o, divine gift for service, 1 Corinthians 12:10; 14:12, 32:

p, and, by metonymy, those who claim to be depositories of these gifts, 2 Thessalonians 2:2; 1 John 4:1-3:

q. the significance, as contrasted with the form, of words, or of a rite, John 6:63; Romans 2:29; 7:6; 2 Corinthians 3:6:

r, a vision, Revelation 1:10; 4:2; 17:3; 21:10.

"Spirit" seems to be an essential element of man by nature, and not merely of man regenerate, 1 Corinthians 2:11.

and soul,—*psuchē* = the breath, then that which breathes, the individual, animated creature; its New Testament uses may be analyzed approximately as follows:

1. the natural life of the body, Matthew 2:20; Luke 12:22; Acts 20:10; Revelation 8:9; 12:11, cp. Leviticus 17:11; 2 Samuel 14:14; Esther 8:11:

2. the immaterial invisible part of man, Matthew 10:28; Acts 2:27; cp. 1 Kings 17:21:

3. the disembodied (or "unclothed" or "naked," 2 Cor. 5:3, 4) man, Revelation 6:9:

4. the seat of personality, Luke 9:24, explained as = "own self" v. 25, Hebrews 6:19; 10:39, cp. Isaiah 53:10 with 1 Timothy 2:6:

5. the seat of the sentient element in man, that by which he perceives, reflects, feels, desires, Matthew 11:29; Luke 1:46; 2:35; Acts 14:2, 22, cp. Psalms 84:2; 139:14; Isaiah 26:9:

6. the seat of will and purpose, Matthew 22:37; Acts 4:32; Ephesians 6:6; Philippians 1:27; Hebrews 12:3, cp. Numbers 21:4; Deuteronomy 11:13:

7. the seat of appetite, Revelation 18:14, cp. Psalm 107:9; Proverbs 6:30; Isaiah 5:14 ("desire"); 29:8:

8. persons, individuals, Acts 2:41, 43; Romans 2:9; James 5:20; 1 Peter 3:20; 2 Peter 2:14, cp. Genesis 12:5; 14:21 ("persons"); Leviticus 4:2 ("any one"); Ezekiel 27:13, of dead bodies, Numbers 6:6, lit., "dead soul," and of animals, Leviticus 24:18, lit., "soul for soul":

9. the equivalent of the personal pronoun, used for emphasis and effect:— 1st person, John 10:24 ("us"); Hebrews 10:38, cp. Genesis 12:13; Numbers 23:10; Judges 16:30; Psalm 120:2 ("me"); 2nd person, 2 Corinthians 12:15; Hebrews 13:17; James 1:21; 1 Peter 1:9; 2:25, cp. Leviticus 17:11; 26:15; 1 Samuel 1:26; 3rd person, 1 Peter 4:19; 2 Peter 2:8, cp. Exodus 30:12; Job 32:2; Hebrews "soul," LXX "self":

10. an animate creature, human or other, 1 Corinthians 15:45; Revelation 16:3, cp. Genesis 1:24; 2:7, 19:

11. "the inward man," the seat of the new life, Luke 21:19 (cp. Matt. 10:39); 1 Peter 2:11; 3 John 2.

With 10 compare:

- *a-psuchos,* soulless, inanimate, 1 Corinthians 14:7.||

With 6 compare:

- *di-psuchos,* two-souled, James 1:8; 4:8:
- *oligo-psuchos,* feeble-souled, v. 14:||
- *iso psuchos;* like-souled, Philippians 2:20:||
- *sum-psuchos,* joint-souled ("with one accord"); Philippians 2:2.

The language of Hebrews 4:12 suggests the extreme difficulty of distinguishing between the soul and the spirit, alike in their nature and in their activities. Generally speaking the spirit is the higher, the soul the lower element. The spirit may be recognized as the life principle bestowed on man by God, the soul as the resulting life constituted in the individual, the body being the material organism animated by soul and spirit, by which alone these can receive impressions from, or communicate impressions to, the material world.

On the other hand, body and soul are the constituents of the man according to Matthew 6:25; 10:28; Luke 12:20; Acts 20:10, body and spirit according to Luke 8:55; 1 Corinthians 5:3; 7:34; James 2:26. In Matthew 26:38 the emotions are associated with the soul, in John 13:21 with the spirit; cp. also Psalm 42:11 with 1 Kings 21:5. In Psalm 35:9 the soul rejoices in God, in Luke 1:47 the spirit. Cp. also the passages referred to under "spirit," *c, d, f, g, h, l,* with those under "soul," *2, 3, 5, 6, 9, 11,* respectively.

Apparently, then, the relationships may be thus summed up, "*Sōma,* body, and *pneuma,* spirit, may be separated, *pneuma* and *psuchē,* soul, can only be distinguished" (Cremer).

Of the corresponding adjectives, *pneumatikos* = spiritual, describes the man in Christ and what pertains to him now, 1 Corinthians 2:15, and in resurrection, 15:44; see also Galatians 6:1.

Psuchikos = psychical, natural, describes the man in Adam and what pertains to him, 1 Corinthians 2:14; 15:44, 46, cp. James 3:15; Jude 19.||

and body—*sōma,* an organism, the instrument of life, as:

- of man, living, Matthew 6:22; Philippians 3:21; Revelation 18:13, "slaves":
- of man, dead, Matthew 27:52:
- of man, in resurrection, 1 Corinthians 15:44:
- of beasts, Hebrews 13:11:
- of grain, 1 Corinthians 15:37, 38:
- of the heavenly hosts, 1 Corinthians 15:40.

The word has also figurative uses, in all of which its essential idea is preserved, see Romans 6:6; 7:24; 1 Corinthians 12:12; Ephesians 1:23, e.g.

In Scripture the human body is called a "sheath" for the spirit, Daniel 7:15, marg.; an "earthen vessel," 2 Corinthians 4:7 (and see note at 4:4, above); an "earthly house," "clothing" (by implication), a "tabernacle," 2 Corinthians 5:14; 2 Peter 1:13; the "outward man," 2 Corinthians 4:16.

By a figure of speech called "synecdoche," in which a part is put for the whole, or the whole for a part, "body" sometimes stands for the complete man, Matthew 5:29; 6:22; Romans 12:1; James 3:6; Revelation 18:13, and sometimes the man is identified with his body, Genesis 3:19, 23; 35:19; 50:2, 26; Acts 9:37; 13:36, and this even in the case of the Lord Jesus, John 19:40–42. But the body is not the man, for, as the metaphors quoted above indicate, the man can exist apart from his body, see also 2 Corinthians 12:2–4; Revelation

6:9; 20:4. The body, however, is an essential part of the man, therefore the redeemed are not perfected until the resurrection, Hebrews 11:40, cp. Luke 13:32, and no man in his final state will be without his body, John 5:28, 29, cp. Daniel 12:2; Revelation 20:13.

The separation of the soul, Acts 5:5, 10; 12:23, *ek-psucho*, ‖ or spirit, Mark 15:37, 39; Luke 23:46, *ek-pneō*, from the body is called death. The body is said to be "mortal," i.e., liable to death, 1 Corinthians 15:53, a term which, with its negative, "immortal," is never in Scripture applied to the soul or the spirit.

On the other hand the body of the believer belongs to God, Ephesians 1:14, with Romans 8:23, and is a temple of the Holy Spirit, 1 Corinthians 6:19, a member of the body of Christ, v. 15, and is under His Lordship, v. 13, and is to be presented to God as a living sacrifice, Romans 12:1, that is to say, its members are to be presented to God as instruments by which His righteous will may be done, Romans 6:13, and that thus He may be glorified in it, 1 Corinthians 6:20, and to this end, since by nature sin works in its members, Romans 7:17, 20, it is to be kept in severe subjection, 1 Corinthians 9:27, cp. James 1:26; 3:2. See further at 4:17.

be preserved—*tēreō*, occurs frequently in the New Testament and is usually translated "keep," as "commandments," 1 Timothy 6:14, the "words" of the Lord Jesus, John 14:24, the "sabbath day," 9:16, etc. The Lord Jesus "kept" His own while He was in the world, John 17:12, and prayed His Father to "keep" them, after He had left it, from the Evil One, vv. 11:15. Jude describes the saints as "kept for Jesus Christ," v. 1, and exhorts them to "keep" themselves, v. 21, cp. 1 Timothy 5:22; cp. 1 John 5:18; Revelation 3:10, where the Lord Jesus Himself is the keeper.

Like "sanctify," "be preserved" is in the "point" tense, and for the same reason, viz., the continuous preservation of the believer is contemplated as a single complete act, without reference to the time occupied in its accomplishment.

The verb is in the singular number, for the man, spirit, soul and body, is the unit, not any one of these apart from the rest.

The spirit needs to be preserved from everything that would defile it, 2 Corinthians 7:1, or hinder the reception of the testimony of the Holy Spirit to the saint's relationship with God, Romans 8:16, or prevent the worship which He seeks, John 4:23; Philippians 3:3.

The soul needs to be preserved from the defilement of evil thoughts, Matthew 15:18, 19; Ephesians 2:3; Titus 1:15, and from the fleshly appetites that war against it, 1 Peter 2:11, and from contention and strife, Hebrews 12:15.

The body needs to be preserved from defilement, 4:3–8; 1 Corinthians 6:12–20, and from evil uses, Romans 6:19, "that the life also of Jesus may be manifested in our body," 2 Corinthians 4:10.

The threefold temptation of Genesis 3:6 was addressed to the three elements in man. The fruit met the need of the body, it was "good for food"; it promised a wider sphere to the spirit, "to make one wise," i.e., to elevate the eater to the divine plane, see v. 5.

entire,—*holokleros,* lit., "whole-lot"; it occurs again in James 1:4, and in LXX it is used of the full week, Leviticus 23:5, and of the unhewn stones of the alter, Joshua 8:31, and of the growing vine tree, Ezekiel 15:5, and of the "sound" of the flock, Zechariah 11:16.||

Holokleros thus = to be complete and sound in every part. Its synonym, with which it is joined in James 1:4, *teleios* = "mature," as in 1 Corinthians 14:20; Philippians 3:15, *et al.* Hence "entire" signifies that every grace should be manifest in the believer that is present in Christ, John 1:16 ("for," *anti* = corresponding to, see note at v. 15); "perfect" signifies that every grace should be developed and matured.

The corresponding noun occurs, Acts 3:16, "perfect soundness," cp. Isaiah 1:6, LXX.||

A close connection exists between this word and the title "God of peace," inasmuch as the Hebrew word for "peace," *shalom,* has for its root meaning wholeness, cp. Joshua 8:31, "unhewn"; see above, Ruth 2:12, "full," Nehemiah 6:15, "finished," Isaiah 26:3, "perfect peace," marg., "peace, peace," Isaiah 42:19, "at peace," marg., "made perfect."

Further, in LXX, Genesis 26:31; 41:16, et. al., *shalom* is rendered by *soteria* (= salvation, see note at v. 9), and what in Hebrew and English is called "peace offering," in Greek is called "salvation offering."

This close association of the ideas of salvation, soundness, and peace, appears also in the words of the Lord to certain whom He had healed, "thy faith hath made thee whole [or, "saved thee," *sozo,* see note at v. 9], go in [lit., "into"] peace," Luke 7:50; 8:48. Cp. also the apostle's aim to "present every man perfect in Christ," Colossians 1:28, and Peter's exhortation "that ye may be found of Him in peace," 2 Peter 3:14.

without blame—*amemptos,* as in 2:10, where, and at 3:13, see notes. There seems to be an ellipsis here which may be thus supplied, "so that ye may be found to be free of blame at the Parousia," where the saints, 2 Corinthians 5:10, and their works, 1 Corinthians 3:13, and the counsels of their hearts, 1 Corinthians 4:5 shall be made manifest before the Judgment Seat of Christ. Thus they were to be unblameable not merely in conduct before men, but in heart before the Lord Himself, cp. Genesis 17:1; Job 1:8, where the corresponding adjective appears in LXX.

at—*en*, lit., "in"; not "until" which would require *achri*, as in 1 Corinthians 11:26; Philippians 1:6; or *eis*, as in Philippians 1:10; or *heōs*, as in 1 Corinthians 1:8; or *mechri*, as in 1 Timothy 6:14.

the coming—*parousia*, see note at 2:19.

of our Lord Jesus Christ.—see note at 1:1.

5:24 Faithful—as in 2 Thessalonians 3:3. God neither lies in making His promises nor repents of them when made, Numbers 23:19, cp. Deuteronomy 7:9; Romans 11:29, but fulfills all His word in His own time, 1 Timothy 6:15, marg.; hence His faithfulness was a favorite theme with the Psalmists, see Psalms 36:5; 119:90, e.g., and He is called the "God of Amen," Isaiah 65:16, marg. Because of His faithfulness the saints are encouraged to confess their sins, 1 John 1:9, and their hope of the coming of the Lord, Hebrews 10:23; to endure trial, 1 Corinthians 10:13, and, generally, to depend upon His promises, Hebrews 11:11.

is He that calleth you,—"the Caller," as in 2:12, where see note; the present participle attracts attention to the person who calls rather than to the calling, cp. the same construction and emphasis in Galatians 5:8.

who will——do it.—there is no object expressed in orig., cp. Psalm 22:31; Isaiah 44:23, where also "it" is supplied by the translators, cp. Ezekiel 36:36. The verb *poieō* has as wide a range in Greek as "do" has in English, cp. Romans 4:21, a parallel passage in which it is translated "perform."

also—*kai*, the order in orig. is "Who also will do," but whereas in Greek *kai* makes the word that follows it emphatic, in English "also" throws the emphasis on the word that precedes it, therefore the order of the words must be changed in translating, that the sense may be rightly expressed. God not only calls the saints to that complete salvation just described, He Himself will accomplish in them His own call.

God is the God of peace, i.e., of wholeness, completeness; with less than perfection in His work He cannot rest satisfied, nor indeed can His saints. But notwithstanding their graces and attainments (for they were elect and beloved, 1:4, to them the gospel had come in power, 1:5, they had suffered joyfully for the Name of the Lord Jesus, 1:6; 2:14, they were sons of light and of day, 5:5, God-taught, 4:9, and able to admonish each other, 5:14) these saints at Thessalonica were not wholly sanctified. Moreover the apostle's words make it plain that God alone could complete this sanctification, and that He would go on perfecting it until the day of Jesus Christ, Philippians 1:6, and that meantime it was proper for the saints to pray one for another that this complete sanctification might be accomplished in them.

5:25 Brethren, pray for us—see notes at vv. 17:3, 10. Paul and his coworkers, their spiritual vigor, gifts, and experience notwithstanding, shared the common need of the sanctifying and preserving power of God, and hence were not independent of the prayers of the saints. Probably "also" should be added, see marg.; cp. 3:6 for another instance of the use of "also" to express reciprocity.

At the beginning of his letters the apostle usually assures his readers of his prayers for them, and at the close requests theirs on his own behalf. Sometimes this request is general, as that he may be helped in his ministry of the word of the Lord, 2 Thessalonians 3:1, of the mystery of Christ, Colossians 4:3, of the mystery of the gospel, Ephesians 6:19; or that he may be delivered from his adversaries, Romans 15:30, 31 (with this added here that his service may find acceptance with the saints at Jerusalem), and 2 Thessalonians 3:2, or from prison, Philippians 1:19 (where a request is implied though not formally made), and Philemon 22 (for he could not visit Colossae until he had been set free at Rome).

The absence of these characteristic references to prayer from 1 and 2 Corinthians and Galatians may be due to the necessity for dealing sternly with the defections of the saints in those places. In 2 Corinthians 1:11, however, their prayers for him are fully acknowledged.

Of the other New Testament writers only John speaks of praying for those to whom he writes, 3 John 2, and only the writer of Hebrews, 13:18, requests the prayers of his readers; though James, 5:13–18, Peter, 1 Peter 3:7; 4:7, and Jude, v. 20 have each something to say about prayer.

Thus far the epistle was written to dictation by an unnamed amanuensis, what follows was added with the apostle's own hand; see Romans 16:22; Colossians 4:16; 2 Thessalonians 3:17.

5:26 Salute—apparently there is an ellipsis of "for me," "in my behalf"; the request is addressed to the elders, the persons who would actually receive the epistle, but see vv. 14, 15, and notes.

all the brethren—elsewhere the apostle wrote "salute one another," Romans 16:16; 1 Corinthians 16:20; 2 Corinthians 13:12.

with—*en*, as at 4:16.

a holy—*hagios*, free from anything inconsistent with their calling as saints, *hagioi*, see note at 3:13, and cp. Ephesians 5:3. In 1 Peter 5:14 the expression is "a kiss of love," *agapē*, as at 3:12, where see note. The words "holy" and "love" invest the salutation with character and meaning and save it from mere idle formality and hypocrisy.

kiss.—*philēma,* the corresponding verb, *phileō,* see note at 3:12, occurs in this sense, Mark 14:44, Luke 22:47; *kataphileō,* a strengthened form = kissed much, also occurs, Matthew 26:49, et al.

The kiss was a common form of salutation between persons of the same sex. The separation of the sexes is part of the historical situation in the light of which Scripture must be interpreted, see, e.g., John 4:27. In Paul's day women were veiled in the assemblies, 1 Corinthians 11:6, and if to be unveiled was a "shame," how much more to do that which "nature itself teacheth," v. 14, to be shameful. The "Apostolic Constitutions," an early Christian writing, compiled about the 4th century A.D., indicates that the men and women sat on different sides of the room (a custom obtaining widely until the present time in Europe, as well as in Asia), and directs the men to salute the men, the women the women, with "the kiss in the Lord."

Christians soon came to be spoken of as evildoers by their enemies, and on this account, lest any should find occasion to speak evil of their good, they were to take pains that their behavior should be seemly and honorable, not only in the sight of the Lord, but also in the sight of all men, 1 Peter 3:16; Romans 14:16; 2 Corinthians 8:21. It is in the light of such considerations as these that the words of the apostle are to be understood.

The essential point was that all should be saluted as was customary among equals, there should be no discrimination against the poor, no partiality for the well-to-do, since all were "brethren beloved of God," 1:4, partakers of a "common salvation," Jude 3, and since all were equally beloved by the person who thus saluted them, cp. 2:11.

5:27 I—as at 2:18; 3:5; the singular pronoun is appropriate to the autograph.

adjure——by the Lord—*enorkizō,* here only in the New Testament; = "I bind you by an oath" (Lightfoot), cp. *horkizō,* Mark 5:7; Acts 19:13, and *exorkizō,* Matthew 26:63, = "I appeal to you by an oath" (ibid). For other passages in which the apostle invokes the Name of God see 2:5, 10; Romans 1:9; 2 Corinthians 1:23; 11:31; 12:19; Galatians 1:20; Philippians 1:8; of the Holy Spirit, Romans 9:1; of Christ, Romans 9:1; 2 Corinthians 11:10. Here the Lord = the Lord Jesus, see note at 3:12.

you—i.e., the elders, v. 12, into whose hands, presumably, the letter would be delivered.

that this [lit., "the"] **epistle**—see Intro. Note.

be read—*anaginōskō,* lit., "to recognize again," and hence = to read, Luke 6:3, and to understand what is read, Luke 10:26, then, to read publicly and aloud, Luke 4:16; Acts 8:28; 1 Timothy 4:13; Revelation 1:3, cp. Nehemiah

8:8, LXX. The epistle would thus be vested with an authority analogous to that of the Old Testament, read in the synagogues of the Jews, see Deuteronomy 31:11; Acts 15:21; 2 Corinthians 3:14, 15. For a similar instruction see Colossians 4:16, cp. Ephesians 3:4. Since at that time there were no facilities for multiplying copies of a writing, and since education was not widely diffused, the public reading of the letter was the only available means of making its contents generally known.

to all the brethren.—to all, that is to say, without distinction, limitation, or exception. There is no secret code in Christianity, no esoteric mystery for the initiated few. All God's spiritual gifts are intended for all God's children. The apostle had a message from God to deliver, 4:15, to all the saints, and each individual believer was, personally and directly, responsible to God for his own hearing and understanding of that message, and for his own obedience to it, cp. Mark 4:23, 24; Romans 14:12.

Further knowledge of the circumstances at Thessalonica as Timothy had reported them to Paul, 3:6-8, would no doubt supply the reason for the use of such vigorous language on this occasion. There were distracting influences at work among the saints, 2 Thessalonians 2:3; an incipient distrust of the elders may be inferred from vv. 12, 13, and, on their part, perhaps some impatience with the disorderly, from v. 14. Some lightly accepted untested teachings, some set prophecy altogether at nought, vv. 19-22; some may have been so overwhelmed with sorrow as to forsake the assembling of the saints, 4:13-18. To help such the epistle had been written, but only such as heard it read could profit by it. Unaccustomed to receive instruction in this form the elders, not recognizing the importance of the communication, might fail to read it to the saints generally, or, out of pique with some, they might read it only to a coterie, cp. 3 John 9; thus garbled reports of its contents might be circulated, and the authority of the apostle claimed for teaching and practices he had not sanctioned. Or, since it was written by another hand, the origin of the letter might be questioned. With these, and perhaps other possibilities before his mind, Paul might well urge strenuously upon the elders that pains be taken to secure that each of the saints hear for himself the very words of the letter. And if Timothy had reported that some were already misusing his name, and pretending to have his authority for their statements, as was certainly the case shortly afterwards, 2 Thessalonians 2:2, the public reading of what he had written would be the best cure for the mischief, and the best preventive of its recurrence.

5:28 The grace of the Lord Jesus Christ be with you.—as "grace" is part of the greeting in each of this apostle's letters, see on 1:1, so "grace" occurs also in the final benediction in each. Cp. also Hebrews 13:25. That the Lord Jesus should be presented as the source of grace (*charis* = free unmerited favor), either alone, as here, cp. Acts 15:11, or in association with God, 2 Thessalonians 1:12, is significant testimony to His deity.

2 Thessalonians

2 THESSALONIANS

CHAPTER ONE

Verses 1–12

1:1 Paul, and Silvanus, and Timothy, unto the church of the Thessalonians in God our Father and the Lord Jesus Christ;

1:2 Grace to you and peace from God the Father and the Lord Jesus Christ—see notes at 1 Thessalonians 1:1, 2.

1:3 We are bound—*opheilō* = to owe, as money, Luke 7:41; to be under obligation to do certain things, as all men are, whether:

- natural, said of all men; not to identify God with any material object, Acts 17:29, to dress becomingly, 1 Corinthians 11:7, 10, to love spouses, Ephesians 5:28, cp. Titus 2:4; or political, Romans 13:7:
- or legal, said of the Jews; to keep the law, Galatians 5:3, or to suffer the penalty for breaking it, John 19:7:
- or religious, said of the priests of Israel; to offer sacrifices for sins, Hebrews 5:3:
- or spiritual, said of all in Christ; not to yield to the impulses of the flesh, Romans 8:12, but to follow Christ, 1 John 2:6, to serve Him without reserve, Luke 17:10, to grow in the knowledge of truth, Hebrews 5:12, to love all saints, 1 John 4:11, to serve them, John 13:14, and even to die for them, 1 John 3:16, to bear with the weak among them, Romans 15:1, to minister in things carnal in return for spiritual benefits received, Romans 15:27, to preach the gospel to all, Romans 1:14, and to forward worthily such as preach it, 3 John 8.

When, in grace, the Son of God undertook the salvation of men, in order that He might accomplish His purpose it was of obligation that He should submit Himself to the limitations and to the sufferings of human life, Hebrews 2:17.

to give thanks to God alway for you, brethren,—the apostle had been so tried at Corinth and on the way thither, and at the same time so filled with apprehension for the converts at Thessalonica, that it seemed to him as though his very life depended on their steadfastness; see at 1 Thessalonians 3:1-8. Receiving confirmation of the former favorable report of their welfare, he acknowledges his own sense of indebtedness to God for what he looked upon as a mercy to himself.

even as it is meet,—*axios* = right on the ground of fitness, becoming; as that labor should be rewarded, Luke 10:7; 1 Timothy 5:17, 18, and sin punished, Luke 23:15; Revelation 16:6. The corresponding adverb occurs at 1 Thessalonians 2:12, where see note.

Apart from the special circumstances under which the apostle felt bound to thank God for them, it was fitting thus to do, for the preservation and development of the infant church at Thessalonica was not to be credited to the missionaries, nor to the converts themselves, nor to those who labored among them, but to the grace and power of God; to God, then, they gave thanks.

for that—*hoti,* introducing the reason for the thanksgiving, as at 1 Thessalonians 1:2–5.

Hoti, which here points to a cause, as at 1 Thessalonians 4:16, sometimes points to an object and is = "that," as in 1 Thessalonians 4:15; 5:2, e.g.

your faith—see notes at 1 Thessalonians 3:2.

groweth exceedingly,—*huperauxano̅,* here only in the New Testament; it is merely a strengthened form of *auxano̅,* which describes the growth of that which lives, as seed, Luke 13:19, flowers, Matthew 6:28, the human body, Luke 2:40, population, Acts 7:17. Figuratively it is used of:

a, Christ in contrast with John the Baptist, John 3:30:

b, the word, or gospel, of God in its results among men, Acts 6:7; Colossians 1:6:

c, the saints individually, Ephesians 4:15; Colossians 1:10; 1 Peter 2:2; 2 Peter 3:18:

d, the churches, Ephesians 2:21:

e, the church, Colossians 2:19:

f, faith, 2 Corinthians 10:15, and here.

Since this growth is the effect of life it is said to be given by God, after the analogy of His operations in nature, 1 Corinthians 3:6; 2 Corinthians 9:10.

In contrast with *f,* above, cp. Luke 17:5, where "increase" represents *prosti-the̅mi* = to add to (from without), as in Acts 13:36, "laid unto."

Since faith is an exercise of the soul, invisible in itself but made visible in its effects, see Mark 2:3–5; James 2:18, ct. Hebrews 3:18, 19, steadfastness in affliction, and unselfish service rendered to others, are evidences of a growing, that is of a living, faith.

and the love—see notes at 1 Thessalonians 3:12.

of each one—thus particularizing the individual.

of you all—thus comprehending the whole; even the "disorderly," 1 Thessalonians 5:14, were neither forgotten nor excluded. Defection in one element does not necessarily indicate that there is defection in all the elements of Christian character, but neither does the vigor of one grace compensate for the absence of another, as some at Thessalonica seemed to think. The whole fruit of the Spirit must be cultivated, Galatians 5:22, 23, that, not in one thing only but in all things, the saints may grow up into Christ, Ephesians 4:15. Even abounding love will not redress the balance where the precepts of God are lightly esteemed, or false ways allowed, Psalm 119:128. Love and mistaken ideas of what God requires may coexist. But no one grace can grow toward perfection save as all the other graces godward and manward, grow with it.

toward one another—as at 1 Thessalonians 3:12; 5:15.

aboundeth;—*pleonazō,* as at 1 Thessalonians 3:12.

Twice in his former letter he had exhorted the converts to see that love abounded among them, now it is his joy to acknowledge their response to his appeal, see 4:1, 10.

There were abuses at Thessalonica as elsewhere, due to ignorance and to self-will, but faith always discerns faith, love always recognizes love, hence the apostle first acknowledges the grace of God in each of them; later, 3:6–15, he deals firmly with abuses. So also in the letters to Corinth, see 1 Corinthians 1:4–7, but not in that to the Galatian churches.

1:4 so that we ourselves—i.e., the missionaries, v. 1, "ourselves" occupies the place of emphasis, thereby implying, first, that others had reported the progress of the church at Thessalonica, and, second, that this progress was so marked that the men who had laid the foundation of the work, and who might, therefore, have been expected to maintain a degree of reticence about it, were constrained to break even so good a rule.

glory—*enkauchaomai,* a strengthened form of *kauchaomai* conveying the same meaning. See note on 1 Thessalonians 2:19, where one of the corresponding nouns, *kauchesis,* occurs.||

in you—*en,* as in Romans 2:17, 23; Galatians 6:13, denoting that which gives occasion to the glorying, cp. Romans 5:2, where *epi* is used, denoting the ground, i.e., hope, on which the believer rejoices in that which is as yet unseen, the glory of God.

in the churches of God—whether by word of mouth in the churches in the neighborhood of Corinth, such as Cenchrea, Romans 16:1, and see 2 Corinthians 1:1, or by letter in those farther away, or both, is not specified.

for—*huper* = on account of; cp. 2 Corinthians 7:14; 9:2, where, in a similar connection, the same preposition is translated "on behalf of."

your patience—*hupomonē*, lit., "abiding under"; the corresponding verb, *hupomenō*, is usually translated "endure."

Patience, which grows only in trial, James 1:3, may be passive, i.e. = endurance, as:

a, in trials, generally, Luke 21:19 (which is to be understood by Matt. 24:13), Romans 12:12; James 1:12:

b, in trials incident to service in the gospel, 2 Corinthians 6:4; 12:12; 2 Timothy 2:10:

c, under chastisement, which is trial viewed as coming from the hand of God our Father, Hebrews 12:2:

d, under undeserved affliction, 1 Peter 2:20:

or active, i.e. = persistence, perseverance, as:

e, in well doing, Romans 2:7:

f, in fruit bearing, Luke 8:15:

g, in running the appointed race, Hebrews 12:1.

Patience perfects Christian character, James 1:4, and fellowship in the patience of Christ is therefore the condition upon which believers are to be admitted to reign with Him, 2 Timothy 2:12; Revelation 1:9. For this patience believers are "strengthened with all power," Colossians 1:11, "through His Spirit in the inward man," Ephesians 3:16.

and faith—see at v. 3.

in all your persecutions—*diōgmos*, the literal meaning of this word may be learned from the use of its verb in 1 Thessalonians 5:15, "follow after," see note there.

and in the afflictions—*thlipsis*, as in 1 Thessalonians 1:6; 3:3, 7, where see notes. "Persecutions" describes the hostile actions of others; "afflictions" are the various forms of injury to body and mind suffered by those who are persecuted.

which ye endure;—*anechomai* = to bear up, as the apostle himself did, 1 Corinthians 4:12, cp. 2 Timothy 3:11.

The present continuous tense indicates that the afflictions which beset them at the beginning, 1 Thessalonians 1:6; 2:14, had been continued or renewed. Confession of Christ had brought upon them the hostility of their fellow citizens, Luke 21:12, cp. Acts 17:5, 6; now they were learning that righteousness and godliness also excite opposition, see Matthew 5:10; 2 Timothy 3:12. In these afflictions, however, they would be sustained by the knowledge that the Lord Jesus regards persecution of His people as of Himself, see Acts 9:4, 5, and cp. Zechariah 2:8, and through grace they would yet learn to rejoice in it, 2 Corinthians 12:10. Moreover to the Christian there is not merely present blessing in persecution, there is also the assurance of future reward, Matthew 5:10–12.

1:5 *which is*—words necessary to complete the sentence in English, but for which there is no equivalent in orig. They are to be understood, not of the persecution itself but of the "patience and faith" in which the persecutions were endured.

a manifest token—*endeigma* = an evidence, a proof, i.e., to themselves. Of this patient endurance they had been incapable until a new power, even the power of the Holy Spirit, had wrought in them this strange experience in which joy went hand in hand with affliction, 1 Thessalonians 1:6. That they had endured patiently and that faith had not failed, was proof of the new life, and a guarantee that, in the end, God would vindicate Himself and them. Thus all thoughts of vengeance would be excluded and a solemn sense of submission to God encouraged instead.

A closely related noun, *endeixis,* is found in Romans 3:25, 26; 2 Corinthians 8:24; Philippians 1:28, where in each case the thought is that of giving proof to others.

of the righteous—*dikazos* = just, without prejudice or partiality. This quality of being right is said to be the foundation of the throne of God, Psalm 89:14; cp. James 1:17; 1 Peter 2:23.

judgment of God;—*krisis* = the act of distinguishing and separating. The word occurs again in Paul's writings, 1 Timothy 5:24, only. In the New Testament it is used of:

a, an estimate of persons or things, John 5:30; 7:24:

b, judicial authority, John 5:22, 27:

c, justice, Acts 8:33; James 2:13:

d, trial before a judge, human or divine, Matthew 5:21; John 5:24; 2 Peter 2:4:

e, an accusation, 2 Peter 2:11; Jude 9:

f, condemnation, Matthew 23:33; John 3:19; Jude 15. (A cognate noun, *krima,* is ordinarily used in this sense, as in Mark 12:40; Rom. 2:2, e.g.):

g, a time of "crisis," John 12:31:

h, just dealing, generally, Matthew 12:18, 20; 23:23; Luke 11:42; Revelation 16:7, and here.

The Holy Spirit convicts the world of (the actuality of) God's judgment, John 16:8, 11. To the children of God present tokens in assurance thereof are vouchsafed to confirm them in times of trial, and these they are taught by the Holy Spirit to discern. But on those who deny that God will judge men, or even that He cares about them, Psalms 10:4–6; 11:13, and who despise alike His goodness to them and His longsuffering with them, that righteous judgment will be revealed in wrath, Romans 2:5 (where *dikaiokrisia,* a compound of the two words used here, appears);|| 1 Thessalonians 5:3.

The words *"which is——*judgment of God" should be read as a parenthesis, i.e., as though they were enclosed in brackets. In v. 6 the apostle returns to the subject thus introduced.

to the end that—some such words as "given you" seem necessary before this phrase in order to complete the sense. This patience and this faith were inwrought in them by God that they might show themselves worthy.

ye may be counted worthy—*kataxioō;* fitness, not merit, is the thought expressed, as also in Luke 20:35; Acts 5:41; see note at v. 3.||

There was no intrinsic merit in the exercise of faith and patience such as would establish a claim to the kingdom of God; their faith and patience testified to the call of God, 1 Thessalonians 2:12, and to the working in them of the powers of that kingdom. It was fitting and right, then, that persons in whom those powers were operating, and in whom consequently a character in harmony with that kingdom was being produced, should be given a place in it at its manifestation.

of the kingdom of God,—i.e., in its future manifestation, see note at 1 Thessalonians 2:12.

for which—*huper,* as in v. 4, where see note = "in the interests of which." They had given their allegiance to a rejected king, see Acts 17:7, assured of the legitimacy of His claims, and of the certainty of His ultimate triumph.

ye—suffer:—suffering with Him now is the condition of reigning with Him then, Romans 8:17, cp. also 2 Timothy 2:12 (vv. 11–13 appear to be the words of an early Christian hymn), and Acts 14:22, "through many tribulations we must enter into the kingdom of God."

also—this word seems to be added to suggest that they were patient in their sufferings, not merely because of their own interests in the rest and glory of that kingdom, but as well from loyalty to it.

1:6 if so be that—expressed by one word, *eiper* = assuming that, as in Romans 3:30; 8:9, 12. Here the apostle returns to the parenthetic statement of v. 5*a,* and proceeds to explain what is involved in the fact that God's judgments are according to righteousness.

it is a righteous thing—lit., "it is righteous," the corresponding adverb occurs 1 Thessalonians 2:10, where see note, and cp. Psalm 129:4; Revelation 16:5.

with God—i.e., in the estimation of God, in the sight of God, as in 1 Corinthians 3:19; Galatians 3:11; Ephesians 6:9.

to recompense—*antapodidōmi* = to give in return for, as at 1 Thessalonians 3:9, where see note; whether between men (but in that case only of good, not of evil, see 1 Thess. 5:15, and note), Luke 14:14, cp. the corresponding noun in v. 12; or between God and evildoers, Romans 12:19; Hebrews 10:30, cp. the noun in Romans 11:9; or between God and those who do well, Luke 14:14; Romans 11:35, cp. the noun in Colossians 3:24. Here both reward and retribution are in view.||

affliction to them that afflict you,—cp. Romans 2:9, the only other passage in Paul's Epistles in which the word is used of retribution to the ungodly in the future, elsewhere it is always used of the present experience of believers, as at v. 4. In either case that which comes upon one from without is intended.

The principle underlying the retribution of God is expressed in Galatians 6:7, "whatsoever a man soweth that shall he also reap," cp. Colossians 3:24, for though these passages refer, primarily, to believers, the principle is of universal application. See further Matthew 26:52; Revelation 13:10.

1:7 and to you that are afflicted rest—*anesis* = a loosing, a relaxation of strain; it occurs again Acts 24:23, "indulgence," 2 Corinthians 2:13; 7:5, "relief," 8:13, "eased," cp. the corresponding verb in Acts 16:26, "loosed." Josephus speaks of the "rest," *anesis,* from plowing and tillage, given to the land in the year of jubilee.||

The apostle did not pray for these afflicted saints that their trials might cease; he reminded them of the certainty of the relaxation of the strain of endurance to which they were subjected because of their allegiance to the kingdom of God. For this easement, however, they were not to look to death, as Job did, 3:17, but to the return of the Lord Jesus.

with us,—though his absence prevented his sharing their griefs the writer was not therefore himself exempt from affliction, see 1 Thessalonians 3:3, 4; nor was he raised by his apostolic office above the experiences common to all saints. On the contrary, he, too, was constrained by trials to long for the relief to which he directed their thoughts. More, he was still filled with the desire for their company so fervently expressed in his previous letter, 3:10, 11. The prospect of its early satisfaction had faded, indeed, but their reunion was assured however it might be delayed.

Here, as at 1 Thessalonians 4:17, he associated himself and them with those who will be alive on the earth at that time; in 2 Corinthians 4:14 he associated himself with those who would pass away before it; see also on 1 Thessalonians 4:15.

The subject immediately before the apostle's mind is not the rest of the saints but the retribution of God on their persecutors. Hence the words, "and to you that are afflicted rest with us," are an incidental extension of the idea of recompense, and are to be read parenthetically, permitting the words that follow to be connected directly with the close of v. 6, thus: "affliction to them that afflict you [and to you that are afflicted rest with us], at the revelation of the Lord Jesus." The time indicated is not that at which the saints will be relieved of persecution, but that at which their persecutors will be punished. The time of relief for the saints had been stated in the earlier letter, 4:15–17; here passing reference to a fact within the knowledge of the readers was all that was necessary. Such extensions of thought are not uncommon in epistolary writings, cp. v. 10, and 1 Thessalonians 1:6; 2:15, 16, and see Intro. Note.

Since, then, the rest of the saints begins with the Lord's descent into the air, which marks also the inauguration of the Parousia, the Parousia itself will intervene before the vengeance of God begins to be executed. Whether the period so termed is to be of longer duration—say extending to years, or shorter—say limited to hours or even to minutes, is not in question here. See note on 1 Thessalonians 2:19; 5:1.

at—_en_, lit., "in," as at 1 Thessalonians 2:19; 3:13; 5:23, where see note. See also 1 Thessalonians 5:3.

the revelation—_apokalupsis_ = an uncovering, an unveiling. It is derived from _apo_ = un-, and _kalupto_ = to cover, cp. Matthew 10:26, "there is nothing covered, _kalupto_, that shall not be revealed, _apokalupto_." In the New Testament it is used of:

_a,_ the drawing away by Christ of the veil of darkness covering the Gentiles, Luke 2:32, cp. Isaiah 25:7:

_b,_ "the mystery," the purpose of God in this age, Romans 16:25; Ephesians 3:3:

_c,_ the communication of the knowledge of God to the soul, Ephesians 1:17:

_d,_ an expression of the mind of God for the instruction of the church, 1 Corinthians 14:6, 26, for the instruction of the apostle Paul, 2 Corinthians 12:1, 7; Galatians 1:12, and for his guidance, Galatians 2:2:

_e,_ the Lord Jesus Christ, to the saints at His Parousia, 1 Corinthians 1:7, 1 Peter 1:7, 13; 4:13:

_f,_ the Lord Jesus Christ when He comes to dispense the judgments of God, here, and cp. Romans 2:5:

_g,_ the saints, to the creation, in association with Christ in His glorious reign, Romans 8:19:

h, the symbolic forecast of the final judgments of God, Revelation 1:1 (hence the Greek title of the book, transliterated "Apocalypse" and translated "Revelation").

For an analysis of the New Testament occurrences of the corresponding verb *apokaluptō,* see at Galatians 1:16.

of the Lord Jesus from heaven—see notes at 1 Thessalonians 1:10; 4:16.

with the angels—*angelos* = a messenger, whether sent by God, or by man, or by Satan, lit., Matthew 11:10; James 2:25, or fig., 2 Corinthians 12:7. It is also used of a guardian or representative in Revelation 1:20, cp. Matthew 18:10; Acts 12:15 (where it is better understood thus than as = "ghost"), but most frequently of an order of created beings, superior to man, Hebrews 2:7; Psalm 8:5, belonging to heaven, Matthew 24:36; Mark 12:25, and to God, Luke 12:8, and engaged in His service, Psalm 103:20. Angels are "spirits," Hebrews 1:14, i.e., they have not material bodies as men have; they are either human in form, or can assume the human form when necessary, cp. Luke 24:4 with v. 23, Acts 10:3 with v. 30. They are usually represented as arrayed in white, and as dazzling the eye with their brightness, Matthew 28:2, 3, cp. 2 Corinthians 11:14. They are called "holy," Mark 8:38, and "elect," 1 Timothy 5:21, in contrast with some of their original number, Matthew 25:41, who "sinned," 2 Peter 2:4 ("left their proper habitation," Jude 6, *oikētērion,* a word which occurs again in the New Testament only 2 Cor. 5:2). Angels are always spoken of in the masculine gender, the feminine form of the word does not occur in the Scriptures.

Angels are frequently associated with Christ in connection with His redemptive and mediatorial work; they announced His birth, Matthew 1:20; Luke 2:8–14, resurrection, Matthew 28:2–6, and return, Acts 1:10; they ministered to Him after His temptation in the wilderness, Mark 1:13, and in Gethsemane, Luke 22:43; they will attend Him at His return to judgment, Matthew 16:27 and here, and are the agents by whom His judgments will be executed, Matthew 13:39, 41, 49; 24:31. In that day they will be called upon to worship Him, Hebrews 1:6, quoted from LXX of Deuteronomy 32:41–43, which reads: "I will render judgment to my enemies, and will recompense them that hate me . . . Rejoice, ye heavens, with Him, and let all the angels of God worship Him"; cp. Psalm 97:7.

of His power—i.e., through whom His power is exercised. "Their mighty strength," Psalm 103:20, is the ready instrument of His will. Cp. Zechariah 14:5.

1:8 in—encompassed with.

flaming fire,—theophanies, i.e., manifestations of God, in Old Testament times were sometimes marked by the presence of fire, cp. Exodus 3:2; 19:18; 2 Chronicles 7:1. If the words are taken with what precedes them, then the fire = the Shekinah, Exodus 40:35, 38. If with what follows them, then the fire = the instrument of the judgment, cp. Leviticus 10:2; Psalm 97:3. There is nothing in the words to decide between these interpretations, unless it be the idea of motion and activity in the word "flame," which would best accord with the latter, cp. also Psalm 50:3, "Our God shall come—a fire shall devour before Him."

The words are quoted, apparently, from Isaiah 66:15, "Jehovah will come with fire."

By describing the Lord Jesus as surrounded with the Shekinah glory and the angels (which He Himself sometimes called God's, Luke 12:8, and sometimes His own, Matt. 24:31), by ascribing to Him the prerogatives of Jehovah in judgment, cp. Deuteronomy 32:36; Psalm 94:1, and by quoting with reference to Him words originally used of Jehovah, the apostle bears indirect but unmistakable testimony to His deity.

rendering—*didōmi* = to give, as at 1 Thessalonians 4:2, 8; in Luke 18:7, a strictly parallel passage, "do," is used (i.e., "avenge," lit., "do vengeance").

vengeance—*ekdikēsis,* lit., "that which proceeds out of justice"; not, as is often the case with human vengeance, out of a feeling of indignation, or a sense of injury. There is thus no element of vindictiveness, of "taking revenge," or of self-gratification, in the judgments of God; they are both holy and right, Revelation 16:7.

to them that know not God,—*oida,* see at 1 Thessalonians 4:5.

The wicked persecution of inoffensive persons was an outcome of the sin of willful ignorance of God, cp. Romans 11:30, where it is implied that this ignorance of God had its origin in disobedience to God.

The judgments of God fall upon men, not merely because of their actions one toward another, but, primarily, because of their attitude toward Himself; cp. Psalm 51:4; 1 John 2:29; 3:10.

and to them that obey not the gospel of our Lord Jesus:—cp. Psalm 79:6; Jeremiah 10:25. God not only entreats men to accept the gospel, He commands them to do so, cp. 2 Corinthians 5:20 with Acts 17:30. Hence those who believe on the Lord Jesus are said to "obey the Son," or "the Faith," John 3:36; Acts 6:7, cp. Romans 1:5; 16:26.

Two classes are intended, as the repetition of the article shows. The first of these includes all Gentiles who have refused such knowledge of God as is to be had from the light of nature, cp. Acts 10:34; Romans 2:10–15. The second includes all, Jews and Gentiles, who, having heard the gospel refused to submit to the claims of God therein declared, cp. Acts 17:32, 33, and see notes at 1 Thessalonians 2:15.

1:9 who—i.e., all who belong to the two classes described.

shall suffer—*tinō* = to pay a penalty.

punishment,—*dikē*, primarily denoting that which is right, a word closely allied to *dikaios,* "righteous," see note at v. 5. In Acts 28:4 *dikē* is the name of a goddess, the personification of justice. Here, and at Jude 7, it is the penalty due on account of willful ignorance and disobedience.||

even **eternal**—*aiōnios*, an adjective derived from the noun *aiōn* = a period of undefined duration, an age, a dispensation, see note at Galatians 1:4. Hence *aiōnios* describes duration, either undefined but not endless, as in Romans 16:25; 2 Timothy 1:9; Titus 1:2; or undefined because endless, as in Romans 16:26 and each of the other sixty-six places of its occurrence in the New Testament

The predominant meaning of *aiōnios,* that in which it is used everywhere in the New Testament save the three places noted above, may be seen in 2 Corinthians 4:18, where it is set in contrast with *proskairos,* lit., "for a season," see Matthew 13:21, end note at 1 Thessalonians 5:1; and in Philemon 15, where only in the New Testament it is used without a noun. Moreover, it is used of persons and things which are in their nature endless, as, e.g., of God, Romans 16:26, of His power, 1 Timothy 6:16, and of His glory, 1 Peter 5:10; of the Holy Spirit, Hebrews 9:14; of the redemption effected by Christ, 9:12, and of the consequent salvation of men, 5:9, as well as of His future rule, 2 Peter 1:11, which is elsewhere declared to be without end, Luke 1:33; of the life received by those who believe in Christ, John 3:16, concerning whom He said "they shall never perish," 10:28, and of the resurrection body, 2 Corinthians 5:1, elsewhere said to be "immortal," 1 Corinthians 15:53, in which that life will be finally realized, Matthew 25:46; Titus 1:2.

Aiōnios is also used of the sin that "hath never forgiveness," Mark 3:29, and of the judgment of God, from which there is no appeal, Hebrews 6:2, and of the fire, which is one of its instruments, Matthew 18:8; 25:41; Jude 7, and which is elsewhere said to be "unquenchable," Mark 9:43.

The use of *aiōnios* here shows that the punishment with which the passage is concerned is not temporary, but final, and, accordingly, the phraseology throughout shows that its purpose is not remedial but retributive.

destruction—*olethros* = ruin. In 1 Corinthians 5:5 it is used of the discipline of an erring believer with a view to his spiritual profit; in 1 Timothy 6:9 of the consequences of the indulgence of the flesh (perhaps referring to physical and temporal, while the accompanying word "perdition," *apōleia,* refers to spiritual and eternal, disaster, see note on "perdition" at 2:3, below); in 1 Thessalonians 5:3, and here, of the effect upon men of the calamities which are to accompany the revelation of the Lord Jesus at the opening of the day of the Lord.

This word like its synonyms, also translated "destroy," "destruction," means, not the destruction of being but of well-being, not annihilation, the putting an end to the existence of a person or thing, but its ruin so far as the purpose of its existence is concerned.

The participle of the corresponding verb is found in Hebrews 11:28 and, but in a strengthened form, *exolethreuō,* in Acts 3:23, a quotation from Leviticus 23:29, LXX; in each case the reference is to the death of the body.||

from—*apo,* which may either = "proceeding from," as in 1 Thessalonians 1:8; Acts 3:19, or "away from," as in 1 Thessalonians 1:9; Matthew 7:23. Each interpretation yields good sense, but the balance of probability is in favor of the latter. The language is taken from Isaiah 2:10, 19, 21, LXX, "hide yourselves in the earth from, *apo,* the face of the terror of the Lord and from, *apo,* the glory of His might, when He shall arise to shake the earth"; cp. Romans 9:3, and see Malachi 3:2; Revelation 6:15–17.

the face—*prosōpon,* as in 1 Thessalonians 2:17, where it is translated first "presence," then "face"; see notes there.

of the Lord—i.e., of the Lord Jesus; in Acts 3:19, where the same phrase appears, God is intended. There, however, the verb used, viz, "come," shows that *apo* = "proceeding from," and *prosōpon* = "presence." It is to be noted that Isaiah speaks of Jehovah in the prophecy from which these words are taken.

and from the glory of His might,—i.e., the outward and visible expression of the inherent personal power of the Lord Jesus, see Matthew 17:2, and cp. note on "fire" above. The punishment here described is thus irrevocable banishment from the presence of the Lord and from the unapproachable light in which He dwells, 1 Timothy 6:16, into the "outer darkness," where, as He Himself said, "shall be the weeping and gnashing of teeth," Matthew 25:30.

1:10 when He shall come—lit., "whensoever He shall have come," referring to the revelation mentioned in v. 7; this language is used because, though the certainty of the coming is assured, its date has not been revealed; see note on 1 Thessalonians 5:2; for "come," *erchomai,* see on 1 Thessalonians 2:19.

to be glorified in His saints,—see note at 1 Thessalonians 3:13. "In," *en,* is not here "by" or "among," but, as in John 17:10, "I am glorified in them," and Galatians 1:24, "they glorified God in me," cp. Isaiah 49:3; 61:3. While the glory of His might destroy the wicked, the glory of His grace is exhibited in His saints, cp. Ephesians 1:6 with Acts 15:11, and in their manifest likeness to Himself, Romans 8:19, 29; Philippians 3:21; 1 John 3:2; cp. also 1 Peter 1:7.

and to be marveled at—expressing the mingled surprise and admiration evoked from the spectators by this manifestation of the love and the grace, the power and the wisdom of God; cp. Psalm 118:23; cp. also Isaiah 52:15, where LXX has "marvel," R.V. margin, "startle." The same event seems to be intended in each passage.

in all them that believed—"point" tense, indicating either that faith has been at this time superseded by sight, or, and more probably, looking back to the moment at which each individual of that host "turned to God," 1 Thessalonians 1:9, see note, and cp. 1 Corinthians 15:2, 11; 2 Corinthians 4:13.

The two expressions "saints" and "them that believed" may describe under different aspects, the whole number of the redeemed who are to accompany the Lord at His coming, i.e., all who are Christ's, whether of this age or of the last, cp. 1 Corinthians 15:23. Or, by the "saints" the redeemed of former ages may be intended, and by "them that believed," "the church which is His Body," Ephesians 1:22, 23. Cp. the two classes of v. 8.

——in that day.—the time referred to is that of the punishment of the wicked and of the glory of the redeemed, the day of the Lord, as in 2:2; 1 Thessalonians 5:2 (where see note) the day of the revelation, v. 7, or coming, of the Lord Jesus.

(because—a parenthesis, in which an extension of the main thought is incidentally expressed, see v. 7, and note there; and for further exx. see 1 Thessalonians 2:15, 16; 5:9, 10; Ephesians 3:2, etc. As at v. 7 so here, the purpose of the parenthesis is to comfort these distressed saints by an explicit assurance that they would be included among those thus blessed at the coming of the Lord.

There is, apparently, an ellipsis here; to complete the sense some such words as "and in you among them" must be supplied before "because." The general statement concerning all who had believed is thus specifically applied to those who had believed at Thessalonica.

our testimony unto you—*marturion*, see note at 1 Thessalonians 2:11. The labors of the missionaries at Thessalonica had been twofold: they had proclaimed certain facts, and they had borne witness to the power of those facts. While preaching (*kērussō*, as in 1 Thess. 2:9, cp. *kērugma* = "thing preached," 1 Cor. 1:21, marg., or "message," Titus 1:3), is objective, i.e., is concerned with that which is external to the preacher, testimony, or witness, is mainly subjective, i.e., is concerned with the preacher's own experience.

was believed)—for whereas, when it is set before them, some refuse the truth altogether, and some while they accept the facts remain unmoved thereby, others not only accept the facts but, submitting thereto in heart, begin to live with a new purpose and to manifest a new character. To the latter class those addressed belonged, "they had become obedient from the heart to that form of teaching whereunto they had been delivered," Romans 6:17, marg.

1:11 To which end—in these words the apostle resumes the subject from which he digressed at the close of v. 5. Verses 6–10, a parenthesis of some length, with its briefer parentheses in v. 7 and v. 10, offers a good example of the characteristically involved style of his writings.

we also pray—_proseuchomai,_ as at 1 Thessalonians 5:17, 25, where see notes. The position of "also" in the sentence marks "pray" as the emphatic word, see note at 1 Thessalonians 5:24.

always for you,—with the object of encouraging them to continue and to abound therein he had warmly acknowledged their faith, love and patience, vv. 3, 4, he had assured them that in due time the strain would be relaxed, v. 7, and had reminded them of the glory of the reward that awaited them, v. 10; but he did more than appeal to them, with the same object in view he also interceded for them with God.

Intercession on their behalf was not inconsistent with his recognition of the tokens that God was working in them, cp. Philippians 1:6; 2:13, nor with the assurance expressed in the words "Who will also do it," 1 Thessalonians 5:24. The certainty of the accomplishment of all the purposes of God does not make prayer either presumptuous or unnecessary. It is His purpose to establish His kingdom upon the earth, yet the Lord Jesus instructed His disciples to pray, "Thy Kingdom come!" Matthew 6:10.

that our God may count you worthy—_axioō,_ as in v. 3, "meet," see note there and at v. 5. The prayer is, not that God would make them worthy but that He would account them so; cp. the same verb in Hebrews 3:3; 10:29. In the bestowal of reward, whether for suffering or for service, grace reigns. At best the servant is "unprofitable," Luke 17:10, yet, because it was in his heart to serve, 1 Kings 8:18, and because he did what he could, Mark 14:8, using what was at his disposal, 2 Corinthians 8:12, according to the opportunity provided, Matthew 25:15, God will reward him not according to the actual attainment or to the work accomplished, but according to the riches of His grace in Christ. To consider the needy may seem a small thing, but such as are approved in this "inherit the Kingdom," Matthew 25:34. See note on "worthily," _axiōs,_ 1 Thessalonians 2:12.

of your calling,—*klēsis,* two callings are mentioned in these Epistles, *a,* that to salvation through the gospel, 2:13, 14, and *b,* that into the kingdom of God in its future manifestation, 1 Thessalonians 2:12, where, and at 5:24, see notes. The latter, *b,* was probably in the apostle's mind here.

and fulfill—*plēroō,* to accomplish, to make effective, as in Romans 8:4.

every desire—*eudokia,* marg., "good pleasure," lit., "good desire" it occurs again of men, but only, as here, of regenerate men, in Romans 10:1; Philippians 1:15; elsewhere of God, Matthew 11:26; Luke 2:14; 10:21; Ephesians 1:5, 9; Philippians 2:13.||

of goodness—*agathōsunē,* as in Romans 15:14; Galatians 5:22; Ephesians 5:9, in each case of regenerate men.||

Neither is this word nor its adjective, *agathos,* good, used of God in the New Testament, save that the latter is found in Matthew 19:17, and in parallels in the other Gospels. In Romans 2:4; 1 Peter 2:3, *chrēstos,* and in Romans 2:4; 11:22; Ephesians 2:7; Titus 3:4, *chrēstotēs* both = "kindness," "benevolence," appear. These words are also used of the regenerate.

The consideration that *agathōsunē* is not elsewhere in the New Testament applied to God, together with the fact that this phrase is coupled with "work of faith," which could only be used of men, is conclusive that the reference is to the desires of the converts themselves, though from Galatians 5:2; Philippians 2:13, it is clear that "desires of goodness" are fruit of the presence of the Holy Spirit in believers.

The phrase may be either, *a,* subjective, = desire characterized by goodness, good desire, or, *b,* objective, = desire after goodness, desire to be and to do good.

and *every* work of faith,—the words are those of 1 Thessalonians 1:3, but the thought appears to be different. There the "work of faith" is the response of the soul to the life-giving Word of God, the initial act in which communion with God is established. Here the word "every," properly repeated in English though not expressed in orig., shows that diversity is contemplated, = "all works of faith." The description applies alike to suffering borne for the Name of Christ, and this was abundant at Thessalonica, and to activities undertaken in the same interest; in this also they had not been lacking, see 1 Thessalonians 1:8; 4:9, 12. Cp. also James 2:18.

with [*en*] power;—*dunamis* = inherent ability; i.e., "fulfill by means of His power." Apart from that living energy of which God alone is the source, Psalm 62:11; Matthew 6:13; Revelation 19:1, and of which the Holy Spirit alone is the minister, Luke 24:49; Acts 1:8, the desire of goodness is impotent, the work of faith is ineffectual. Paul himself was conscious that all his own labor was vain save as that power worked in him, Colossians 1:29, where "mightily" is, lit., "in power" as here. Genesis 39:3; Psalm 1:3, may be compared, and Ephesians 3:20.

1:12 that the name of our Lord Jesus—name suggests character, Exodus 34:6, 7; Psalm 9:10; John 17:6, rank, Hebrews 1:4, authority, Mark 9:39; John 5:43; 1 Corinthians 5:4, power, John 17:11, 12; Acts 4:10, cp. v. 7, each or all. Sometimes indeed, it is put for the person, as in Leviticus 24:11; Joel 2:32 (where it is used of God; the passage is quoted in Rom. 10:13 of the Lord Jesus), Luke 1:49; John 1:12; Romans 1:5; Revelation 15:4. His Name is what He is, it is Himself.

may be glorified—_endoxazomai,_ as in v. 10; see notes on "glory," v. 9, and 1 Thessalonians 2:6, 12, 20. Verse 10 refers to the future, here the present is intended, cp. John 17:10, etc. Cp. Isaiah 66:5, LXX, "speak ye . . . to them . . . that the name of the Lord may be glorified."

in you,—i.e., in their daily conduct, in their "desires of goodness," their thoughts, and in their "works of faith," their acts.

The new faith differed from the religion it had displaced in the hearts of the converts in that it is centered in a person. The essence of their faith lay in this, not that they had embraced a new creed merely, but that they had become so closely identified with the Lord Jesus that their conduct either caused His name to be reviled, cp. Isaiah 52:5; Ezekiel 36:20, 21, or to be honored, see Matthew 5:16; 2 Corinthians 9:13; 1 Peter 2:9, 12. Since His honorable Name had been called upon them, James 2:7, marg., they lived not unto themselves but unto the Lord, Romans 14:7, 8, cp. Philippians 1:20.

and ye in Him,—there is an ellipsis here, "and that ye may be glorified in Him." The phrase affords still another illustration of the apostle's style, see on vv. 7–10; he had been speaking of the present, but, at the mention of the glory of Christ, he abruptly interrupts himself to extend his thought into the future, and to speak of the glory that awaits the believer because of his union with Christ. Believers who die in Christ do thereupon enter into rest with Him, Philippians 1:22–24, cp. Revelation 6:11; 14:13, though death is not set before them as their proper hope in these epistles, nor, indeed, in the New Testament, see v. 7. But not until the resurrection at the Parousia will they be glorified; then their bodies are to be "fashioned anew," i.e., to be endued with new life, to be endowed with new properties and new powers, and so to be "conformed to His glorious body," Philippians 3:21, cp. 1 Corinthians 15:49; 1 John 3:2. At the close of the Parousia believers, in these changed bodies, are to accompany the Lord in His revelation to the world, and thus to manifest and to share His glory, Colossians 3:4; 1 Peter 5:1.

according to the grace—this phrase is to be taken with each of the preceding clauses; with the first since it is the grace of God that instructs believers to live to the glory of their Lord, Titus 2:11–14, and enables them so to do, Romans 6:14, cp. 2 Corinthians 9:8; 12:9; Hebrews 4:16; with the second since the glory in prospect is to be bestowed upon them in fulfillment of the purpose of God, 1 Peter 1:10, 13, the climax of His gracious dealings with them, cp. Romans 5:15–21; Ephesians 2:5–7.

of our God and the Lord Jesus Christ.—See note at v. 1.

1:7b–10 concerning the righteous recompense of God, may be analyzed thus:

- its time—at the revelation of the Lord Jesus from heaven . . . in that day when He shall come to be glorified in His saints, and to be marveled at in all them that believed;
- its circumstances—with the angels of His power in flaming fire;
- its purpose—rendering vengeance;
- its objects—to them that know not God, and to them that obey not the gospel of our Lord Jesus;
- its character—who shall suffer punishment, even eternal destruction from the face of the Lord and the glory of His might.

2 THESSALONIANS

· CHAPTER TWO ·

Verses 1–17

2:1 Now we beseech you, brethren,—the apostle thus passes to the main theme of the epistle.

touching—*huper,* see note at 1 Thessalonians 5:10; here = in the interest of, i.e., "with a view to correcting your thoughts about."

the coming of our Lord Jesus Christ,—*parousia,* as at 1 Thessalonians 2:19.

and our gather together—*episunagōgē,* as in Hebrews 10:25, where it is used of the present assembling of companies of believers on earth, cp. Acts 20:7. Here it refers to the "rapture" of the saints into the air to meet and to be forever with the Lord, see 1 Thessalonians 4:17.||

The article appears before *parousia* and is not repeated before *episunagōgē,* indicating that these are complementary elements in one event.

unto him;—Christ is the divinely-appointed center of gathering whether for local companies of believers during this age, Matthew 18:20, or for all that are His of every age at His Parousia, 1 Thessalonians 4:17, cp. John 14:3, or for Israel, Genesis 49:10, cp. Psalm 50:5, or for the nations, Isaiah 11:10.

2:2 to the end that—these words are to be connected with "we beseech you." In the previous letter he had reassured them concerning the future of their departed, here he reassures them concerning their own present experiences; the afflictions they were enduring were not evidence that the day of the Lord had set in.

ye be not——shaken—*saleuō,* in the New Testament ordinarily = to agitate, to excite, Luke 6:38; Acts 17:13, but in Greek authors also = "to move away from," as a ship in a tempest from her moorings; the latter is apparently the meaning here and in Acts 2:25.

quickly—i.e., hastily, responding readily to an impression without waiting to consider, cp. the close parallel in Galatians 1:6, and see note there.

from your mind,—i.e., from sobriety, either to excitement or to anxiety. Believers are not to be controlled by the emotions, whether of dread or of desire, but by the mind, enlightened by the revelation of the mind of God.

Nous, mind, is the seat of the understanding, as in Luke 24:45; Revelation 13:18; 17:9, where only it occurs in the New Testament outside the epistles of Paul; it bears the same meaning in Romans 1:28; 14:5; 1 Corinthians 14:14, 15, 19; Ephesians 4:17; Colossians 2:18; 1 Timothy 6:5; 2 Timothy 3:8, 9; Titus 1:15, and cp. Philippians 4:7. It also = purpose in Romans 11:34; 12:2; 1 Corinthians 1:10; 2:16; Ephesians 4:23. In Romans 7:23, 25, where it is set in contrast with "the flesh," the principle of evil which dominates fallen man, *nous* = the new nature which belongs to the believer in Christ in virtue of the new birth.

Here = either, *a,* settled conviction, or, *b,* the purpose based thereon; i.e., either, *a,* the confidence that the day of rest and recompense will come, or, *b,* the purpose to endure affliction based upon that confidence. The latter is, of course, involved in the former.

nor yet—i.e., not even, not so much as.

be troubled,—*throeō,* as in Matthew 24:6; Mark 13:7.||

The things to which he was about to refer were not only not to be permitted to move them away from their convictions and purposes of mind, they were not even to be permitted to disturb its peace. The difference between "shaken" and "troubled" seems to be that the former refers to the shock sustained, the latter to the consequent disturbance.

either by spirit,—by metonymy for those who claimed to be depositories of spiritual gifts, cp. 1 John 4:1–3. All such claims were to be closely scrutinized, see notes at 1 Thessalonians 5:20, 21.

or by word,—*logos,* i.e., by reasoning, or by statement not professing to be a divine revelation, or by a pretended verbal message from the missionaries.

or by epistle—i.e., a written message, pretending either to contain the teaching of the missionaries as delivered elsewhere, or to be written for them, as this was, see 3:17.

as—as if, purporting to be.

from—*dia,* with the genitive case = through, by means of. Paul did not claim to be a source of knowledge in himself; he was merely a channel through which God revealed His mind to men.

us,—the use of the plural here shows further that Paul did not claim to be the sole channel through which revelations were given. Doubtless the old principle of the double witness still held good, as it did in the case of the Lord Himself, John 5:31; 8:17; cp. Romans 16:26 with Ephesians 3:8. But, further, any revelation from the same source, through whatever channel it might come, would certainly be consistent with what they had already received, and if any pretended revelation failed to satisfy this test it must be rejected as originating elsewhere than with God, Galatians 1:6–9. The apostle did not say that such messages had been delivered to them or received by them. He was aware that something had disturbed them, but apparently he had not had full information on the point, hence he warns them against possible devices whereby they might be deceived.

as that—i.e., representing that.

the day of the Lord—see notes at 1 Thessalonians 5:2. Although in his previous letter the apostle had not said anything to suggest the identity of the Parousia with the day of the Lord, his readers were apparently confused in mind about them. That they are distinct periods, the following considerations go to show:

_a_, whereas the day of the Lord is a subject of the Old Testament prophecy the Parousia is not:

_b_, the scene of the day of the Lord is the earth; the scene of the Parousia is the air:

_c_, the day of the Lord, since it is a period of judgment and punishment, is to be anticipated with dread; the Parousia, since it is a period of rest and reward, is to be anticipated with joy:

_d_, from the day of the Lord believers are to be delivered, saved; in the Parousia they are to meet the Lord and to be with Him:

_e_, angels are prominent in connection with the day of the Lord; they are not mentioned in connection with the Parousia:

_f_, the aim of the apostle here is to clear away the confusion existing in the minds of the converts by further defining the circumstances attending the day of the Lord; these are different from the circumstances of the Parousia.

is _now_ **present;**—_enistēmi_, as in Romans 8:38; Galatians 1:4 (where see note); Hebrews 9:9. Their heavy afflictions seemed to point to this conclusion, which, however, the apostle proceeds to show was unwarranted.

2:3 let no man beguile you—_exapataō_, a word elsewhere used of the influence of sin, Romans 7:11, and of self-deception, which is not distinguishable from sin, 1 Corinthians 3:18; of Satan, 2 Corinthians 11:3; 1 Timothy 2:14_b_, and of men his instruments, Romans 16:18. It is a strengthened form of _apataō_, 1 Timothy 2:14_a_, which may be paraphrased, "Adam was not beguiled at all, but the woman, being thoroughly beguiled, etc."||

This warning exhortation is an echo of the words of the Lord, "let no man lead you astray" _(planaō);_ indeed, since the Lord probably spoke in Aramaic, and since the Greek words are synonyms, it may well be that the apostle is here translating and quoting what He actually said.

in any wise:—lit., "according to any manner," cp. Romans 3:2; Philippians 1:18; i.e., neither in the ways just specified nor in any other that might be devised.

for—*hoti* = because, as at 1:3, where see note; introducing the reason for his emphatic assertion that the day of the Lord had not already set in.

it will not be,—words necessary to supply the ellipsis in orig.; = "the day of the Lord will not set in." Such ellipses are a feature of the epistolary style, cp. Romans 4:16; 2 Corinthians 8:13, e.g., and see note at 1:12, above.

except the falling away—*apostasia,* occurs in LXX of Joshua 22:22, "rebellion," 2 Chronicles 29:19, "trespassed," Jeremiah 2:19, "forsaken." In Joshua 22:23 it is defined as a "turning away from following Jehovah," and in Hebrews 3:12 as "falling away from the living God"; cp. the defection of Israel in the wilderness, Acts 7:39–41. The believing Jews at Jerusalem were apprehensive that Paul's gospel would have the effect of encouraging the Jews of the Dispersion to apostasy from the law of Moses, Acts 21:21.||

The article may serve a double purpose, viz, to indicate *a,* that this apostasy would not be an isolated case, the defection of individuals, as in Acts 20:30; Romans 16:17, 18; 1 Corinthians 16:22, e.g., but a movement of a more general character than any that preceded it; and *b,* that it had been the subject of a former oral communication, see v. 5.

All apostasy is essentially religious, i.e., it is revolt against God. This apostasy is not merely a revolt against God, it is a denial of the existence of any being, or order of beings, superior to man. It is the claim of man to absolute supremacy not only in the world but in the universe.

The time of this apostasy from Christ of which the apostle speaks is not indicated. The centuries since the words were written have not produced the person here described as displaying fully the characteristics of the apostasy. The conclusion that the prophecy awaits fulfillment seems inevitable.

come first,—i.e., before the day of the Lord.

and the man of sin—this is a Hebrew idiom used to describe a predominant characteristic, cp. "man of knowledge," Proverbs 24:5, "man of sorrows," Isaiah 53:3, but the expression in fullness and intensity of meaning is really without parallel. The word "man," *anthrōpos,* is not elsewhere used of other than a human being, hence the phrase cannot be read as = sin personified, nor as = the incumbents of a certain office, such as a line of emperors or popes. Probably, therefore, it is to be understood of a man over whom sin will have absolute dominion, the willing and efficient instrument of sin, cp. Romans 6:16. A various reading, is "man of lawlessness"; for this there is considerable manuscript authority, it agrees, moreover, with the words of vv. 7, 8; cp. also the statement of John "sin is lawlessness," i.e., "sin" and "lawlessness" are interchangeable terms, 1 John 3:4.

Sin, *hamartia* = "a missing of the mark," is very common in the New Testament; lawlessness, *anomia* = "a breaking of law," is used again by Paul in Romans 4:7; 6:19; 2 Corinthians 6:14; Titus 2:14, cp. Matthew 7:23; Hebrews 8:12. In Psalm 89:22; Zechariah 5:8, LXX, the latter occurs and is translated "wickedness," which, on the whole, better represents it than "lawlessness" does, since what is meant is actual transgression of law, see also Ezekiel 15:50, "abomination." Here, perhaps, the word is extended to include the idea of contempt of [divine] law. If Antichrist denies the existence of the lawgiver he is not likely to respect His laws.

be revealed,—*apokaluptō,* see on 1:7; the tense is momentary, lit., "have been revealed"; the word is applicable to that which is present at any given time but hidden from general knowledge. Its use elsewhere in the New Testament suggests also the operation of a superhuman power in this unveiling.

The order in orig. is, "and there be revealed the man of sin," thus emphasizing the verb, and bringing together the descriptive words applied to the mysterious being who is the subject of the paragraph.

the son of perdition,—*apōleia,* see note on "destruction," 1:9; the same words were used of Judas by the Lord Jesus, John 17:12. This also is a Hebrew idiom, sometimes expressing character, as in "son of peace," Luke 10:6, and sometimes destiny, as in "son of death," 1 Samuel 20:31, LXX. If "man of lawlessness" refers to character, then "son of perdition" refers to the proper destiny of such a one, who, like Judas, must "go to his own place," Acts 1:25, cp. Philippians 3:19, and Revelation 17:8, 11. See also on 1 Thessalonians 5:5.

The meaning of *apōleia* may be learned from its use of material things, such as ointment, Matthew 26:8, and money, Acts 8:20. Like *olethros,* see at 1:9, it is a general term for disaster, material and spiritual, temporal and eternal. In no one of its New Testament occurrences is the idea of cessation of being necessarily involved.

2:4 he that opposeth—*antikeimai* = "to be set over against"; it is used of those who opposed the Lord Jesus, Luke 13:17; of those who oppose His people, 21:15; 1 Corinthians 16:9; Philippians 1:28; 1 Timothy 5:14; or His doctrine, 1 Timothy 1:10; and also of the mutual antagonism between the Holy Spirit and the flesh in the believer, Galatians 5:17. In LXX it is used of Satan, Zechariah 3:1, and of men, Job 13:24; Isaiah 66:6.||

The grammatical form here, i.e., the participle with the article, makes a descriptive title = "the opponent." John, writing long afterwards, called the same person "Antichrist" = "the opponent of Christ," 1 John 2:18; thus the later title supplements and defines the earlier.

and exalteth himself—*huperairō*, as in 2 Corinthians 12:7, "exalted over much"; so here = "greatly exalteth." The words are a quotation from Daniel 11:36.

against all that is called God—or, "against all that is said to be Divine," i.e., against the conception of deity, whether pagan, 1 Corinthians 8:5, Jewish, Deuteronomy 6:4, or Christian, 1 Corinthians 8:4, 6; cp. the equally comprehensive language of Daniel 11:36, 37; this similarity points to the identification of this mysterious person with the "willful King" of that chapter, cp. also 8:25; Ezekiel 28:2.

or that is worshiped;—*sebasma* = "an object of reverence," as in Acts 17:23.||

A corresponding verb, *sebazomai*, occurs only in Romans 1:25; another, *sebomai*, in Acts 13:43; 19:27, et al.; both = "to worship"; neither is used of men or angels, but only of gods, or idols, or of God. Thus religion in every form, idolatry as well as the worship of the true God, will fall under the ban of Antichrist.

so that—to such a length will his opposition to God and his self-exaltation carry him.

he—strongly emphatic, for *a*, the pronoun is expressed in orig., *b*, it stands at the beginning of the clause.

sitteth—point or momentary tense = "he takes his seat," as in Mark 16:19; Ephesians 1:20.

in—*eis*, lit., "into"; presenting this as the culminating act in his rebellious course.

the temple—*naos*, among the heathen = the shrine wherein the idol was put, Acts 17:24; 19:24; among the Jews = the sanctuary in the temple *(hieron)* at Jerusalem, Matthew 23:35, called also "the house," Luke 11:51 (marg.) only, and "the Holy [place]," Hebrews 9:2; into it only the priests could lawfully enter, Luke 1:9; Hebrews 9:6.

The entire edifice, with its courts, etc., was called the *hieron*, Matthew 4:5; 24:1, cp. Acts 19:27. Since He was of the tribe of Judah, and so not a priest at all while He was upon the earth, Hebrews 7:13, 14; 8:4, the Lord Jesus did not enter into the *naos;* it was in one of the courts of the *hieron*, to which all the people had access, that He sat and taught daily during His visits to the city, Luke 21:38; John 18:20. Of the two words *naos* only is used figuratively in the

New Testament The Lord Jesus used it of His own literal body, John 2:19, 21; Paul used it of the church, the mystical body of Christ, Ephesians 2:21, and of the church, the believers at Corinth, 1 Corinthians 3:16, 17; 2 Corinthians 6:16, and of the present body of the individual believer, 1 Corinthians 6:19. This is the word translated "temple" throughout the Revelation.

of God,—this further definition excludes any reference to a heathen temple. The words have been understood, *a,* literally, of the temple at Jerusalem; *b,* of a Christian building corresponding to the temple of the Jews; *c,* of all buildings throughout the world intended for Christian worship; *d,* figuratively, of the whole body of Christians on the earth at the time of the revelation of Antichrist.

In favor of *d* it may be urged that elsewhere the apostle speaks of the temple of God only in a figurative sense, and thus there is a presumption that he does not intend the phrase to be taken literally here. But on the other hand the Christians on the earth at any given time are not in the New Testament viewed as an organized body and are not called "the Temple of God." The figurative uses of the expression are noted above. Antichrist certainly could not in any conceivable sense "take his seat" in the church the body of Christ, which, while it is complete in the purpose of God, will not be manifested until the revelation of the Lord Jesus, 1:7–10, cp. Colossians 3:4, the time of his destruction, v. 8. And if he were to assert himself in any one company of Christians, he would command only local and limited attention, whereas it is implied in the passage that he will occupy the world stage and exert a worldwide influence.

Inasmuch as there is no other reference in the New Testament to any Christian ecclesiastical building, whether "temple" or "church," *b* and *c* may be dismissed.

Against the literal interpretation, *a,* may be urged the fact, already noted, that the phrase is not elsewhere used literally by the apostle Paul. That, however, does not preclude him from using it also in its current sense, Matthew 26:61.

More cogent, perhaps, is the consideration that the temple at Jerusalem was demolished by the Romans within twenty years of the writing of this epistle, while the Antichrist has not been manifested yet. But the temple in which the Lord taught, and the demolition of which he foretold, Matthew 24:2, was not that built by Solomon in obedience to divine command, 1 Chronicles 22:9, 10, but one built by Herod in succession thereto, yet the Lord Himself spoke of it as "My Father's House," John 2:16, 17. Old Testament prophecy pointed to a rebuilding of Solomon's temple which cannot have been fulfilled in Herod's, and which must, apparently, be still future, Ezekiel 37:26. If, and when, another temple is built at Jerusalem, it also will be "the Temple of God." On the whole, therefore, it may be concluded that the temple at Jerusalem was in the mind of the apostle, cp. Daniel 11:31; 12:4; Matthew 24:15.

setting himself forth—*apodeiknumi*, continuous tense; this is the course he will pursue after he has entered into and taken his seat in the temple of God. The word was in common use for the proclamation of a sovereign on his accession, or of an official on his entry into office. It occurs in 1 Corinthians 4:9 of a public spectacle. That this will not be an unsupported claim is implied in the word, cp. its use in Acts 2:22; 25:7, "approve," and "prove"; the corresponding noun is translated "demonstration" in 1 Corinthians 2:4. For Antichrist's "demonstration" see v. 9.||

as God.—lit., "that he is God"; the words do not mean that Antichrist will claim to be the God of the Bible, the God worshiped by the Jew and the Christian; had that been intended the article would probably have been inserted. Neither will he merely declare himself one among gods and lords many, as the Roman emperors did. Years before the apostle wrote, Julius Caesar was called "god made manifest . . . and savior of mankind," and Nero, years after, "the good god." Indeed it had become the custom for each successive Caesar to deify himself and Caesar worship was the state religion, from which dissent was not tolerated. Antichrist, following and improving upon this precedent, will, apparently, claim absolute and exclusive deity. Cp. the words of the Lord Jesus in John 5:43.

2:5 Remember ye not, that, when I was yet with you, I told you these things?—"told" is continuous tense, "I used to tell." A reproof, albeit of a kindly sort, and in tone different from that of Galatians 1:6; had they remembered his teaching they would not have been disturbed by these alarms.

Having dealt with the subject during his brief stay at Thessalonica, he was able when writing to avoid making definite statements which, had the letter fallen into the hands of their vigilant enemies, would have exposed the converts to charges of intriguing against the government. At the time of the disturbance which brought the visit of the missionaries to an abrupt termination, the charge made against them was political, namely, that they had said, "there is another king, one Jesus," Acts 17:7. This charge may have been based upon garbled reports of the apostle's teaching concerning the "willful King," and the king of God's kingdom, cp. 1 Timothy 1:17; Revelation 11:15–17. He had, perhaps, expounded and expanded such Scriptures as Psalm 2; Isaiah 32:1; Daniel chh. 8 and 11, in the light of the words of the Lord Jesus, such as those recorded in Matthew 16:28, and under the guidance of the Holy Spirit, who came for this very purpose, John 14:26; 16:13–15.

The difference between a letter and a treatise is that in the latter all that is necessary to make the writer's meaning clear is categorically stated, whereas in the former much that is common knowledge between the writer and those whom he addresses need only be alluded to. The letter, however, has this disadvantage that to those who do not share that knowledge the references and allusions are necessarily obscure. The obscurity in this instance is, no doubt, overruled to further larger ends, and it also makes dogmatism on the interpretation of the passage futile and foolish. The difficulties are further enhanced by the fact that, alike in form and in matter, the passage is without parallel in the other writings of this apostle. His own words "we know in part and we prophesy in part," 1 Corinthians 13:9, convey a salutary warning here.

The visit of the missionaries to Thessalonica was of short duration, but brief as was their time with the young church, part of it was given to this subject. Similarly, when the apostle John addresses the "little children" of the family of God, i.e., the young Christians, he also dwells on the Antichrist and the antichristian spirit, 1 John 2:18–27. Christianity is not a code of morals however spiritual. In Christ men are brought into communion with God; which is to say that in the new life the believer enters intelligently into God's purposes, becomes antagonistic to God's enemies, and joyfully anticipates God's ultimate triumph over all the forces of evil.

2:6 And now—the words may be understood, _a,_ in a temporal sense, in contrast with "his own season," cp. John 4:18; 16:22; _b,_ logically = "well, then," resuming the subject interrupted by the parenthesis, v. 5; cp. 1 John 2:28.

ye know—_oida,_ see notes at 1 Thessalonians 4:5; the oral instruction they had received would enable them to perceive the meaning of the apostle's words.

that which restraineth,—_katechō_ = to hold fast, actively and purposively, see note at 1 Thessalonians 5:21, and its use of things in 1 Corinthians 7:30; 2 Corinthians 6:10, and of a person in Philemon 13, cp. Romans 7:6; hence it also means "to restrain," as the multitude sought to restrain the movements of the Lord Jesus, Luke 4:42. There is a suggestive parallel to the present passage in Romans 1:18, which may be paraphrased, "unrighteous men who, in spite of what they know, or might know if they cared to learn, restrain the spread of truth by their unrighteousness." Here it is lawlessness that is said to be restrained in its development. The neuter participle is used, lit., "the restraining [thing]."

to the end that he—i.e., Antichrist, in whom the lawless spirit, now under a measure of restraint, will be fully developed and displayed.

may be revealed—see at v. 3.

in his own season.—i.e., then, and not before; the time will be ripe, the hour will come and the man with it. The word used is _kairos,_ see at 1 Thessalonians 5:1, for not the date but the characteristics of the period are in view. And since "the times and the seasons" are among the "secret things" of Deuteronomy

29:29, cp. Acts 1:7, speculations and calculations therefore are forbidden and are vain; see at 1 Thessalonians 5:2, and cp. 1 Timothy 6:14, 15.

2:7 For—introducing the reason why restraint is necessary and, by implication, accounting for their afflictions. Wherever the gospel is preached and believed there the lawless spirit begins its active opposition.

the mystery—*musterion,* in the New Testament = something that lies beyond human ken, and, consequently, that can become known to man only by revelation, including God, Job 11:7, and His ways, whether in providence, Romans 11:33–36, or in grace, Ephesians 3:8, 9. Hence it is associated with such words as "made known," "revealed," "manifested," "preached," "understanding," "dispensation," each of which declares the publication of the mystery with which it is associated. Indeed the apostle himself defines a mystery, in Romans 16:25, as that "which hath been kept in silence . . . but now is manifested . . . and made known." It is never = what cannot be known, or what is incomprehensible or "mysterious" in the usual sense of that word.

In the New Testament *musterion* is used of:

a, spiritual truth generally, as revealed in the gospel, 1 Corinthians 13:2; 14:2. Among the ancient Greeks "the mysteries" were religious rites and ceremonies practiced by secret societies into which anyone who so desired might be received. Those who were initiated into these "mysteries" became possessors of certain knowledge, which was not imparted to the uninitiated, and were called "the perfected," cp. 1 Corinthians 2:6–16 where the apostle has these "mysteries" in mind and presents the gospel in contrast thereto; here "the perfected" are, of course, the believers, who alone can perceive the things revealed, cp. John 3:3. The corresponding verb, *mueomai,* occurs only in Philippians 4:12, which may be paraphrased, "I have been initiated into the mystery of contentment."

b, Christ, who is God Himself revealed under the conditions of human life, Colossians 2:2; 4:3, and submitting even to death, 1 Corinthians 2:1–7, but raised from among the dead, 1 Timothy 3:16, that the will of God to coordinate the universe in Him, and subject it to Him, might in due time be accomplished, Ephesians 1:9, cp. Revelation 10:7, as is declared in the gospel, Romans 16:25; Ephesians 6:19:

c, the church, which is His, Christ's body, i.e., the union of redeemed men with God in Christ, Ephesians 5:32:

d, the rapture into the presence of Christ of those members of the church which is His body who shall be alive on the earth at His Parousia, 1 Corinthians 15:51:

e, the operation of those hidden forces that either retard or accelerate the kingdom of heaven (i.e., of God, see note at 1 Thessalonians 2:12), Matthew 13:11; Mark 4:11:

f, the cause of the present condition of Israel, Romans 11:25:

g, the spirit of disobedience to God, Revelation 17:5–7, and here, cp. Ephesians 2:2.

of lawlessness—lawlessness is not necessarily confusion and disorder, the idea intended is that it is the aim of the Devil and of "the spiritual hosts of wickedness in the heavenly places," Ephesians 6:11, 12, to overthrow the divine government.

doth——work:—*energeomai,* as in 1 Thessalonians 2:13.

already—i.e., even when these words were written the forces of evil had begun to draw together with this end in view, cp. 1 John 2:18.

only—introducing the explanation why the forces of evil do not manifest themselves, and prescribing the limit set to their operation.

there is—words inserted to complete the sense in English; the marginal rendering is "only until he that now restraineth be taken out of the way."

one that restraineth now,—lit., "the restrainer." This may refer either, *a,* to an individual, cp. such titles as "the Deliverer," 1 Thessalonians 1:10, "the Tempter," 3:5; or *b,* to a number of individuals presenting the same characteristics, cp. "the believer," i.e., all believers, Romans 9:33; 1 John 5:10, et al.

In v. 6 a principle is referred to, here that principle is presented as embodied in a person or persons. Illustrative parallels occur in Romans 13:3, 4, "the power . . . he is a minister of God," i.e., the power is wielded by the ruler, and 2 Timothy 2:16, "shun profane babblings: for they will proceed further in ungodliness," i.e., those who babble profanely will proceed, etc. So here, "that which restraineth" = the restraining principle; "he that restraineth" = the person or persons in whom it is expressed. For further illustrations see Daniel 7:17, 23; Matthew 13:18–23; and Galatians 1:5, 9, where see note.

until he be taken—*ginomai,* as in 1 Thessalonians 1:5, where it is translated, first, "came," and second, "shewed"; lit., the words run, "until he, or it, become"; the tense is momentary.

out of the way.—*ek mesou,* lit., "out of the midst." In every other New Testament occurrence the accompanying verb signifies removal, as in 1 Corinthians 5:2; Colossians 2:14, "take," 2 Corinthians 6:17, "come," here it does not, see above.

Many attempts have been made to identify this restraining power, but the conditions are such that these can be little more than speculative. The following suggestions, among others, have been made:

a, The Man of Sin is Nero; the restrainer the wise Seneca, his tutor, whose death he ultimately procured. This is quite inadequate; moreover, what is restrained is not the Man of Sin but the lawless spirit which finally produces him.

b, The restrainer is the Holy Spirit; that which restrains is the church; the time of the taking away is the rapture described in 1 Thessalonians 4:13–17. This interpretation is without support in other parts of the New Testament Matthew 5:13 has been appealed to, "ye are the salt of the earth," but the idea expressed in the remainder of the saying is, not that the salt shall be removed, but that it may lose its distinctive character and thus cease to hinder corruption. Neither is it elsewhere stated or implied that the Holy Spirit will leave the earth at the rapture of the saints, for after that event there will be those upon the earth who will witness for God, see Revelation 11:3, 4; 13:7, etc., in the energy of the Holy Spirit, see Joel 2:28, 29. Yet this interpretation demands not merely that the Holy Spirit change the mode of His operations but that He leave the world entirely. Moreover had the Holy Spirit and the church been in the writer's mind there does not appear to be any reason why he should not have said so plainly; see note on v. 5. The suggestion seems to be of quite modern origin, there is, apparently, no trace of it in early writings on the subject.

c, The restrainer is God, that which restrains, the countless operations of His providence. This interpretation is not embarrassed with the difficulty that the verb *ginomai* seems quite incapable of the translation "removed," "be taken." Moreover it gives a good sense to the passage as rendered in the second of the paraphrases suggested in the first paragraph of the note at v. 8. The difficulty here also is to find a reason why the apostle did not express himself in plain terms if this is what he meant.

d, The restraint is the Roman Empire and policy; the restrainer, the Roman emperors and their representatives. But the Roman Empire has passed away and yet the Antichrist has not been revealed, nor has the Lord Jesus come.

e, It may be, however, that the apostle alluded to Gentile dominion, the course of which had been outlined by the Prophet Daniel: "Thou, O King . . . unto whom the God of heaven hath given the kingdom, the power, and the strength, and the glory, and wheresoever the children of men dwell, . . . hath made thee to rule over them all: . . . And after thee shall arise another kingdom . . . and another third kingdom . . . and (a) fourth kingdom . . . it shall be a divided kingdom . . . And in the days of those kings . . ." Daniel 2:37–44. In due time the Babylonian Empire, to whose king the words were spoken, was succeeded by the Persian, that by the Grecian, and that again by the Roman, which flourished in the apostle's day, and which was afterwards divided into a number of separate states, as Daniel foresaw would be the case. Nevertheless dominion remains in the hands of the Gentiles, and will remain "until the times of the Gentiles be fulfilled," Luke 21:24. The laws under which these states maintain their existence were inherited from Rome as Rome inherited them from the empires that preceded her. Thus the existing authorities are ordained of God, Romans 13:1–7; 1 Peter 2:13–17. "Law is for the lawless," 1 Timothy 1:9, i.e., constituted authority is intended to act in restraint of lawlessness. The Lord Jesus Himself reminded the Roman governor of this fact when he was about to abuse the trust committed to him, see John 19:11. The local representatives of Roman authority interposed to save Paul from mob violence at Corinth, Acts 18:12–17, and at Jerusalem, 21:27–36, and protected him at Thessalonica, 17:9; fear of it quelled the excited populace at Ephesus, 19:40; and to its highest tribunal, Caesar himself, Paul, fearing miscarriage of justice at Jerusalem, made his appeal, 25:6–12.

If, then, constituted government was in his mind, the wisdom of indefiniteness is obvious; he would not again give their alert and unscrupulous enemies ground on which to base a charge of political intrigue.

It is true that the Roman emperors, men of the type of Nero, presented some of the characteristics of the Antichrist. Themselves the representatives of the law, they were yet at heart lawless, aiming to assert a personal supremacy over law, though with never more than trifling success. The individual ruler passed, but the state, based on and ordered by law, remains. When the appointed days of Gentile dominion have run their course, Luke 21:24, this restraint will cease, and the individual, probably a Jew, see Daniel 11:37, "Neither shall he regard the gods [so R.V.] of his fathers," does not seem sufficient ground for the deduction that the Antichrist must be of Jewish race, sufficiently gifted to recognize the opportunity and to seize it, will assert a personal ascendancy over the law, and, finally, "raising the standard of atheistic pantheism will proclaim himself the incarnation of the Absolute," and so become at once the political head of the nations, and the object of their worship.

2:8 And then shall be revealed the lawless one,—see at vv. 3–7.

For two reasons the English versions of these words cannot be called successful translations; *a,* as already noticed, *ginomai* never elsewhere means "to be removed," and, *b,* its nominative is not expressed in orig. Hence this is a case in which any translation is bound to be an interpretation. It would be possible to paraphrase thus: "only [there is] a restrainer now [who will restrain] until out of the midst [of the human race] there come to be, and then [come] to be revealed, the Lawless One." Or thus—"only [there is] a restrainer now [who will restrain] until it, i.e., lawlessness, show itself (as at 1 Thess. 1:5), out of the midst [no longer an influence working in secret but a characteristic of the age], and then shall be revealed the Lawless One." These alternative translations, however, do not solve the problem of the reference of the apostle; either would be quite consistent with the interpretation suggested above.

whom the Lord Jesus—the personal name, emphasizing the identity of Him who dispenses this judgment with the One who "was born under [the] law," Galatians 4:4, cp. Matthew 3:15.

shall slay—or, as in marg. and in A.V., "consume," a "various reading," cp. Jeremiah 25:30, 31.

with the breath of His mouth,—quoted from Isaiah 11:4, LXX, "with the breath of His lips shall He slay the impious one"; a vivid metaphorical statement of the effect of His voice, cp. Job 4:9; Psalm 29:3-6; 33:6.

and bring to nought—*katargeō* = to render inactive, or useless, as the barren fig tree did the ground it occupied, Luke 13:7, and as the death of Christ makes ineffective, prospectively, the power of the Devil, Hebrews 2:14.
    Elsewhere in the New Testament this word occurs only in Paul's writings; he uses it of:
    a, the transitory brightness on Moses' face, 2 Corinthians 3:7, 11, 13, and of the symbolic veil wherewith it was hidden, v. 14:
    b, the effect of maturity of mind on the interests of childhood, 1 Corinthians 13:11:
    c, the end of physical appetite, 1 Corinthians 6:13:
    d, the transitory character of gifts in the churches, 1 Corinthians 13:8, 10:
    e, the effect of a husband's death on a marriage contract, Romans 7:2, cp. v. 6:
    f, the effect of the death of Christ upon the religious barrier between Jew and Gentile, Ephesians 2:15:
    g, the effect of death with Christ upon the body of sin in the believer (the body of sin = sin viewed as an organized power acting through the members of the body; but the seat of sin is in the will, not in the body), Romans 6:6:
    h, the effect of the ultimate triumph of Christ upon all rule that does not own direct allegiance to God, 1 Corinthians 15:24, cp. 2:6; 1:28:
    i, the ultimate triumph of Christ over death, 1 Corinthians 15:26; 2 Timothy 1:10:
    j, the effect of seeking justification by works upon the relation of men to Christ, Galatians 5:4; and the effect of preaching it upon the Cross, the essential element in the gospel, v. 11:

And with a negative, of:

k, the effect of the preaching of salvation by faith upon the law, Romans 3:31:

l, the effect of the giving of the law on the preceding covenants and promises of God, Romans 4:14; Galatians 3:17:

m, the effect of the unbelief of men on the faithfulness of God, Romans 3:3. Here it is used of the effect upon the Lawless One of the appearing of the Lord in glory.||

by the manifestation—*epiphaneai*, English "epiphany," lit., "a shining forth"; it was used of the appearance of a god to men, and of an enemy to an army in the field, etc. In the New Testament it occurs of:

a, the advent of the Savior when the word became flesh, 2 Timothy 1:10:

b, the coming of the Lord Jesus into the air to the meeting with His saints, 1 Timothy 6:14; 2 Timothy 4:1, 8:

c, the shining forth of the glory of the Lord Jesus "as the lightning cometh forth from the east, and is seen even unto the west," Matthew 24:27, immediately consequent on the unveiling, *apokalupsis*, of His Parousia in the air with His saints, Titus 2:13, and here.||

The corresponding verb, *epiphainō*, is used of the stars, Acts 27:20, and of the grace, Titus 2:11, kindness and love, 3:4, of God made manifest in the coming of His Son for the salvation of men, see also Luke 1:79.||

of his coming;—*parousia*, as at 1 Thessalonians 2:19; this event brings the period so termed to an end and ushers in the millennial reign of the Lord Jesus.

The contrast is vividly presented: the presumption and arrogance of the Man of Sin, paralyzed by a look and a word from the Lord Jesus!

2:9 *even he,* **whose coming**—*parousia;* the italicized words supply the subject which the writer had not expressed; the context makes the reference to the Lawless One quite evident.

The apostle, having carried his readers directly to the climax toward which the forces of evil and of good are even now working, returns to indicate the hidden source of the Antichrist's power, and to describe the way in which he will manifest it, and the effect upon men generally. Antichrist's "parousia," in strict accord with the meaning of the word, is the period of his supremacy, beginning with his revelation to the world, vv. 6–8, and ending as just described.

is according to the working—*energeia*, English "energy"; cp. the corresponding verb in v. 7. The same word is used of the power of God at work in the resurrection of Christ, Ephesians 1:19; Colossians 2:12; and in the call and induement of the apostle Paul, Ephesians 3:7; Colossians 1:29; and of the power of Christ, universally, Philippians 3:21, and in the church particularly, Ephesians 4:16. See also v. 11, below.||

of Satan—see at 1 Thessalonians 2:18, and cp. Daniel 8:24, "but not by his, i.e., Antichrist's, own power." Here is revealed the instigator and energizer of all the evil that now works in secret, and that is shortly to be developed as already described.

with all—in every kind of.

power—*dunamis,* as in 1:11.

and signs—*sēmeion,* a token or indication, whether given by man to man, 3:17; Matthew 26:48; or appointed by God to be observed by man, as circumcision was, Romans 4:11; or whether given by God in natural phenomena, Luke 21:25, or in the trend of human affairs, Matthew 16:3, or through His Son, John 2:11; 20:30, or His servants, Acts 5:12; 7:36; or whether given by Satan through his agents, Matthew 24:24; Revelation 16:14, and here.

and——wonders,—*teras* = something strange, exceptional, causing the beholder to marvel.

These words occur together concerning the works of the Lord Jesus, Acts 2:22, and of His apostles, Romans 15:19; 2 Corinthians 12:12; Hebrews 2:4. They describe the same act or event from different standpoints. "Power" declares its source to be supernatural; "sign" expresses its purpose and appeals to the understanding, "wonder" describes its effect upon the observer and appeals to the imagination. The last is the least important idea and hence "wonder" is never used save in association with "sign," though "sign" and "power" are each found alone, Mark 6:5; John 6:26, e.g.

lying—*pseudos,* false; not that the miracles will be fraudulent, produced by clever trickery; they will be real miracles, but their purpose will be to deceive men into acknowledging Antichrist's spurious claim to deity. The words may be paraphrased: "with a display of every kind of power, that is to say, with signs and wonders calculated to deceive," cp. Revelation 13:13–15.

2:10 and with all [lit., in every] **deceit of unrighteousness**—Antichrist and his servants will not be restrained by any scruple from words or acts whereby men may be deceived. "Unrighteous" and "lawless" are synonyms.

for them that are perishing;—lit., "the perishing," present continuous tense, as in 1 Corinthians 1:18, etc.; cp. note on the corresponding noun, "perdition," at v. 3 above. Antichrist and his deluded supporters, since they share a common character and shall share a common doom, are appropriately described by the same term.

because—*anth'hōn*, introducing the reason why "the perishing" are so readily deceived. The phrase, which is an infrequent one, conveys the idea of recompense; cp. "because he gave not God the glory," Acts 12:23.

they received not—*dechomai*, see notes at 1 Thessalonians 1:6, and 2:13, "accepted." Cp. "them that obey not," 1:8; in both places it is evident the apostle had in view those who had had the gospel declared to them.

the love of the truth,—i.e., love for the truth, described more fully as "the word of the truth of the gospel," Colossians 1:5. Absence of desire for truth is evidence of moral obliquity, and is thus to be distinguished from failure to attain to, or to receive, the knowledge of truth. Cp. the following:

- knowledge of the truth, Hebrews 10:26:
- belief of (the) truth, v. 13, below:
- obedience to (lit., of) the truth, 1 Peter 1:22:
- manifestation of the truth, 2 Corinthians 4:2.

(In this latter passage there is, perhaps, an allusion to Exodus 28:30, where for "Urim and Thummim" LXX has "manifestation and truth".)

that they might be saved.—cp. 1 Thessalonians 2:16. Having no love for the truth they remain in ignorance alike of their danger and of the way of escape therefrom. "Smooth things," Isaiah 30:10, such as "peace and safety," 1 Thessalonians 5:3, are more agreeable to men, Jeremiah 5:31, than is the stern truth of the certainty of the judgment of God.

2:11 And for this cause—i.e., their distaste for truth, their love for darkness rather than for light, John 3:19.

God sendeth them—the present tense is used because the mystery of lawlessness is already working and this retributive judgment of God is even now in force; cp. Romans 11:8, and ct. 2 Corinthians 4:4.

a working—*energeia*, as in v. 9; contrast the working of the truth in those who accept the message of the gospel, 1 Thessalonians 2:13. Cp. Isaiah 30:28.

of error,—as at 1 Thessalonians 2:3, where see note. When men persistently refuse to obey the truth they soon become incapable of perceiving it. It was because men refused to have God in their knowledge that He gave them up to a reprobate mind, i.e., a mind bound to lead them astray, inasmuch as it was no longer controlled by Him, Romans 1:28. But plainly more is intended than merely to say that God permits men to be deceived, cp. Ezekiel 14:1-9, and 1 Kings 22:19-23. The retributive justice of God is not arbitrary; sin and its punishment are related as cause and effect. Every violation of God's laws brings inevitably its own peculiar consequences. And inasmuch as God is the source of the laws under which men live, He is also the source of all the consequences to men of their violation of those laws.

that they should believe—lit., unto the believing, i.e., with the foreseen and intended result that they should believe.

a [lit., the] **lie**—with specific reference to the lie of v. 4, viz., that man is God; cp. also Genesis 3:5, and Romans 1:25. See also John 8:44, lit., the lie. Cp. Revelation 17:17.

2:12 that—*hina*, in order that, see at 1 Thessalonians 5:4.

they all might be judged—the verb here, *krinō*, corresponds with the noun used in 1:5; its use in the New Testament may be analyzed as follows:
    a, to assume the office of a judge, Matthew 7:1; John 3:17:
    b, to undergo process of trial, John 3:18; 16:11; 18:31; James 2:12;
    c, to give sentence in a suit, Acts 15:19; 16:4; 21:25:
    d, to condemn, John 12:48; Acts 13:27; Romans 2:27:
    e, to execute judgment upon, here and Acts 7:7; Revelation 18:20.
    f, to be involved in a lawsuit, whether as plaintiff, Matthew 5:40; 1 Corinthians 6:1, or as defendant, Acts 23:6:
    g, to administer affairs, to govern, Matthew 19:28, cp. Judges 3:10:
    h, to form an opinion, Luke 7:43; John 7:24; Acts 4:19; Romans 14:5:
    i, to make a resolve, Acts 3:13; 20:16; 1 Corinthians 2:2.

who believed not the truth,—i.e., because they refused to believe it; the negative, *mē*, used here, expresses more than the fact that they did not believe the truth, what exposed them to this judgment was their refusal to believe it; cp. 1:8.

but had pleasure—as in 1 Thessalonians 2:8 = free and deliberate choice. Cp. Romans 1:32, and ct. 1 Corinthians 13:6.

in unrighteousness.—the sin that involves men in this catastrophe is not intellectual, unwillingness to exercise the reasoning powers; it is moral, the love of evil. Distaste for the truth leads to its rejection; God in retributive justice sends a working of error to those who love error, this they gladly accept, yielding themselves to it and cooperating with it until they are overtaken by the climax in which the righteous judgment of God is expressed.

    In this section of the epistle are foreshadowed the final developments of the two great spiritual forces that have been at work in the world from the beginning, and their final conflict and its result. In the little that emerges from the obscurity that necessarily enshrouds the future it may be discerned that the evil continues to simulate and to oppose the good. The Trinity of persons in the Godhead, 2 Corinthians 13:14, is travestied by an operative trinity of evil, Revelation 16:13; Antichrist is Satan's counterfeit of, and substitute for, the Christ of God. Their motives and objects are as the poles apart; the mystery of godliness is expressed in Christ, 1 Timothy 3:16, the mystery of lawlessness in Antichrist, v. 7. Christ humbled Himself; Philippians 2:8, Antichrist exalts himself, v. 4; Christ came to serve and to save, Mark 10:45; John 10:10, Antichrist comes to domineer and to destroy, Daniel 11:39; John 10:10; Christ came to do His Father's will, John 4:34, Antichrist comes to do his own, Daniel 11:36. The true Christ wrought miracles, Acts 2:22, but by the power of the Spirit of God, Matthew 12:28; Acts 10:38; Antichrist will work miracles, but by the power of Satan, v. 9. The true Christ is to be king, but for God, and He will rule in righteousness, Psalm 2:6; Isaiah 32:1; Antichrist will be a king, but for the Evil One, Revelation 13:2, 12, and he will rule in arrogant selfishness, Daniel 11. Christ is the holy and righteous One. Acts 3:14, Antichrist is the Man of Sin, the lawless one. The symbols of the Apocalypse declare them each in his true character: Christ is the lamb, Antichrist is a wild beast.

2:13 But we are bound to give thanks to God alway for you,—as at 1:3; here, however, the nominative, "we," is expressed in Greek, and where this is the case it is usually intended to bear emphasis. The apostle may intend to suggest a comparison between himself and his companions on the one hand, and those who persecuted the converts at Thessalonica on the other. In view of the ultimate issue just described, the missionaries gave thanks to God for those who, since they were the objects of His grace and of the love of the Lord Jesus, would escape the doom of Antichrist.

brethren beloved of the lord, cp. 1 Thessalonians 1:4. "Lord" = Christ, see note at 1 Thessalonians 3:12. That the love of God is the love of Christ, cp. Romans 8:35 with v. 39. A further contrast is thus suggested; though men might hate them, they were the objects of the love of Him who will one day triumph over all His and their enemies; the safety of the beloved of the Lord is thus assured, cp. Deuteronomy 33:12.

Whereas in the New Testament the world is frequently said to be the object of the love of God, John 3:16; Romans 5:8, e.g., it is never said to be the object of the love of Christ. His love to the world was expressed in His death, indeed, but, save in the incident recorded in Mark 10:21, His love is always mentioned with reference to those who believe, whether individually, Galatians 2:20, or collectively, the local church, Revelation 3:9, and the church which is His body, Ephesians 5:25.

for that—*hoti,* as at 1 Thessalonians 2:13, see note at 1:3.

God chose you—*haireomai* = to choose for oneself; the tense is momentary. The word occurs again at Philippians 1:22; Hebrews 11:25, but in each case of human choice. Paul's usual words are *proorizō*, lit., to mark out beforehand, as in Ephesians 1:5, and *eklegomai*, as in Ephesians 1:4; for the latter see note at 1 Thessalonians 1:4. *Haireomai* is found in Deuteronomy 7:6, 7; 26:18, LXX, as here, of the divine choice.||

At 1 Thessalonians 2:13, the reason ascribed for thanksgiving was that the gospel message had been accepted as from God; here the apostle, penetrating into the secret of the divine sovereignty, gives thanks because God had chosen those who had accepted the message. They had chosen God, indeed, but only because God had first chosen them; cp. Philip who found Christ, but not until Christ had first found Philip, John 1:43–45.

from the beginning—*ap'archēs*, two interpretations are possible, *a*, that the words refer to the first preaching of the gospel at Thessalonica, "the beginning of the gospel," cp. Philippians 4:15; and, *b*, that God's eternal counsels are intended, cp. Revelation 13:8 (where marg. is to be preferred, cp. 17:8). Against *a* is the fact that Paul does not elsewhere speak of the election of men unto salvation taking place in time; what takes place in time is God's call, see next verse. In favor of *b* is the fact that this idea is common in his writings, though, indeed, he does not elsewhere use this expression, preferring others such as "before the ages," 1 Corinthians 2:7, "before the foundation of the world," Ephesians 1:4, "before times eternal," 2 Timothy 1:9.

There is, however, an alternative reading, which is well supported and gives a good sense. This is *aparchēn (aparchē)* = "firstfruits." Though the English word is plural in each of its occurrences save Romans 11:16, the Greek word is always singular. Two Hebrew words are thus translated, one meaning the chief or principal part, Numbers 18:12; Proverbs 3:9, et al.; the other the earliest ripe of the crop or of the tree, Exodus 23:16; Nehemiah 10:35, et al.; they are found together in Exodus 23:19, et al., "the first of the firstfruits." The term is applied in things spiritual:

a, to the presence of the Holy Spirit with the believer as the firstfruits of the full harvest of the Cross, Romans 8:23:

b, to Christ Himself in resurrection in relation to all who have fallen asleep believing in Him, 1 Corinthians 15:20–23:

c, to the earliest believers in a country in relation to those of their countrymen who believe later, Romans 16:5; 1 Corinthians 16:15:

d, to the believers of this age in relation to the whole of the redeemed, here and James 1:18. Cp. also Revelation 14:4.||

unto salvation—see on 1 Thessalonians 5:9; here, as there, with reference to the delusions of Antichrist, and the doom of the deluded.

in sanctification—*hagiasmos,* see note at 1 Thessalonians 4:3.

of the Spirit—notwithstanding the absence of the article in orig. the reference is to the Holy Spirit as in Romans 8:9; 1 Corinthians 2:4; and see the parallel passage, 1 Peter 1:2, where "Spirit" is again without the article but where the mention of the Father and the Son make it plain that the Holy Spirit is intended. See note at 1 Thessalonians 1:5.

The Holy Spirit is said to be the agent in sanctification in Romans 15:16; 1 Peter 1:2, and here, only, cp. also 1 Corinthians 6:11. Here and in 1 Peter 1:2 the sanctification of the Spirit is associated with the choice, or election, of God; it is a divine act preceding the acceptance of the gospel by the individual. The other passages are best understood in harmony with these.

The fuller statement of 1 Peter 1:2 may be paraphrased thus: "to those who were elected according to the foreknowledge of God the Father, and set apart by the Holy Spirit that they might obey the truth [see v. 22] and so come under the shelter of the sprinkled blood of Jesus Christ."

and belief of the truth:—lit., "of truth"; where the article is present the particular fact or facts presented to the mind are in view; where it is absent the moral quality of these facts is the point. The will to believe truth is the necessary condition precedent before any work of God can begin in the soul; cp. the words of the Lord Jesus, "if any man willeth to do His will He shall know of the teaching," John 7:17.

The faculty whereby truth is recognized grows with its exercise; on the other hand the ministry of the Holy Spirit, which begins with revealing the truth of the gospel to the individual, continues to guide the believer into all truth, John 16:13, "renewing him unto knowledge," Colossians 3:10; hence the apostle's prayers for the converts in Philippians 1:9, 10; Colossians 1:9, which see. When they were called through the gospel, it was that they "might know the truth and that the truth might make them free," John 8:32. Only love of truth can save a man from the working of error.

2:14 whereunto—lit., into which, i.e., into which salvation.

He called you—like "chose" above, "called" is in the point tense, describing a single act. Ct. the present tense, "calleth," in 1 Thessalonians 2:12; 5:24.

through our gospel,—i.e., by means of the gospel preached by us; see notes at 1 Thessalonians 1:5; 2:2. This refers to the time when God in His providence brought His servants to Thessalonica, and made His electing grace effectual through their ministry.

to the obtaining—as at 1 Thessalonians 5:9; these words with those that follow define the "salvation" of the preceding clause; the grace that laid the foundation in eternity past will crown the edifice in due season.

of the glory—*doxa*, as at 1:9, 1 Thessalonians 2:6, 12, 20; the range of meaning of the word in the New Testament is wide, here = the outward and visible expression of what is inward and essential.

of our Lord Jesus Christ.—New Testament references to the glory of the Lord Jesus may be classified as those which speak of, *a*, that glory which is His in virtue of His Deity, *b*, that which He displayed during "the days of His Flesh" and, *c*, that which is His because of accomplished redemption. To *a* belong such passages as Luke 9:32; 2 Peter 1:17, His transfiguration, when what was veiled was permitted to shine forth, and Luke 9:26, His unveiled appearing in the heavens at His return; this is the glory He had with the Father before the world had any existence, John 17:5, cp. 1:1, 2. To *b* belong John 1:14; 2 Corinthians 3:18, where the moral expression of what He is essentially is intended, cp. Revelation 22:23. To *c* belong Philippians 3:21, the glory of His resurrection body, 1 Timothy 3:16, the circumstances attending His ascension, and Luke 24:26; John 17:24; Hebrews 2:9; 1 Peter 1:21, the glory given Him by the Father therein.

Here the reference is to the glory of the revelation of the Lord from heaven, 1:7-10, in which the believers are to share, see Colossians 3:4. Unlike their afflictions, which would pass, this glory would be their abiding possession, in prospect whereof the apostle comforted and stimulated himself, 2 Corinthians 4:17, and others, Romans 8:17, 18; 2 Timothy 2:10. For the whole passage cp. 1 Peter 5:10, and note its correspondence with Romans 8:29, 30:

foreknown and ⎫ foreordained ⎭ chosen	
called	called
justified	in belief of the truth
glorified	obtaining of glory

In the light of its use in the Old Testament with the ineffable name, Jehovah, and particularly of such passages as Isaiah 48:11, the association of "glory" with the Lord Jesus in the New Testament is clear testimony to the apostolic belief in His deity; cp. "King of glory," Psalm 24:7-10, "God of glory," Psalm 29:3; Acts 7:2, and "Father of glory," Ephesians 1:17, with "Lord of glory," in 1 Corinthians 2:8; James 2:1.

2:15 So then, brethren,—since they were assured of the sovereign grace of God in their election, and of its certain issue in glory, the apostle urges upon them the reasonableness of ordering their lives in accordance with the eternal purposes of God rather than with the antagonistic spirit of lawlessness, under the temporary ascendancy of which they suffered.

stand fast,—lit., "stand," continuous tense; see note at 1 Thessalonians 3:8. Here he puts positively what he had expressed negatively at the opening of the section, v. 2, "be not quickly shaken."

and hold—*krateō*, lit., "to exert strength upon," whether by the hand, Matthew 9:25; 28:9, or by the mind, Mark 7:3; 9:10, "kept," or by authority, John 20:23, "retain," or by other means, Luke 24:16. Believers are to hold, i.e., to grasp firmly in the mind and the affections:

- Christ, the Head of the Church, Colossians 2:19:
- His Name, Revelation 2:13:
- His sayings, Mark 9:10:
- the confession of Christ, Hebrews 4:14:
- the hope of which He is the object, Hebrews 6:18:
- the apostolic teaching, here, and cp. Revelation 2:25.

See also note on "hold fast" at 1 Thessalonians 5:21, where, however, the Greek word is *katechō*, for which see note on "restraineth," v. 6.

the traditions which ye were taught,—*paradosis*, lit., "a handing on," is used in the New Testament of the teachings of the Jewish rabbis, Matthew 15:2; Galatians 1:14; Colossians 2:8, whose interpretations of the Old Testament were transmitted orally from one generation to another, and were only committed to writing at a much later period.

Its use, by the apostle, of Christian doctrine is at once a denial that what he preached originated with himself and a claim for its divine authority; cp. his use of the corresponding verb, *paradidōmi*, to transmit, to hand over, and the complementary verb, *paralambanō*, to receive, in 1 Corinthians 11:23; 15:3. He received the doctrine he taught, not from man but "through revelation of Jesus Christ," Galatians 1:12. In this way, whether through Paul or through the other apostles, was "the faith . . . once for all delivered, *paradidōmi*, unto the saints," Jude 3.

At the outset, and for twenty years thereafter, there is no evidence that anything was committed to writing whether by the apostles or by their colleagues, but before the last of the apostles had passed away each book of the New Testament had been written and was in circulation, more or less wide, among the churches. Not until a later date, however, were the separate books brought together to form one volume.

The whole of the apostolic "teaching," Acts 2:42, or "tradition" (the words cover the same ground in this connection) that has been preserved for the churches in the providence of God, is contained in the Canonical Scriptures of the New Testament Each book thereof has a well established claim to its place, and for no other writing has it ever been possible to establish even a doubtful one.

Nor has any new revelation been made to men since the close of the apostolic age. Teachings, oral and written, which have claimed to come from God, either contradict the plain teaching of the Canonical writings, in which case they stand condemned, or merely repeat what is contained therein, in which case they are superfluous.

Here the "traditions" are matters of doctrine, in 3:6, they are instructions concerning everyday conduct, and in 1 Corinthians 11:2 concerning the gatherings of the saints. Thus the word occurs in this good sense only in the early writings of the apostle. In his latest epistles he speaks of the doctrine as "the deposit," 1 Timothy 6:20; 2 Timothy 1:12, 14 (in each case the marg. is to be preferred).

whether by word,—i.e., during the visit of the missionaries.

or by epistle—i.e., since that visit; cp. v. 2. He refers here to the first epistle, and particularly to the section 4:13–18, concerning which see note on "word of the Lord," v. 15.

of ours.—these words are to be joined with both "word" and "epistle," not merely with the latter. Two important deductions may be made from this exhortation; first, that the era of the oral transmission of the faith was passing in favor of the more secure literary transmission; and, second, that the "traditions" were not separate and distinct from the written word; the former gave place to the latter, the latter contained the former. There is therefore no body of authoritative tradition separate and distinct from the Bible, as some claim to be the case.

2:16 Now—*de*, lit., but, as at 1 Thessalonians 3:11; 5:23, where see notes.

our Lord Jesus Christ himself, and God our Father—as at 1 Thessalonians 3:11; 5:23, so here, "Himself" occupies a position of emphasis, and for the same purpose. The powers of evil so far outmatch the saints in subtlety and strength that the fullest knowledge of the progress of evil and the doom of Antichrist would itself avail them little. Once again, therefore, the apostle commends them to God that they might be by Him directly cheered and maintained in the evil day.

At 1 Thessalonians 3:11, "Himself" refers to the Father, here to the Lord Jesus, which is yet another indication of the place He held in the thoughts of the apostle. Here, moreover, the name of the Son precedes that of the Father, as in 2 Corinthians 13:14; it is by the grace of the Son that the revelation of the Father is made, cp. Matthew 11:27.

which loved us—*agapaō*, as at v. 13, where see note. Here the momentary tense refers, not to any definite period, nor to any historical manifestation of love, but to the love of God viewed as timeless and immutable, as in Ephesians 2:4, "God . . . for His great love wherewith He loved us." The verb is singular, and though it might properly be connected with "God our Father" alone, yet it is perhaps better to take it as referring to both, cp. v. 13, "beloved of the Lord," and 1 Thessalonians 1:4, "beloved of God."

The love of God the Father is seen in this, that He sent His Son to be the propitiation for our sins, 1 John 4:10, and in that He quickened us with Him, and raised us up with Him, and made us to sit in the heavens in Christ Jesus, Ephesians 2:4–6. The love of the Son is seen in this, that He laid down His life for us, 1 John 3:16.

and gave us——through [lit., in] **grace,**—i.e., freely, not in discharge of obligation but without constraint of any kind. The tense again is "point," fixing the attention on the time when the love was manifested in the coming of Christ into the world. Had the reference been to the preaching of the gospel at Thessalonica "you" would have been the appropriate word, not "us."

eternal—as at 1:9; the future of the afflicted is thus set in contrast with that of their persecutors. Moreover, the affliction is transient, the recompense is permanent; cp. Romans 8:18.

comfort—*paraklēsis*, as at 1 Thessalonians 2:3, "exhortation"; cp. also note *c* on the corresponding verb at 1 Thessalonians 2:11. Here it means not merely alleviation of grief, it carries also the thought of encouragement.

Sources of encouragement to the believer are:

a, God, 2 Corinthians 1:3:

b, Christ, Philippians 2:1:

c, the Holy Spirit, Acts 9:31, cp. John 14:16:

d, the Scriptures, Romans 15:4:

e, the brethren, 2 Corinthians 7:6, 7; Colossians 4:11.

and good—*agathos*, as at 1 Thessalonians 5:15, and cp. "goodness," 1:11. The hope is said to be good because of its cheering and sustaining effect on him who cherishes it.

hope—here, as in the great majority of its occurrences in the New Testament, describes, *a*, the happy anticipation of good; in two places it seems rather to indicate, *b*, the ground upon which hope is based, Acts 16:19; Colossians 1:27 (where "in you,"); and in a few others, *c*, the object upon which the hope is fixed is intended, see Acts 23:6; 26:6, 7; Galatians 5:5; Ephesians 1:18; 2:12; 4:4; Colossians 1:5, 23; 1 Timothy 1:1; Titus 2:13.

The element of uncertainty, with the consequent possibility of disappointment, which is of the essence of all hope among men, has no place in the hope of the Christian, cp. "we know" with "this hope" in 1 John 3:2, 3.

Three adjectives are used to qualify "hope," in the New Testament: "good," here, and "living," 1 Peter 1:3, where hope belongs to *a* above; and "blessed," Titus 2:13, where it belongs to *c,* above, and points to the "appearing of the glory of our great God and Savior Jesus Christ."

2:17 comfort—see note *c* at 1 Thessalonians 2:11, and on v. 16 above. Notwithstanding that two names are united to form the subject, this verb is in the singular number, as is "stablish," below. For the inference as to the deity of the Lord Jesus Christ see note on "direct" at 1 Thessalonians 3:11.

your hearts—see note at 1 Thessalonians 2:4.

and stablish them—see note at 1 Thessalonians 3:2; ct. "shaken," v. 2, above.

in every good—as above = beneficial, useful, helpful.

work and word.—the order is significant, practice should precede precept, cp. Philippians 2:15, 16, "among whom ye are seen as lights—holding forth the word," and the testimony concerning the Lord Jesus, Luke 24:19; Acts 1:1, cp. 10:38. The phrase comprehends the whole of Christian conduct, private and pubic; in this connection the reverse order, "word—deed," is found only in Colossians 3:17.

2 THESSALONIANS

▪ CHAPTER THREE ▪

Verses 1–18

3:1 Finally, brethren,—see note at 1 Thessalonians 4:1.

pray for us,—see note at 1 Thessalonians 5:25.

that the word of the Lord—i.e., of Christ; see note at 1 Thessalonians 1:8.

may run—a metaphor expressive of free and rapid progress, found also in Psalm 147:15; the same idea is expressed negatively at 2 Timothy 2:9. Cp. the saying "the King's writ runs in such a place," i.e., the King's authority is acknowledged there.

and be glorified,—the preceding word expresses the apostle's desire that the authority of God might be acknowledged in the submission of men to His claims as declared in the gospel, this expresses His desire that its power may be exhibited in them. At Antioch of Pisidia the Gentiles "glorified the Word of God," i.e., they were moved to some measure of thanksgiving to God for His mercy, though the language used suggests that not all thus impressed turned to God, Acts 13:48. Here, probably, the apostle means more than Luke meant, viz., the evident effect of the word of God in turning men to righteousness; cp. Matthew 5:16; Titus 2:10.

even as also *it is* **with you;**—as he had joyfully declared in 1 Thessalonians 1:6–10. At Corinth, whence he wrote, the gospel had not met with the reception the Thessalonians had given it, as the narrative of Acts 18 shows. Later, however, the word of the Lord did run and was glorified there. Did the Thessalonian believers respond to the apostle's request for prayer, and was this the answer?

3:2 and that we may be delivered—as at 1 Thessalonians 1:10; the apostle put the interests of the gospel first, but the human instinct of self-preservation was strong in him, hence this prayer, cp. Romans 15:30, 31. The fact that he had already received the divine assurance of personal safety while he remained in Corinth did not make him independent of the prayers of the saints to this very end. The knowledge of God's will and purpose does not render prayer superfluous, rather it encourages thereto, cp. Ezekiel 36:37.

from unreasonable—*atopos,* lit., "out of place"; perverse, truculent, seems to be the meaning intended here, men capable of outrageous conduct. This word refers to behavior, as the next refers to character.

and evil men;—*ponēros,* as at 1 Thessalonians 5:22. The presence of the article, making the meaning "these unreasonable and wicked men," indicates that the apostle had a particular class in his mind, and one his readers would at once recognize. Now the troubles that beset them in the different cities visited, with the exception of Philippi, Acts 16:19-24, were always traceable to the malignity of the Jews, and even as he wrote they were adopting a threatening attitude at Corinth. To the Jews, therefore, these words seem to refer, cp. 1 Thessalonians 2:14-16.

for all have not—i.e., few have; cp. Romans 10:16, where the quotation from Isaiah 53:1, "who hath believed?" shows that "not all" = but few; so here, the Jews generally "opposed themselves and blasphemed," but not all, there were exceptions such as Titus Justus, and Crispus and his house, Acts 18:5-8. Thus in the dispensation of the gospel, as in that of the law, the faithful are always "a little flock," Luke 12:32.

faith.—lit., as marg., "the faith"; see at 1 Thessalonians 3:10.

3:3 But the Lord is faithful,—in Greek the order is "not all have faith, faithful, however, is the Lord," the juxtaposition of the words emphasizing the antithesis between faithless men and the faithful God, cp. 2 Timothy 2:13. In 1 Thessalonians 5:24 God is named; here by "the Lord" Jesus is intended, though indeed it may well be that the apostle did not make any conscious distinction in his own mind as he wrote.

who shall stablish you,—as in 2:17; here the writer returns from his own dangers, to which he had for a moment digressed, to those to which his readers were exposed.

and guard you—*phulassō,* as God guarded Noah through the Flood, 2 Peter 2:5, and as the Lord Jesus guarded the disciples in the days of His flesh, John 17:12. The word is a synonym of *tēreō,* see 1 Thessalonians 5:23 and note there.

from the evil *one,*—*tou ponērou* may be either masc. gender, = the Evil One, i.e., Satan, or neuter, = evil generally. This form of the word occurs again in Paul's writings only in Ephesians 6:16 where Satan is certainly meant. In Romans 12:9 there is no such ambiguity, it is plain that evil generally is intended, the principle, not the persons in whom it is expressed, for Christians are not to abhor any but to love all. In 1 Corinthians 5:13 the English versions are evi dently right in supplying "man," though the Greek may be either masc. or neuter.

In Matthew 5:39, which is similarly ambiguous, "the evil man" is intended (for we are told to resist the Devil that he may flee from us, James 4:7) and in Matthew 13:38; 1 John 3:12, Satan. There does not seem to be any adequate reason why in Matthew 5:37; 6:13; John 17:15, and here, Satan should not be understood.

Satan had already been indicated as the instigator of opposition to the gospel, present and prospective, 2:9, cp. 1 Thessalonians 2:18; 3:5; it is fitting, therefore, that while he urged the converts to stand fast in the face of human enmity, the apostle should commend them to the Lord for protection from the archenemy. In so doing he had in mind, perhaps, the words of the Lord recorded in Matthew 6:13 and John 17:15.

3:4 And we have confidence in the Lord touching you,—with the addition of the characteristic Christian formula "in the Lord," these words correspond with those of 2 Corinthians 2:3, "having confidence in you all." It seems clear, then, that the meaning is "we have confidence in you, not indeed because of any natural stability of character but because of your relationship with the Lord, the sufficient source of power for all His people." Cp. Galatians 5:10, where the same thought is expressed, and Philemon 21.

that ye both do and will do—hitherto he had had no occasion to question the general loyalty of the converts, and he anticipated none in the future; cp. 1 Thessalonians 4:10.

the things which we command,—_parangellō_, as at 1 Thessalonians 4:11, see note at 4:2. The words concerning prayer are rather a request than a command: he had laid many commands upon them during his stay with them, and in his previous letter, and to these he was about to add, vv. 6–13.

3:5 And the Lord—i.e., the Lord Jesus, see note at 1 Thessalonians 3:12.

direct—as at 1 Thessalonians 3:11.

your hearts—see note at 1 Thessalonians 2:4.

into the love of God,—three interpretations of these words seem possible, _a_, that they might learn to love God, _b_, that they might apprehend the love of God toward them, _c_, that they might love each other, and all men, after the pattern of His love, see note at 1 Thessalonians 3:12. The comprehensiveness of the term is probably designed to include every aspect of the love of God, and every possible effect of that love upon the believer.

and into the patience of [the] **Christ.**—here also three interpretations seem possible *a*, the patient waiting for Christ, so. A.V. paraphrases the words *b*, that they might be patient in their sufferings as Christ was in His, see Hebrews 12:2, *c*, that since Christ is "expecting till His enemies be made the footstool of His feet," Hebrews 10:13, so they might be patient also in their hope of His triumph and their deliverance.

While a too rigid exegesis is to be avoided, it may, perhaps, be permissible to paraphrase: "the Lord teach and enable you to love as God loves, and to be patient as Christ is patient."

3:6 Now we command you, brethren, in the Name of our Lord Jesus Christ,—i.e., by His authority, see note at 1:12. The apostle here turns from the troubles that had come upon the converts from without, to deal with the troubles which had arisen among themselves; such have never been lacking in the "churches of the saints."

that ye withdraw yourselves—*stellō*, a word used of the furling of a sail, and hence, metaphorically, of shrinking from any person or thing, it occurs again in 2 Corinthians 8:20. A compound, *hupostellō*, is used in the same sense in Galatians 2:12, where see note.‖

from every brother that walketh—*peripateō*, as in 1 Thessalonians 2:12.

disorderly,—*ataktōs*, cp. the corresponding adjective in 1 Thessalonians 5:14.

and not after [i.e., according to] **the tradition**—as at 2:15.

which they—i.e., the disorderly ones. The grammatical discord, "every brother——they," seems to have led some ancient copyists to correct "they" into "he" or "ye"; see marg.; "they," however, is probably what was originally written.

received of us.—*paralambano*, the word which refers rather to the outward ear, cp. notes at 1 Thessalonians 2:13.

3:7 For yourselves know—*oida*, i.e., from your observation of our ways; cp. 1 Thessalonians 1:4, 5; 2:1, where see notes.

how—i.e., in what way, by what kind of conduct. It was not really necessary, the apostle seems to suggest, to describe the manner of life becoming to a Christian, they had seen it exemplified in the ways of the missionaries.

ye ought to imitate us:—see note at 1 Thessalonians 1:6; there the apostle referred to the initial step which made them Christians, here he exhorts them to pursue steadfastly the course upon which they then set out.

for we behaved not ourselves disorderly among you;—see note at 1 Thessalonians 5:14.

3:8 neither did we eat bread—by synecdoche = "were we maintained." This is a common Hebraism, see 2 Samuel 9:7; Psalm 41:9.

for nought—*dōrean,* lit., "as a gift," gratis, cp. Matthew 10:8; Romans 3:24; 2 Corinthians 11:7; Revelation 21:6; 22:17; the same word = "without a cause" in John 15:25; Galatians 2:21.||

at any man's hand,—lit., from any. This was apparently an element in the disorderliness with which the apostle is dealing.

but in labor and travail, working night and day, that we might not burden any of you:—cp. 1 Thessalonians 2:9, and see notes there. The sentence is incomplete, the ellipsis to be supplied is, of course, "we maintained ourselves."

3:9 not because we have not the right,—i.e., the right to be maintained by those among whom they labored, for this they had, cp. 1 Corinthians 9:3, 14, and indeed the whole section, vv. 1–18. This "right" stood in virtue of the "authority" given by the Lord Jesus, cp. Matthew 10:10; Luke 10:7, and 1 Timothy 5:17, 18.

The word *exousia,* here translated "right," is, first, freedom to do anything, and then, authority to do it. Thus God is free to do as He wills, Acts 1:7, and has made man free also, 1 Corinthians 7:37. Then it has pleased God to delegate responsibility in certain matters to others, who are thus said to have "authority." He gave authority to His son while upon earth in humiliation, Matthew 9:6; Mark 1:22; John 10:18, as well as in resurrection, Matthew 28:18; John 17:2, and cp. 5:27.

The angelic hosts, good and evil, are said to be "authorities" or to have "authority," Acts 26:18; Ephesians 1:21; 1 Peter 3:22, because all hold their freedom to act from God Himself however some of them may have abused it. The same is true also of human governments, Romans 13:1, cp. Matthew 8:9; Luke 12:11; John 19:11; Titus 3:1.

Satan offered to delegate his authority over the kingdoms of the earth to the Lord Jesus, Luke 4:6, Who, well aware of His right thereto, refused, awaiting the time when He shall receive all that, and infinitely more, from the only source of authority, God, Revelation 12:10.

The Lord Jesus also gave authority to His apostles to do certain things, Luke 9:1; 2 Corinthians 10:8, and here.

Again, *exousia* is used of an inherent or self-evident right, as in Acts 5:4; Romans 9:21; and of privileges conferred by God on those who fulfill conditions prescribed by Him, John 1:12; Revelation 22:14.

Finally, in a few passages in the Revelation, alone in the New Testament, *exousia* is used to express the idea of strength, 9:3, 9, 10.

Its principal synonym is *dunamis*, see at 1:11; the two may thus be distinguished: *dunamis* is power, *exousia* is freedom to use it.

but to make ourselves—cp. 1 Thessalonians 2:8, and 2 Corinthians 8:5; lit., and with the ellipsis supplied = "but waived it in order to give."

an ensample unto you,—as at 1 Thessalonians 1:7; cp. Philippians 3:17; 1 Timothy 4:12; Titus 2:7; 1 Peter 5:3, where the word appears again in the same connection.

that ye should imitate us—as at v. 7. In 1 Thessalonians 2:5-11 the apostle referred to his manual labors to prove the freedom of the missionaries from self-interest, here he refers to them as an example for the converts.

3:10 For even—i.e., even before the writing of the earlier epistle, in which he had little more than hinted at abuses concerning which he now speaks plainly. The words may, perhaps should, be translated "for also," in which case the meaning is, "we not only set you an example, we gave you a command also."

when we were with you, this we commanded you,—the missionaries during their brief stay at Thessalonica had evidently noted the idle tendencies of some of the converts and, in view of the threatening danger, had chosen to labor for their own support.

If any will not work,—i.e., is not willing to, refuses to work.

neither let him eat.—the rabbis had a saying current in similar if not identical terms; with them it was perhaps a deduction from Genesis 3:19. The apostle forbade the mistaken charity which encourages indolence and degrades those who receive it.

3:11 For—introducing his reason for referring to the subject at all.

we hear of—cp. 1 Corinthians 1:11; 11:18, where, however, he gives the name of his informant, here he withholds it. The bearer of the tidings which called forth this second letter would tell him much concerning the believers at Thessalonica.

some that walk among you disorderly,—see at v. 6.

that work [*erazomai*] not at all, but are busybodies [*periergazomai*].—the play upon the words used cannot be reproduced in a literal translation though it may be attempted in a paraphrase, such as "some that are not busy people, but are busybodies," or "some that are not busy in their own business but are over-busy in other people's business."||

This figure of speech is called paronomasia, and is used to give "cheerful liveliness to the language, or greater emphasis to the thought." It is of frequent occurrence in Paul's epistles; "using," *chraomai*, and using it to the full, *katachraomai*, 1 Corinthians 7:31; "read," *anaginōskō*, and get to understand fully, *epiginōskō*, 2 Corinthians 1:13; "known," *ginōskō*, and "read" *anaginōskō*, 3:2; "having," *echō*, and "possessing," *katechō*, 6:10; "number," *enkrinō*, and "compare," *sunkrinō*, 10:12; "concision," *katatomē*, and "circumcision," *peritomē*, Philippians 3:2, 3, are instances.

The evils against which the apostle had sought to guard the converts in the earlier epistles, see 4:11, 12; 5:14, had become aggravated. When, on any presence, Christians cease to occupy their time and dispose of their strength legitimately, they soon begin to do things that are first superfluous and then mischievous. Cp. 1 Timothy 5:13, where the corresponding adjective, *periergos*, occurs, and Acts 19:19, where it is significantly translated, "curious."||

Concerning idleness see the Lord's parable in Luke 19:11–27.

3:12 Now them that are such we command—as he was entitled to do in virtue of his apostolic office, cp. Philemon 8.

and exhort—i.e., to obey that command. Exhortation was unnecessary at v. 6, for there he addresses those on whose readiness to obey he could count.

in the Lord Jesus Christ,—see at 1 Thessalonians 4:1; here, however, both "command" and "exhort" are to be connected with "in the Lord."

that with quietness—*hēsuchia*, see note on the corresponding verb at 1 Thessalonians 4:11. Here, as there, the contrast is with the noisy activity of the busybodies.

they work and eat their own bread.—see at v. 8. The rabbinical teaching was not dissimilar. "When a man eats his own bread he is of a quiet and orderly turn of mind, whereas if he devours the bread of his parents or children, to say nothing of that of other folks, he is less quietly disposed."

3:13 But ye, brethren,—returning now to the orderly members of the church whom he had addressed in vv. 1–6.

be not weary—*enkakeō,* in view of the danger of failure in perseverance; the word is used again:

a, of prayer to which the answer seems deferred, Luke 18:1:

b, of the ministry of the word in its purity, when some modification might make it acceptable, 2 Corinthians 4:1:

c, of the same, in spite of the fatigue and physical suffering involved, 2 Corinthians 4:16, cp. Ephesians 3:13:

d, of Christian conduct in the face of evil example and the temptation to laxity, here and Galatians 6:9.||

in well-doing.—*kalopoieō,* a compound of *kalos,* see at 1 Thessalonians 5:21, and *poieō,* see at 1 Thessalonians 5:24. The words occur, but separately, not in a compound, in Galatians 6:9, and also in Romans 7:21; 2 Corinthians 13:7; James 4:17.||

The preceding admonitions were directed not against activity but against disorder. The more sober might misunderstand this, and some might even appeal to the apostle's words to excuse indolence in a good cause, such as gospel preaching, visiting the distressed, or what not, hence this parenthetic sentence is added.

3:14 And if any man obeyeth not our word by this epistle,—the exhortation of 1 Thessalonians 4:11 had been disregarded by some who, perhaps, claimed to be better exponents of the apostle's mind than the recognized leaders of the church, and who refused to acknowledge the authority of a letter. With such the apostle deals explicitly, the letter had all the authority of the spoken word.

note that man,—continuous tense, suggesting that no hasty conclusion was to be drawn from an act, but that the course and general conduct was to be observed.

that—this word is inserted in the English translation in order to complete the sense.

ye have no company with him,—*sunanamignumi,* = to mingle with and among, i.e., to hold free intercourse with, as in 1 Corinthians 5:9, 11, in a similar connection.||

to the end that he may be ashamed,—i.e., seeing that the godly leave him alone, he may look to his own ways for the reason.

3:15 And *yet—kai,* lit., "and"; care must be taken that the one under this discipline is not treated as "the Gentile and the publican," Matthew 18:17.

count him—*hēgeomai,* as at 1 Thessalonians 5:13.

not as an enemy,—i.e., not as one who is opposed to Christ, cp. Philippians 3:18; to do otherwise would drive a true believer to despondency, or to hostility, rather than lead him to repentance.

but admonish him—*noutheteō,* as at 1 Thessalonians 5:12.

as a brother.—not = "as though he were," but = "because he is"; cp. Leviticus 19:17. The purpose is to "gain," or win, him over to better ways, cp. Matthew 18:15. Believers may stray or stumble, but since they have been born anew they continue to be children of God, and brethren in the Lord, and where reproof is necessary they must be reproved as such. Hostile feeling mars discipline, which, if it is to be effectual for restoration, must have love for its evident motive.

The discipline of this section falls short in severity of that enjoined in the very different case of 1 Corinthians 5. Evidently "have no company with" = "withdraw from," v. 6, and neither expression seems appropriate to describe excommunication, or, indeed, formal action of any kind.

The end of all discipline is restoration, see 1 Corinthians 5:5, and prevention of the spread of evil among the believers, see 1 Timothy 5:20; Titus 1:13, and only such as are "spiritual" are qualified to exercise it, Galatians 6:1.

3:16 Now—*de,* as at 1 Thessalonians 5:23; have endeavored to induce tranquility of mind in all, and to reduce to sobriety of conduct the disorderly among them, the apostle turns, as his manner is, to his sufficient resource in every perplexity.

the Lord of peace—cp. 1 Thessalonians 5:23; as the title "God of peace" refers to the Father, so "Lord of peace" is best understood of the Son.

Himself—see note at 2:16.

give you peace—cp. Numbers 6:26; John 14: 27; 16:33; the prayer is not for the cessation of persecution, nor yet of the internal disorders from which they suffered, but for that calm of heart which comes of faith in God and is independent of circumstances.

at all times—*dia pantos* = through all, continually, Luke 24:53; Hebrews 9:6; 13:15, *et al.*

in all ways.—*en panti tropō,* lit., "in every way," cp. the similar phrase in 2:3. A various reading is *topō,* "place," but the text is to be preferred.

The Lord—i.e., the Lord Jesus.

be with you all.—the prayer is based upon His promises, Matthew 18:20; 28:20, and accords with His Name, "Immanuel," 1:23; indeed, but a little while before the words were written the apostle had heard the voice of the Lord saying to him, "I am with thee," Acts 18:10. Thus with comfort wherewith he had himself been comforted the apostle sought to comfort others, 2 Corinthians 1:4.

The same advance from the gift to the giver is made in Philippians 4, cp. v. 7 with v. 9.

3:17 The salutation of me Paul with mine own hand,—so far the letter had been written by another, here the apostle takes the pen himself. Signatures were not usual at the end of ancient oriental letters, cp. Acts 15:23–29; 23:26–30.

which—i.e., the autograph attached, not the form of words, which varied both in substance and in length, see references.

is the token—*sēmeion,* as at 2:9; his autograph attested the authenticity of his letters.

in every epistle: so I write.—the autograph does not appear in 1 Thessalonians, perhaps more recent experiences of forged letters may have suggested the precaution, in which case this is to be understood as a purpose rather than a custom, = "as I do now, so I intend to do in future." It appears elsewhere, however, only in 1 Corinthians and Colossians; Galatians and Philemon seem to have been holographs. The absence of the signature from all the other epistles ascribed to the same writer is capable of different explanations; the assurance of their authenticity rests upon quite different grounds.

The language certainly suggests that the apostle had been accustomed to write letters and intended to continue to do so, see Philippians 3:1. There is no reason to assume that everything he wrote has been preserved. It is not impossible, e.g., that the gifts from the Philippian church received at Thessalonica and elsewhere were acknowledged by letter, as was that received at Rome ten years later. And just as in 2 Corinthians 7:8 he refers to 1 Corinthians, so in 1 Corinthians 5:9 he refers, in the same words, to a previous epistle which has not been preserved. Very little of the activities of Paul or of any of the apostles has been put on record, as, indeed, might have been anticipated, cp. John 21:25. Whether in the case of the master or of the servants, however, the providence of God has secured for subsequent ages all that is necessary to acquaint us with the facts of the gospel and with their meaning, so that we "may stand . . . fully assured in all the will of God," Colossians 4:12.

3:18 The grace of our Lord Jesus Christ be with you all.—see on 1 Thessalonians 5:27, 28. Here, and in v. 16, the word "all" is added, for while he had commended some and censured others, his final word of benediction is for all. The same reason may have led to the inclusion of the same word in 1 Corinthians 16:24; 2 Corinthians 13:14, but not in Romans 15:33.